INSTRUMENT OF WAR

OSPREY
PUBLISHING

Other books by Dennis Showalter:

Railroads and rifles: Soldiers, technology and the unification of Germany
Little Man, What Now?: "Der Sturmer" in the Weimar Republic
Tannenberg: Clash of Empires, 1914
The Wars of German Unification
Patton and Rommel: Men of War in the Twentieth Century
Hitler's Panzers: The Lightning Attacks that Revolutionized Warfare
Frederick the Great: A Military History
Armor and Blood: The Battle of Kursk: The Turning Point of World War II

WITH HAROLD C. DEUTSCH
If the Allies Had Fallen: Sixty Alternate Scenarios of World War II

WITH B.W. COLLINS
The Wars of Frederick the Great

DENNIS SHOWALTER

INSTRUMENT OF WAR

THE GERMAN ARMY 1914–18

First published in Great Britain in 2016 by Osprey Publishing,
PO Box 883, Oxford, OX1 9PL, UK
1385 Broadway, 5th Floor, New York, NY 10018, USA

E-mail: info@ospreypublishing.com

Osprey Publishing, part of Bloomsbury Publishing Plc

A CIP catalog record for this book is available from the British Library.

Dennis Showalter has asserted his/her right under the Copyright, Designs and Patents Act, 1988,
to be identified as the Author of this Work.

ISBN: 978 1 4728 1300 8
PDF e-book ISBN: 978 1 4728 1302 2
ePub e-book ISBN: 978 1 4728 1301 5

Index by Angela Hall
Typeset in Adobe Garamond Pro
Originated by PDQ Media, Bungay, UK
Printed in China through Worldprint Ltd.

16 17 18 19 20   10 9 8 7 6 5 4 3 2 1

Osprey Publishing supports the Woodland Trust, the UK's leading woodland conservation charity.
Between 2014 and 2018 our donations are being spent on their Centenary Woods project in the UK.

www.ospreypublishing.com

Imperial War Museums Collections

Many of the photos in this book come from the huge collections of IWM (Imperial War Museums)
which cover all aspects of conflict involving Britain and the Commonwealth since the start of the
twentieth century. These rich resources are available online to search, browse and buy at www.iwm.
org.uk/collections. In addition to Collections Online, you can visit the Visitor Rooms where you can
explore over 8 million photographs, thousands of hours of moving images, the largest sound archive
of its kind in the world, thousands of diaries and letters written by people in wartime, and a huge
reference library. To make an appointment, call (020) 7416 5320, or e-mail mail@iwm.org.uk

Imperial War Museums www.iwm.org.uk

CONTENTS

INTRODUCTION
AND
ACKNOWLEDGEMENTS

The Imperial German Army is one of World War I's defining institutions. It is also arguably the most protean: presented from a prism of perspectives that can be as confusing as enlightening. The army is described in social contexts: contributing fundamentally to Germany's development as a militarized state and a militarized culture, with a resulting century of global-scale catastrophes. The army can be depicted in political contexts, as fatally unbalancing an already fragile state system, taking it down the road of military dictatorship in the Great War and eventually guiding it into the Third Reich. The army can be studied as a social institution, analyzing its internal dynamics from the grass roots to the general staff. The German Army can be presented as the "other," the opposition to the British, French, and Americans, as mysterious as it was dangerous. Finally, sometimes almost as an afterthought, the German Army can be considered as a fighting force, whose plans, institutions, and fashions were so admired before 1914 that for a while American cavalrymen in remote western outposts turned out for dress parade wearing spiked helmets. And if its combat performance from 1914 to 1918 continues to be trenchantly and appropriately criticized, the German Army is also credited with inflicting a disproportionate number of casualties on the Allies—no small benchmark for a conflict whose memory and mourning is heavily understood in a context of lives lost.

This work seeks to integrate the spectrum of approaches to tell the story of the German Army of 1914–1918 as an institution: an instrument of war that, in the developing context of a total war, found itself overextended from before the war's beginning. It displayed less a genius for war than a gift for improvisation: meeting unexpected challenges with limited resources, making the best tactically and operationally of questionable strategies and policies until the machine broke down and the men had nothing more to give. In that sense this is less a history than a story—an elegy, perhaps, for an institution that, however dubious might have been its cause, gave the last full measure to attain it.

This work is also intended for general readers. Documentation has been kept to a minimum. The endnotes are generally intended as guides to further reading on particular points and arguments. For the sake of user friendliness, whenever possible I have cited English translations. All the mistakes and misjudgments are my responsibility.

This book has been a long time coming. I am professionally indebted to Osprey for giving me the opportunity. As a boy I put a lot of my discretionary money into Osprey publications, and used to dream of writing for them myself. Well, it's never too late to fulfill a dream! I thank particularly Kate Moore for her sharp eyes and endless patience. I owe academic debts as well to Madeleine Engel for her course work on the German treatment of shell shock, and to Christopher Goodwin for his extremely useful Norwich MA thesis on the roots of Prussian masculinity.

It is on the personal side, however, where the debts mount. Kathy Barbier and Paul Thomson proved time and again that a sympathetic ear on the other end of a phone can be almost as good as an arm across the shoulders. Brandy Lachocki proofread and corrected the manuscript, saving a myriad of grammar errors and typos. And Clara Anne—thanks as always for everything!

Since coming to Colorado College in 1969, I have amassed an unpayable debt of gratitude to the staff of the library. Diane Armock in particular supplied the endless list of interlibrary loan requests that enabled my research on project after project. And the rest of the staff—whether filling orders, answering questions, or renewing overdue books, have smoothed my path in too many ways to thank. This book is dedicated to all of them, with respect, admiration, and appreciation.

CHAPTER I

PORTENTS
AND
PRELIMINARIES

In 1898 the *Berliner Illustrierte Zeitung*, a leading popular magazine, polled its readers on the most significant events and personalities of the last hundred years. The choice of the Nineteenth Century's greatest thinker was none other than Helmuth von Moltke. In an era of philosophers like Hegel, authors like Tolstoy, and scientists like Darwin, selecting the chief of Prussia's Great General Staff in hindsight reads at best like a bad joke. Taken as a meme, it reinforces the familiar image of Imperial Germany as a society comprehensively defined by its military culture, as specifically expressed in the army. When Frank House, US President Woodrow Wilson's advisor, wrote from Berlin in April 1914 of "militarism run stark mad," he was not reacting as an innocent abroad. Germany's European neighbors might agree on little else, but by the early Twentieth Century a strong consensus had developed that even by the continent's increasingly prevalent, increasingly comprehensive standards of military planning and military posturing, Germany was in a class by itself.

I

That development was by no means irrational. At seventh and last Germany had been united by force of arms. A century's dream had been fulfilled not by politicians or philosophers, intellectuals or industrialists, but by soldiers. Moreover unification's price in lives and money had been cheap. Even during the Franco-Prussian War of 1870–71, total deaths amounted to around 30,000. In contrast with the Crimea or the American Civil War, most had been recorded. Increasing numbers were listed on local public monuments. Unlike their Civil War and World War I counterparts, Germany's veterans developed nothing like a mythology of sacrifice and victimization. Instead the war deaths had an opposite effect, providing groups and cohorts, whether university classes or soldiers' associations, with foci for a nostalgia that increased as time passed.

Nor did unification have a high direct cost. If the South German states had their share of financial problems, Prussia had been able to underwrite victory in 1864 and 1866 by conventional means: the state treasury and the international finance market. Loans and public subscriptions carried the major burden of 1870/71, with the French indemnity coming in to balance the books. War seemed good business financially as well as psychologically. It made little difference that in fact the indemnity contributed heavily to the overheated economy and the speculative boom that in 1873 triggered two decades' worth of economic depression throughout Europe. Instead the "Promoters' Panic" was projected as the work of liberals and Jews, or internalized as a punishment for seeking profit without working for it.[1]

Internationally too, the Wars of Unification seemed an unadulterated triumph. A Prussia that for over a century had been a great power only by the courtesy of its neighbors now stood at the apex of Europe: not a hegemon definitely, but a fulcrum with arguably more leverage to come. No longer were the Reich's lesser states clients to be bought, used, and discarded, as in the days of Louis XIV and Napoleon. An army that in 1860 had been described as embarrassing the profession of arms now set global standards for doctrine, tactics, and even uniforms, as spiked helmets appeared on the parade grounds of the American West. Small wonder that Max Weber prized his status as a reserve officer alongside his position as Germany's foremost economist.

The Wars of Unification made German geopolitically legitimate. Such once-credible alternatives as the Confederation established at the Congress of Vienna, with its joint Austro-Russian hegemony, or the German-dominated Central European Confederation advocated during the 1850s by philosopher/politician Constantin Frantz, had neither support nor viability. In Austria, itself reconfigured in 1867, the end of the old order generated some nostalgia, but the outcome of the Franco-Prussian War was a clear sign that hopes of a Habsburg-dominated Greater Germany centered north of the Inn River no longer existed. The Wars of Unification had demonstrated to the lesser German states the advantage—arguably the necessity—of participation in a large-scale military and economic system, particularly since the federal organization of the Second Reich meant that local mores and local power structures were respected if not privileged.[2]

Factionalism also posed no significant problems, immediate or long-term. Liberal and progressive elements felt themselves so well satisfied with the new Imperial system that by most accounts they offered too little resistance to Bismarck's political manipulations during the 1870s. Of the Reich's ethnic minorities, the Poles had nowhere else to go, since no prospects for reestablishing Polish independence existed outside the context of cataclysmic war. The integration of Alsatians into the new state was more successful for a longer period than French nationalism has been willing to concede. Jews had participated in the war enthusiastically in every capacity from riflemen to surgeons. Their behavior, while motivated primarily from conviction, reflected as well the hope that—finally—they would be recognized as fully equal citizens.[3] They embraced the new Reich with an enthusiasm that denied an anti-Semitism the influence of which up to 1914 was in any case limited enough to seem trivial in retrospect. Catholics made up a one-third religious minority in a state the dominant ethos of which was moving towards Protestantized secularism. But even the bitter *Kulturkampf* of the 1870s was not enough to alienate them permanently from the Empire for which their sons too had fought. An emerging working class had almost to be driven out of the Imperial consensus by the anti-Socialist legislation of the 1880s. Social Democratic leader August Bebel asserted that the Prussian Guard, 90 percent socialist, would nevertheless shoot him dead if given the order. Bebel may have been exaggerating for effect, but there is no question in 1914 Socialists reported for duty with no significant protest, individual or collective.

The common denominator in each of these cases was that no particular element of German society, whether defined in economic, political, or ethnic terms, felt itself sufficiently excluded or sufficiently victimized to reject its chances in the system. Bismarck's demonstrated virtuosity at manipulating interest groups and creating new ones, usually described in negative terms, offered hope as well of improving one's place in the hierarchy.[4]

The Wars of Unification provided a common symbolic structure for a German public culture that was increasingly entropic and increasingly locally focused since the 1648 Peace of Westphalia, if not the Protestant Reformation. Munich's *Oktoberfest,* inaugurated in 1816, was a typical example. Elsewhere in Europe military plays had flourished during the Nineteenth Century. Initially intended to show the power of the post-Napoleonic state, they were evolving as well into celebrations: safe enough for children; respectable enough for families; and with no admission charges, social, religious, or financial.

In imperial Germany the occasions for these events were overwhelmingly military—less from popular belligerence than because those were the only events the new Reich had in common. Sedan Day on September 1, the Empire's defining holiday, combined contemporary celebratory patriotism designed to encourage national identity with a spectrum of local initiatives confirming local traditions. Parades, bands, and speeches by generals became part of carnivals, harvest festivals, and church consecrations in the same pattern of synergy, generally acceptable to a broad spectrum of public opinion. By 1914 even a hard-core Social Democrat might expect forgiveness from his party comrades for taking his family to the show and stopping for a beer or two.[5]

The military system that developed after the Wars of Unification became central as well to gender self-identification—for women arguably no less than for men. The bipolar structure of male fighters and female helpmates had been affirmed and reinforced by the Wars of Unification. They had been short, and competently waged, offering limited motives for opposition based on the examples of Desdemona and Lysistrata. They had largely been fought away from homelands, providing limited opportunities for women to be thrust into the roles of victim or heroine. The low levels of loss and sacrifice created limited opportunity for women to establish status as healers and nurturers in the pattern of the American Civil War. As it developed in Germany's midcentury experience, women's function in war was to symbolize its opposite: the peace the Empire proposed to maintain indefinitely and intended to restore promptly when necessary.[6]

The Imperial German Army was an army of mobilized civilians. Almost half the men in every active regiment at war strength were reservists; entire divisions and army corps were also composed of these hostilities-only soldiers. The Germans were far ahead of their contemporaries in accepting the martial virtues of the citizen in uniform. Unlike the French and Russians, who treated reserve formations as second-line troops suited only for garrison duty or subsidiary missions, the Germans proposed using their reserve units alongside the active ones, giving them the same tasks and assuming the same levels of proficiency.

Sustaining a conscript citizen army on the German model of "everyone a front-line combatant" had two essential prerequisites. The first was that the vast majority of men could be made into soldiers by compulsion and killers by necessity. The second was that, having passed through the crucible of modern war, these men could return to civilian life without permanent, massive psychological damage. A parallel function of the army was to establish paradigms of war-fighting that provided links with order and connections to society by channeling and controlling individual and collective energies.[7]

Most recruits reported in early autumn, just after the harvest. Fall and winter were devoted to "The school of the soldier:" instruction in wearing and maintaining uniforms and personal equipment, close-order drilling, less with an eye to parade-ground display than to developing skill in group movements, physical training, marksmanship, and not least standards of order, cleanliness, and hygiene vital for health in barracks that were at best close and spartan quarters.

Time and patience played a much larger role in German training than familiar accounts and mythologies credit. Most conscripts remained in the companies where they were trained; the sullen and the intractable could not simply be passed along like low cards. Effectiveness as an instructor was not only a serious responsibility but a fundamental criterion of retention and promotion among both NCOs and officers. They were given wide latitude in securing results—a peacetime exercise of the individual initiative so important in German operational doctrine. Latitude, however, did not mean license. Too many black eyes and split lips on parade, too many entries in a company punishment book, and the responsible authority could usually count on an unpleasant session with his own superior, centering negatively on his career prospects if the situation continued.

In early May the recruits were inspected: most of them were assigned to full time duty in their original companies. The rest of the spring and summer was devoted to battalion and regimental training, then maneuvers. Most were working-day affairs at corps and division level; the showpiece was the Imperial maneuvers pitting corps against corps, observed—and under William II increasingly muddled—by the kaiser himself. In autumn another fresh class of recruits—"*Hammel*" (castrated sheep, or dummies) for their short haircuts and clueless bewilderment—crowded the barracks. The newly-minted reservists invested in souvenirs, checked travel schedules, and looked forward to intimidating the younger generations with peacetime war stories.

A system designed for instrumental purposes developed a wider social and cultural context as well. The German Army emerged as the nation's primary male rite of passage. Masculinity is fundamentally a social characteristic: a male is a man when he is accepted as such by other men. The criteria for that acceptance usually involve some kind of initiation process specific to the group, from dueling fraternities for university students to *Wanderjahre* ("journeymen years") for aspiring craftsmen. These rituals, however, were likely to carry little external weight. The drastic changes in German society since the mid-Eighteenth Century had in any case marginalized many of them. In the Second Reich military service developed as a replacement, an alternative common denominator. Going through the conscription process, even without actually being assigned to active duty, certified male adulthood. It validated claims to permanent employment, to a seat at the men's table in the *Gasthaus*, to think even of starting a family.

German youth was part of a society that laid significant stress on stereotyped and distinct sex roles. It was described by a contemporary sociologist as male-defined: patriarchal, rigid, militaristic—but one that also enabled the questioning of that pattern just enough to generate male societies in which the feminine element in men could be legitimately—and safely—expressed in same-sex, but not overtly sexual, situations. Old soldiers bullied the new ones, but usually in the sense of showing them their place in this new world, as opposed to the comprehensive, efflorescent brutality that characterized the Soviet Union's armed forces in the regime's final years. From the army's perspective, hazing that became more than an uncomfortable game was bad for discipline. From the old timers' point of view, hazing could be expensive in other ways. A man on the down side of his active service, someone who knew the ropes and judiciously shared them, seldom had to pay for his schnapps and cigars.

Few conscripts had not experienced something similar as boys and adolescents. In Germany, as indeed throughout Europe, for young men to be caned, slapped, and beaten by parents, teachers, clergymen, employers, and neighbors was an experience so general that even to the victims it appeared natural and necessary in the maturing process. The rigors of army initiation were further mitigated by the sure knowledge than one's own turn on top would come with the passing of time. Few thought of complaining; fewer still acted on the thought. Only a *Muttersöhnchen* (mama's boy, or sissy) who occasionally found himself in the barracks instead of paying for the privilege of serving one year as a volunteer and living off post, complained.

The collective and temporary experience of military service worked against conscripts forming particular friendships, but that was not essentially different from civil life. On the farm, in the factory or the shop, even the schoolroom, participants came and went with increasing frequency in an increasingly mobile society. But in the army, more than in the workplace, comradeship was generated by need. The government provided little in the way of institutionalized services. That meant a middle-class son who received generous packages from home was expected to share out. A man apprenticed as a tailor or cobbler in civilian life, a clerk who wrote legible letters home for the less articulate, a farmhand or a domestic servant able to shine leather and clean uniforms was welcome in barracks even as a recruit.

The army's place in that meme is best expressed in nicknames. The captain was "the father of the company." The *Feldwebel*, the first sergeant, was the "company mother." The accepted reply by a recruit asked what he wanted to become in the army was "an orphan!" But the underlying reality the images implied was more than their sarcastic dismissal in a universally familiar joke. Historian Ute Frevert, anything but an admirer of the "nation in barracks," speaks of the peacetime regiment as a family. And if its potential for nurturing individual development was limited, the same is true for all families.

Two or three years in the German active army was no easy rite of passage. Behavior by the NCOs, a boxed ear, a kicked backside, a tirade of imaginative comments on a soldier's ancestry and character, could be complemented systematically by burdensome extra duty involving kitchens, latrines, and, even in the infantry, stables. The conscripts' new world invited dissociation from emotional and behavioral traits associated with the subaltern domesticity that defined and limited young men's civilian experience. Smoking, drinking, idleness—all the things good mothers warned against—were barracks norms. Sexual talk, rigorously suppressed by parents, teachers, and pastors, was "theme number one" for previously repressed young adults. As for action, at least in Berlin it was not unusual for the girl to pay for a date—particularly if the man served in an elegantly-uniformed regiment.

Army life nurtured a particular masculine culture socially as well as sexually. Relationships with fellow soldiers of the regiment, the company, and the barracks formed and defined an individual's identity. Draftees usually spent their entire service in the same unit. A reputation once established was correspondingly difficult to change or shed, and could make the difference between nostalgia and nightmare. Self-control, endurance, grace under pressure largely defined that reputation. *Ein ganzer Kerl* or "a real man" was expected to "stand his man" against anything the army threw at him—to do his duty but "take no shit," as one Social Democratic official advised a group of conscripted party members. As one piece of army doggerel expressed it, anyone who had not spent three days in the guardhouse on bread and water for some breach of regulations, or for angering a sergeant, could hardly call himself a soldier. At the same time good officers and NCOs understood when to look away, to laugh or swear at the infinite ability of young men to pitch tents on Fool's Hill.

Active service, moreover, could be a positive experience. German standards of comfort, particularly among countrymen and the working classes, were sufficiently spartan that army food, army beds, and army routines did not represent a steep decline in quality of life. Military service, moreover, could salve the perceived wounds of modernization. Traditional conservatism and modern liberalism alike postulated a direct connection between effort and result. Individuals and groups achieved success through their own efforts. In the course of the Nineteenth Century, however, industrialization and agribusiness steadily diminished the relationship between that meme and economic reality. The alienation of wage labor in mines and factories or on landed estates was paralleled in towns and cities by an emerging and subaltern class of white-collar employees trapped behind counters and desks and in the country by a peasantry that might be legally emancipated, but whose economic position was steeply and visibly declining. Hard work now pitted men against machines that wore them out and broke them, or against complex, impersonal systems impossible to comprehend, much less master.[8]

That matrix nurtured Marxist and *Völkish* ideologies, both to the Second Reich's detriment. The army, however, was different. It was fundamentally designed to enable success. Like a university, a corporation, a church or a hospital, it existed to *do* something. No system, however, can function if a significant portion of its members cannot meet the system's standards. The German Army, moreover, was a secondary institution. The demands of rifle marksmanship and physical training, the drill ground and the route march, might be high but could be met—and not only by a chosen or privileged few. If many German men spoke with favor of their military service, it was because they achieved there the kind of visible, recognized triumphs denied them the rest of their lives. A cigar from the captain, a chance to win one of Kaiser William's prize medals, promotion to *Gefreiter* (private first class), towards the end of one's time as an incentive to reenlist, might not seem much—but the reward was in the context.

The army also had a way of challenging conventional civilian hierarchies. A laborer good at drill, an artisan with an impeccable uniform, was more likely to be well regarded by the officers and NCOs than a well-off merchant's son with two left feet and perpetually dull boots. And if a blundering Gymnasium student earned the whole squad or platoon extra drill or extra duty, the offender was likely to receive a midnight "visit from the Holy Ghost," a beating administered by his barrack-mates as an unofficial motivational exercise.

Contemporaries before World War I and scholars afterward have described Imperial Germany as ultimately ruled more by the sword than the scepter. The dominant consensus has been that the army that was built on the victories of the Wars of Unification expanded its influence in state and society, to an extent making the soldiers fundamentally, if not entirely, responsible for a diseased *Sonderweg* ("special path") that led to two world wars, the rise of Nazism, and the destruction of a European order that, while imperfect, was in its openness, its tolerance, and its opportunities preferable to the German-generated alternative.

In fact, whatever may have been the dreams of some of its generals, the army of the Second Reich remained a subaltern institution. To a degree this was structurally determined. The increasingly contentious relations between Otto von Bismarck and Helmuth von Moltke during the Wars of Unification are too often misrepresented in the context of friction in a parliamentary system between a prime minister and the armed forces, along the lines of Winston Churchill and his generals in World War II. In this view, Moltke's claims for autonomy in the conduct of military operations, his challenges to Bismarck's proposals and decisions, represented a move to undercut civilian political authority.

Reality was a good deal more complex—and to a great degree the product of a compromise. A decade-long constitutional conflict over the army's status was resolved in the aftermath of Prussia's victory over Austria in 1866. Bismarck accepted Parliament's rights as a legislative body; Parliament in turn acknowledged the king's autonomous relationship with the cabinet ministers and his independent position as commander in chief of the army.

It was a Solomonic decision, reflecting a widespread belief that neither party could resolve the issue in its favor at an acceptable political and social cost. A cabinet model had characterized Prussia's government since the Eighteenth Century, *de jure* and *de facto*. Both Bismarck and Moltke saw themselves functioning in its contexts. Thus in terms of his own perspective Bismarck was closer to a cabinet secretary on the US model than to a prime minister directly answerable to the Prussian parliament. The system was also flexible enough that Moltke was by 1870 *de facto* a full member, despite his (increasingly nominal) structural subordination as chief of staff to War Minister

Albrecht von Roon. Relationships were collegial, with the hierarchy of influence largely determined by circumstances and personalities. By 1870 Bismarck and Moltke were the alphas. But the positions of both men ultimately depended on the decisions of the executive. Moltke did not regard Bismarck in the same way a French general of the Third Republic regarded the premier. A more appropriate parallel would be the relationship between the departments of State and Defense in the US cabinet during the Cold War and later. And King William of Prussia was hands-on, sufficiently conscious of his power and position to use them sparingly; he was a good deal shrewder than history often acknowledges, anything but a catspaw of over-mighty or over-ambitious subordinates.

Prussia's bequest to the new Reich was also Bismarck's legacy. Bismarck after 1871 had worked consistently and successfully to nurture and exacerbate institutional, as opposed to situational, conflicts within the military. In particular he separated the War Ministry, the General Staff, and the Military Cabinet in charge of personnel matters, reporting directly to the kaiser and functioning as a back channel. Bismarck's intention was to set the three against each other as a means of limiting the soldiers' direct involvement in politics. The result was a command structure sufficiently divided internally that the army's influence on German policy, foreign and domestic, remained not only limited, but sufficiently diffuse in many cases to be best described as random.[9]

William II, Germany's emperor after 1888, head of state and primary public symbol, was obsessed with the trappings of war-making, almost at the expense of his other responsibilities combined. One of his first acts on assuming the throne was to issue a proclamation emphasizing his "special relationship" with the army. Within a matter of months, however, the kaiser had established a reputation as a poser and a *flaneur*, interfering randomly in everything from the conduct of annual maneuvers to the appointment of senior officers. Alfred von Waldersee, Moltke's successor as chief of staff, described the kaiser as lacking knowledge and experience, with no impulse to improve because "he thinks he knows everything very well and better than anyone else."

Considered in the army's internal contexts, William's behavior was more irritating than consequential. His incapacity in military matters was so widely acknowledged that most of the time he could be sidestepped, neutralized, even ignored in matters more serious than the details of uniform or a regiment's honorific title. And when that did not succeed the emperor made a handy scapegoat. His decades-long preoccupation with a globe-girdling navy to underwrite a vaguely-defined *Weltpolitik* further distracted William's attention and strained his capacity for focused decision making.

And yet the vacuum at Germany's power apex was not filled by the army—neither by default nor assertion. In 1875 and again between 1887 and 1888 it was Bismarck who held the ring. Leo von Caprivi, Bismarck's successor as chancellor, then Caprivi's successors, Hohenlohe, Bülow, Bethmann-Hollweg, kept fundamental, if at times uneasy, control of the Second Empire's fundamental decisions: war or peace. The notorious War Council of December 1912 produced bluster but not decisions. While the respective degrees of responsibility are hotly debated, it is increasingly clear that in the summer of 1914 Bethmann and William made the fateful decisions that brought Germany, and arguably Europe, into the Great War. For all his decades of bloviating, at crunch time William never advocated preventive war. Indeed at the ultimate sticking point he compelled the soldiers to delay the occupation of Luxembourg while awaiting a final word from Britain.[10]

What then of the generals? In early July 1914, probably around the 6th, the military began to check the readiness of the armed forces. The cross-talk as recorded in diaries and memoirs shows significant discussion as to whether the developing international situation was favorable or unfavorable to Germany. There is no evidence, however, of groupthink patterns involving either support for a preventive war or open-ended support for Austria-Hungary. The latter situation indeed inspired as much reserve as enthusiasm: Habsburg military effectiveness was not highly regarded in higher German military circles. Prussian War Minister Erich von Falkenhayn, for example, was present at the meeting of July 5 when William first discussed his pledge of support to Austria, but more as a spear carrier than an advisor. His declaration that the army was ready was unsurprising in context. It was the sort of pumping-up by now second nature to generals dealing with William. Even more to the point, for Falkenhayn to say anything else was tantamount to offering his resignation. That day he wrote Moltke, currently on leave, that he expected nothing to come from this latest contretemps.[11]

Moltke responded by continuing his cure. His deputy, Georg von Waldersee, was on compassionate leave due to a death in the family. On July 8 Bethmann-Hollweg advised him to take some additional time to recover health shaken by recent surgery. Waldersee would not return to Berlin until July 23. Wilhelm Gröner, head of the vital Railway Section of the General Staff, was visiting Bad Kissingen for his health.

Not until July 25 did Moltke return to Berlin. Indeed, not until the Austro-Hungarian ultimatum to Serbia and the breaking off of Austro-Serbian diplomatic relations, and the proliferating reports of Russian military preparations, did Germany's generals begin taking seriously the prospect that the long-projected Great European War might indeed be upon them. The ultimate trigger of a war-focused consensus was the increasing number of reports of Russian military preparations, coming from external sources like Sweden, as well as German intelligence, that began coming in on July 28.

II

Might all this have been an elaborate deception plan to lure Europe into a false security? It is difficult to imagine conspirators having that kind of insouciant confidence in the face of a long-anticipated Armageddon. Instead, when reduced to basics, the generals' consistent contribution to high German politics in the July crisis was to assure the emperor and his ministers that the army was prepared to be about its fundamental task, and that the army could deliver. But "never let your mouth write a check your hands can't cash" is as fundamental a principle in starting a world war as a street brawl. How did the army's accounts and credits stand as the guns of August began rolling into place?

Diplomats by their nature prefer to avoid wars. Politicians are ambivalent. Soldiers take wars as a given, and focus on how to win them. Soldiers in 1914 were also the ones with detailed knowledge of the increasing complexities of mobilization. This gave them leverage in any small-group discussions. Since civilian authority, Bismarck increasingly concluded, accepted the army as "competent by definition" far more than did their counterparts in the other great powers, these reassurances were welcome—arguably necessary—to the diplomats and politicians.

The question of the army's military effectiveness was exacerbated by the army's success as an instrument of socialization. That success was underwritten by year after year of peace. The continued growth of the population, combined with lower death and disability rates in a safer, healthier society, steadily increased the raw numbers of potential soldiers. At the same time, Germany's political parties might agree on very little, but as a rule they saw, albeit for varying reasons, no reason to expand the army budget sufficiently to make universal service come close to a reality.[12]

The conscription system correspondingly developed an increasingly broad spectrum of loopholes. Its definitive legal statement, conscription remaining in force until 1914, was the Military Service Law of 1888. That provided for three years of active service, reduced to two in 1893, and five in the reserve. Those not inducted were assigned to a Supplementary (Ersatz) Reserve for a twelve-year term: this reserve included all men temporarily unfit, or excused for specific reasons. Grounds for exemption metastasized. Men who were the sole support of families or elderly parents, men able to make a case that service would threaten a family, business, or profession, self-employed craftsmen, small shopkeepers—all could be excused active service. Unwilling warriors in the universities were known to benefit from wink-and-nudge diagnoses of things like flat feet from fraternity brothers graduated as doctors of medicine.

By 1914 almost half the Empire's eligible conscripts met one or another of those categories. In other words, an ever-smaller percentage of the males eligible for conscription actually performed active service. The army had no room for them. Military authorities seldom challenged a system that enabled exempting the kind of men experience suggested would be more trouble than it was worth to make into effective soldiers. And that included as well urban recruits whose family or employment profiles suggested sympathy with Social Democracy; Poles and Alsatians with nationalist profiles; and similar potential troublemakers.

The result was that by 1914 around half of the men theoretically eligible for military service at most spent a token amount of time with a Supplementary Reserve learning nothing they might reasonably be expected to retain. And that figure generated some awkward questions. To a significant degree the active army and its reserves were self-selected, drawn from those who for some reason did not seek to pull threads to escape. Would the socializing and conditioning aspects of military service be as effective on men from the other half of the spectrum?

No less to the point, the Prussian/German system had developed after 1871, and as far as the army had been concerned, in an environment of profound peace. Whatever threats might cause *frissons* in newspaper headlines, government offices, and military headquarters, seldom excited the barracks. But might actual war bring the social contract to a breaking point? Could a citizen army prepare to fight a war when half its soldiers had performed only nominal service? Would men whose training and conditioning was based on drill and maneuvers—in plain words, on playing soldiers—be able to rise to the demands of high-tech industrial war?[13]

III

The army's position in Imperial Germany was ambiguous. On one hand it assumed, sought, and was assigned the role of a primary social institution, demanding ultimate loyalty from and control over its personnel while on active duty, but the army was also a secondary institution. It existed to *do* something. In armies, corporations, or universities, abstract claims, whether of justice, compassion, or equity, tend to be balanced against a need for results. The ultimate issue for a secondary institution is not doing the right thing, but doing the thing right.

Could the German Army do the thing right? Did the professionals understand the next war well enough to win it? From the Peace of Frankfurt in 1871 to the outbreak of World War I in 1914 it was generally accepted both at home and abroad as embodying a particular gift for making war. Current scholarship, however, increasingly describes that army as consciously plunging Germany into war knowing it would not and could not be the short conflict that was the only kind of war the Second Reich stood a chance of winning and surviving. "Suicide from fear of death" is one historian's mordant verdict on a military system that preferred risking annihilation to existing in a "modern, pluralistic, industrial society."[14]

The theorists and the field soldiers responsible for developing war plans and attitudes understood war not as an end in itself, nor as an opportunity for displaying either the soldiers' *virtu* or the patriotic zeal of the German people. War was a rationally calculated extension of state policy. Moltke the Elder described the best practical method of waging modern war as prophylactic: keeping conflicts short by a combination of quick victory and prompt negotiation. As the Nineteenth Century progressed, however, that concept was influenced by an increasingly apocalyptic understanding of war. The research of uniformed scholars comprehensively stressed confusion, panic, horror, and blind chance at all levels. The infantryman's life in particular was understood as solitary, nasty, brutish, and above all short. As early as 1895, a general staff officer prepared a memorandum evaluating the prospects of a German offensive against France. Given current technologies and force structures, he concluded the best to be expected was a limited advance followed by tactical stalemate. Army and people must understand that the "most offensive of spirits" would achieve no more than a step-by-step advance, demanding as the price a nightmare's worth of blood.[15]

How could the turn-of-the-century German Army best address that problem? One approach, closely associated with the Conservative party and conservative movements, was relatively broad-gauged. It developed along the lines of a "dual militarism," with the army striking an unstable, arguably contradictory, balance between maturing into a relatively limited force committed to upholding the domestic status quo, and evolving towards an ideologized mass instrument able to overshadow the navy in implementing a German drive for world power.[16]

A second paradigm, more operationally focused, addressed the tensions between quality and quantity. In this model, the army was torn between externally focused militarists advocating total national mobilization at whatever domestic cost, and technocrats supporting higher levels of material preparation at the expense of mere numbers.[17] At planning levels these concepts were not mutually exclusive. A force that could engage domestic enemies immediately and wholeheartedly and an army that could cross frontiers decisively from a standing start were hardly mutually exclusive. Alfred von Waldersee, appointed Moltke's deputy in 1882 and his successor in 1888, believed Germany needed every possible force multiplier, without being particularly specific. Waldersee's successor, Alfred von Schlieffen, defined his responsibility for maximizing Germany's military capacity as concentrating on operational planning and enhancing operational readiness. Germany's geography, its domestic structure, and its level of military preparation all called for prompt operations. Instead of playing to its enemies' strengths by a series of frontal encounter battles, Schlieffen argued, the German Army must seek to force the next war's pace to the point where its opponents would be able to do nothing except react. General Staff exercises in the 1890s increasingly tested the possibilities of a lesser force defeating a larger one by concentrating against an enemy's flank, then driving against his lines of retreat. Among Germany's probable enemies, France was most vulnerable to this kind of shock and speed. Geographic and political considerations impelled its concentration forward, along the frontier, where its army could be fixed and destroyed by superior German fighting power. Russia in turn could receive the same treatment at more leisure, if it did not conclude peace on German terms. Armies, not peoples, were the targets of German theory and German doctrine; a battle of annihilation was not the prequel to a war of annihilation.[18]

That position addresses a major recent specialist controversy in the German historical community. It begins with the fact that social Darwinist ideas were prevalent, arguably dominant, in military circles. It continues by describing a relationship between Imperial German colonialism and Nazi German racial policies. It concludes by asserting a direct connection between the uniquely brutal, at times genocidal, behavior of the German military in China and Africa and their successors' comprehensive contributions to the Third Reich's crimes.[19] The syllogism is intellectually satisfying and politically correct. The middle, however, is missing. At no time before 1914 did the German Army pay serious, systematic attention to the Reich's colonial experience. The army in particular was fixated on Europe. Its "Africans" were few in number and marginal in status. Nothing developed remotely resembling the "colonial" cities in France and Italy, or the "Asiatic" one in the Russian Army. Preparations for and conduct of imperial operations were haphazard and inefficient. Colonial operations were discussed in domestic political contexts: the stuff of newspaper articles, election campaign literature, and parliamentary rhetoric. They were never incorporated into either the principles or the practices of planning for "real" war in continental Europe. The motives for and the links between the German Army's behavior in the world wars are better sought elsewhere.[20]

The army's institutional response to Germany's perceived grand strategic situation was to focus the Second Reich's war-making capacities ever more closely on ending the "next war" as rapidly as possible, even if it took *just* a bit longer than public and political opinion might wish. From the field army's perspective, whether in General Staff circles or at rifle-company level, managed war appeared to be the Reich's best means to that end. Limiting participation in the greater worlds of policy and diplomacy, the soldiers concentrated their energies downwards. Operational effectiveness became the multiplier expected to override geography and politics.

Between 1890 and 1914, the German Army increasingly concentrated on three focal points: intelligence, mobility, and firepower. All were material based. All appeared susceptible to the bureaucratic and technocratic virtues of management and control. All appealed to an officer corps whose mentality was increasingly influenced by a belief in technological progress as complementing rather than challenging traditional martial virtues. Taken together, they offered the possibility of reconciling innovations with institutions at, respectively, strategic, operational, and tactical levels. Thus they fit, perhaps too well, the army's search for vectors strong enough to guide the way into a new military century.

In a quick-war scenario like that developing in Germany, forewarned was forearmed. Preparing to fight outnumbered and on two fronts required the broadest possible spectrum of accurate information on all possible enemies. That meant the kind of bureaucratized processes increasingly natural to the German Army. Signal interceptions, attachés' reports, and above all evaluation of the increasing amounts of printed information about armed forces placed in the public domain by parliamentary debates, journalists, and specialized publications, offered relative freedom from the catch-as-catch-can world of spies and counterspies. It was like constructing a castle from toothpicks.[21] Most of the material by its nature dealt with details of armament, organization, and doctrine. As a consequence, it facilitated the development of intelligence in Germany as an operational tool, as opposed to facilitating the political aspects of strategic planning. Unpleasant surprises were still possible. They could now, however, be quickly evaluated and promptly normalized. As 1914 approached, the "fog and friction" that had so often hobbled the offensives of 1866 and 1870 seemed increasingly susceptible to dissipation through diligence.

In the east, Walter Nicolai had established a formidable reputation for his success, developing a combination of electronic intelligence built around the radio station in Königsberg and a solid network of field agents, mostly disaffected Poles and Jews supplemented by Russian officers with problems of fast women, slow horses, and low cards. It even included sabotage teams in position to destroy key rail bridges. In 1913 Nicolai was promoted to chief of Abteilung IIIa, the military secret service and counterintelligence bureau, and assumed responsibility for another well-established network of agents and observers across the French and Belgian borders. Here, however, his successes proved limited. The Germans seemed to have acquired detailed knowledge of French war plans into the Twentieth Century. Increasingly, however, in reaction to the intelligence fiasco that triggered the Dreyfus Affair, the French plugged old leaks and prevented new ones. The Germans found out little about Plan XVII—which was only adopted in April 1914—or the changes in post-mobilization deployments.

That information gap only encouraged a growing downward focus in German planning. Collecting estimates of French intentions was less important than enhancing the Reich's operational abilities. An even clearer, arguably far more significant, example of that development involved Austria-Hungary. Even before the conclusion of the Dual Alliance in 1879, German military attachés were deeply embedded in the Habsburg information structure. Their comprehensive reports included perceptive and accurate evaluations of the shortcomings of Vienna's military system. The Entente's prewar experience suggests frank communication and focused financial assistance from Berlin could have significantly improved Habsburg military effectiveness before 1914. Instead the General Staff and the Foreign Office alike systematically ignored information that at least might have made Austria's catastrophe less of a surprise.

By 1914 German military intelligence was so narrowly focused that not until July 23 were the intelligence officers of the eastern corps districts officially informed that Berlin was interested in keeping abreast of military events in the tsar's empire. Not until the 25th did Nicolai explain to his immediate subordinates that a war was likely and the department was expected to keep an eye on France and Russia. Nicolai's office began receiving a significant number of reasonably verifiable reports of Russian military preparations the next day, presumably forwarded from various desk drawers and pigeonholes. Whether he is interpreted as an alarmist or a war hawk, he saw that the data moved immediately into decision-making circles.

Moltke remained skeptical—until shown an official Russian placard proclaiming mobilization. Across the other frontier, observers and agents described increasing and public Belgian defensive measures. Initially the country's proposed mobilization might have been in principle a "defense in all directions," directed against France as well as Germany. But Belgian preparations focused heavily on reinforcing the fortress of Liège—the crucial immediate barrier to any projected offensive involving large-scale violation of German neutrality.[22]

Intelligence thus played a significant role in justifying Germany's mobilization and Germany's declaration of war. It did so, however, in an operational context rather than a strategic one. And that confirmed the Reich's emphasis on its rail network. Railroads are usually interpreted in strategic contexts. In Germany by 1914 they were an operational instrument. Their ability to move men, equipment, and supplies into a theater of war had been clearly demonstrated during the Franco-Prussian War. Over the next four decades improvements in track design and roadbed configuration enabled ever-greater concentrations of heavy, high-speed traffic on a given set of lines. Improved communications facilitated control and timing of traffic. The growing bureaucratization of Germany's railway system provided an organization increasingly capable of collaborating effectively with the military on long-range planning. So important, indeed, did railroads become in the everyday routine of the General Staff that the latter's ethos began taking on some of the creed of railroad procedure: continued, reliable, predictable service independent of any specific individual.

The nature of modern railway systems fostered an offensive approach to war in two ways. Most obvious and most often cited was the encouragement of war by timetable. The schedules of train movements, prepared in peacetime with such increasingly elaborate care, could not be altered lightly. Quite apart from the actual difficulties involved in such a process, the years of time and effort spent developing the administrative structure of mobilization generated their own momentum and their own mindset. The most familiar illustration of this came on August 1, 1914, when William II, his spirits temporarily buoyed by hopes of French neutrality, announced to his chief of staff that now all Germany needed to do was concentrate its entire strength against Russia. Moltke the Younger, insisting that the result would be mass chaos, responded with a nervous collapse. After the war, a senior officer on the General Stairs Railway Section, outraged by the implied slur against his bureau, demonstrated in a Teutonically learned monograph that such a shift had indeed been possible: in theory.[23] But when facing an ultimate professional challenge, officers who had spent careers shaving kilometers and hours from train schedules were psychologically unlikely to imagine, much less seriously consider, scrapping their life's work in response to a mere change in external circumstances.

Firepower, last on the list, was also most familiar. Since the days of Frederick the Great, the Prussian/German Army had ample opportunity to learn that lead was deadlier than steel. That lesson was incorporated in the twenty-five active army corps that were the army's heart. A German corps was big and power-laden: two divisions, each of two infantry brigades with two regiments apiece, and an artillery brigade of seventy-two pieces. But the dirty work was still done by the foot soldier. A German infantry regiment included just over three thousand of them, in three four-company battalions. They carried a rifle a cut below the best available. The Gewehr 98 was a Mauser design. Sturdy and reliable, it was bulkier and clumsier than the British Lee-Enfield and the US M1903 Springfield, neither as rapid-firing as the British weapon nor as accurate as the American. These points were, however, less significant in an army much less interested in individual aimed shots than in producing concentrated, controlled bursts at the right time. Field tests, even under artificial peacetime conditions, demonstrated time after time that an exaggerated emphasis on individual marksmanship, the approach fostered by imperial awards to the army's best shots, was less important than volume of fire, with the first round placed somewhere near the target and the rest more or less in the same place.

An even clearer indication of the German Army's appreciation of the potential of massed small-caliber fire was the new organization most regiments were taking into the field: a company of six water-cooled Maxim automatic machine guns. The machine-gun companies were unique in two ways. They represented concentrated firepower, in contrast to the diluted version provided by the two guns per battalion standard in other armies. And unlike most such new creations, which are built on the discards of other units, the machine-gun companies usually had not only first-class cadres, but no fewer than four officers for around a hundred men—only one officer fewer than a rifle company two and a half times as large.

This complementing of organic firepower with organizational flexibility reflected the German Army's focus on the machine gun less for its defensive potential, generally understood, but for its perceived uses in preparing and supporting the offensive. The company's six guns were the "essence of infantry," able to work in two-gun platoons in direct support of battalions and companies, no less able to concentrate fire on an objective until the very moment an assault was pushed home, even after the artillery had to cease for fear of hitting its own men.[24]

Since the Franco-Prussian War, German artillerymen had emphasized method over speed. The field entrenchments that had been challenging obstacles in 1870 were becoming increasingly formidable—as demonstrated in the Russo-Turkish War of 1878–79. Black-powder low-power shells could be expected to have a correspondingly limited effect—particularly in the broken, built-up country of eastern France, expected to be the primary theater of operations. German gunners were expected to cope by reconnoitering firing positions carefully, ranging their targets systematically, and making few changes in position once the fighting started. The replacement of gunpowder by cordite in the 1880s did not change the principles of methodical destruction of enemy field works and methodical preparation of friendly infantry attacks. Nor did the improved recoil mechanisms introduced during the 1890s affect the

German artillery's emphasis on system. The introduction of the Model 1896 field gun, with cordite rounds and an effective range of 7,800 meters, seemed a triumph of a quarter-century of technical and doctrinal development—until the French unveiled their paradigm-shifting "75" a year later.

A decade's worth of tinkering produced between 1905 and 1907 the Model 96 nA (neuer Art). Its shorter range and slower rate of fire than its French rival reflected the continued German conviction that artillery was best used in masses to deliver well-aimed, well-directed fire over extended periods of time from concealed positions. Training put increasing emphasis on observation, on shooting from maps, and on maintaining communications among observers, guns, and infantry. Each division had its own artillery brigade: two regiments, each with six six-gun batteries. And in 1899 the gunners received a major reinforcement. The 10.5-cm field howitzer 98 was the end product of years of debate. Critics said its range was too short and its technology too primitive to be effective against modern field entrenchments. But its shell was twice as heavy and had twice the explosive force of the C 96: German gunners learned to love it. An updated version had an improved recoil mechanism, improved ammunition, and a shield to protect its crews. In 1912 the initial allotment of one battalion per corps was increased to one per division—the highest of any army in Europe except the British.

At the same time the foot artillery was acquiring a new lease of life. Originally restricted to siege and garrison roles, it had paid increasing attention to providing support for the field army as well, but was handicapped by the weight and clumsiness of its guns, and the army's reluctance to provide draft horses. With the new century, however, not only horses were made available. The firm of Alfred Krupp and the army's gun designers combined to introduce a 15-cm heavy howitzer that was the counterpart of the French 75 in terms of bringing increased firepower to the battlefield. It could throw a 90-pound explosive shell 7,500 meters. In its improved and shielded versions, the heavy field howitzer 13, dubbed "crump" and "Jack Johnson" by the British, would drive the backbone of Germany's artillery in World War I and become the model for a broad spectrum of imitations. By 1914 each active army corps had a battalion of them: four four-gun batteries, a mailed fist for the corps commander, whose crews prided themselves as able to take their three-ton pieces anywhere the light artillery could go and demolish anything that blocked the path of the infantry.[25]

Like the infantry, in short, the German artillery went to war with an integrated system of weapons, doctrines, and attitudes based on a defensible evaluation of past experiences and expected conditions.

The firepower evolution even affected the cavalry. The most professionally and socially conservative of the army's branches, it began gradually modifying its historic role of deciding battle by mass charges as the Nineteenth Century waned. After 1900 and the introduction of machine guns, the mounted arm's principal role shifted to reconnaissance and screening. Almost half its regiments were assigned to the infantry for close work. The eleven cavalry divisions the army took to war were expected to ride ahead of the main formations, some providing information and security, and, of no less significance, others launching raids and pursuits as opportunity offered: this was the cavalry's contribution to keeping the front fluid and the offensive moving.

The mission harked back to the days of Seydlitz and Murat, but the means were fundamentally different. While cavalry was still expected to do most of its work on horseback, the amount of time given to serious marksmanship training increased. The final version of the traditional carbine, the Kar 98, competed reasonably with the US Springfield, and was good enough to remain, slightly modified, as the standard German infantry rifle throughout World War II. Each cavalry division had four radio stations for communication, and a machine-gun detachment of six Maxims.[26]

The army also had a number of Jäger battalions: elite light infantry whose four rifle companies were supplemented by a cyclist company and a machine-gun company with six Maxims. The battalion also included a truck column, the ten vehicles of which were enough to keep the unit supplied and to run a shuttle service enabling the foot soldiers more or less to keep pace with the troopers under field conditions. This embryonic combined-arms battle group was hardly a breakthrough instrument, but a cavalry division or corps could usually count on having up to three of them attached to do the heavy lifting.

The German Army's emphasis on the tactical offensive was in no sense an unconsidered decision. The difficulties accompanying attack under modern conditions were recognized and accepted in Germany long before the first rounds were fired from the guns of August. But no army, however confident in its generals' abilities, could afford to base its doctrines on the assumption that enemies would be obliging enough to dash themselves to pieces on one's own rifles, artillery, and machine guns. Some time, somehow, it would be necessary to go forward and get through.

In war, as in so many other human endeavors, the necessary tends to become the possible. German doctrine did not assert advancing was easy, only that it was still feasible under the right conditions. Troop movements and fire support must be exactly coordinated. Attacks must be precisely timed. Reserves must be at hand immediately, when and where required, to bolster a weakening position and even more to exploit victory. In the absence of reliable short-range communications, even lieutenants must strike a fingertip balance between dispersion and control, keeping their men from bunching up on a skirmish line yet keeping them in hand for the final, decisive rush. Not romanticism but hard, practical considerations led the Second Reich's army to concentrate as heavily as it did on human factors.[27]

In this respect, paradoxically, the industrial revolution offered increasing grounds for optimism. Images of the Nineteenth-Century industrial worker frequently assert factory routines dulled the mind. The reverse was far more likely to be the case. Participation in a modern industrial plant demanded high degrees of alertness and cooperation. The miner, the mill hand, the iron worker, could rarely detach his mind from what his hands did, or from what his workmates were doing.[28] What civilian employers could do, the German Army saw itself able to do even better. In particular the revised drill regulations of 1906, which set the prewar infantry's doctrines and subtexts, recommended in paragraph after paragraph the need to develop inner assertiveness, the compulsion to reach an objective no matter the risks and costs, with orders or in their absence.[29] And the long distrusted, often despised factory workers might well set the example—Social Democrats or not!

The German Army's morale was more than the creation of blaring bands and cheering civilians. It was more than the belligerence of ignorance. German men who took the field in August 1914 were part of a society with a long tradition of compulsory military service. They were overwhelmingly either serving soldiers or men who had worn uniforms sometime earlier in their lives, however briefly. American military writer S. L. A. Marshall once declared that when a soldier is known to those around him, he has reason to fear losing the one thing he is likely to value more than life: his reputation as a man among men. The structure of the 1914 German Army was designed to foster this mutual knowledge and to take advantage of it.

IV

But how was this instrument of war to be best employed? The focus of that question, the Schlieffen Plan, has been challenged, and dismissed, as a military construction riddled with internal contradictions, a product of post-World War I myth making, and as something that never existed at all. To make sense of this debate, it is necessary to establish its basic perceptual context. Germany after 1871 had established itself as Europe's primary power. But did this mean Bismarck's "honest broker" or the casino croupier who takes a house percentage on every play? After Bismarck's dismissal in 1890, increasingly vocal social and economic pressure groups called for assertive global policies. This *Weltpolitik*, initially vaguely defined, was given a focal point by Alfred von Tirpitz, who proposed using sea power to make the Second Reich a superpower.

The army viewed the growing popularity of that vision with serious reservations. Inter-service rivalry and social conservatism played roles in establishing the trope of doubt. The key question, however, was the probable effect of this paradigm shift in policy on a continental strategic position that, in a worst-case scenario all too obvious, uncomfortably resembled a watermelon caught between two steel plates since the Russo-French alliance of 1894. Nor are the records innocent of evidence that in the run up to 1914 political and military leaders alike in Paris and St Petersburg accepted the premise that conflict was inevitable if their respective countries proposed to achieve their foreign policy objectives. Senior Russian officials from Tsar Nicholas down openly discussed hoped-for gains when Austria-Hungary finally disintegrated. French Colonel Cherles Mangin advocated raising a "black army" in sub-Saharan Africa for the purpose of restoring Lorraine to France. Such fulminations and prognostications were hardly *prima facie* evidence of warmongering. But neither were they exactly soothing in Berlin. Even Fritz Fischer, hardly an apologist for the Second Reich, conceded that after the completion of the Entente in 1907 Germany lived perpetually under the threat of a war on two fronts.[30]

The army's institutional response has been described above. The perceived consequence was a major contribution to the increasing concern for continental "encirclement," exacerbated by the highly predictable failure of *Weltpolitik*, the no less predictable decline of Germany's Austrian ally, and the wild card of Russia's perceived economic development and military recovery after the debacle of 1904–05. It is in those contexts that the first avatar of what for custom and convenience would be referred to as the Schlieffen Plan emerged.

Terence Zuber's highly controversial and intensively debated assertion that Schlieffen's original *Denkschrift* (memorandum) was not a genuine war plan, to say nothing of a prescription for a preemptive war, has obscured his more defensible position that the document is best considered as a position paper, intended to demonstrate Germany's precarious military position and argue for—what else?—substantial increases in the army's strength. The memorandum, moreover, did not advocate a tunnel-vision all-or-nothing drive on Paris. It incorporated a spectrum of scenarios, albeit scenarios with a common structure of a major operation against France. Based on the premise reasonable at the time that Russia would be out of the strategic equation for the near future, the prospect of a one-front war so enticed Schlieffen that he advocated a first strike against France in 1905 whose most logical course would have been an envelopment of the French left flank, in turn operationally calling for movement through the Low Countries.[31]

The Schlieffen Plan, in other words, was a war plan. It did exist. In later years its author significantly altered it to meet changing circumstances—including a French offensive followed by a German counterattack. But Schlieffen wrote from retirement, and his successor was anything but a mouthpiece. Helmuth von Moltke the Younger has been sufficiently mocked personally and excoriated professionally so that anything offered in mitigation seems revisionist.[32] To begin, the two chiefs faced the same threats, problems, and perspectives. Both were required to prepare, with smaller than optimal forces, solutions to an encirclement that was not only strategic but increasingly diplomatic. The army's institutional focus and its subaltern position in the Reich's political system meant that the solution would have a military focus, with policy aspects at most limited. It was scarcely surprising that their specific plans had a common paradigm: to wage not a two-front war, but two one-front wars in immediate succession: one involving a cavalry sword against a dueling epee, the other a rapier against a bludgeon. For all its acknowledged positive qualities, moreover, the French Army was to Germany what the German Navy was to Great Britain: a challenge no one doubted could be overcome, and overcome expeditiously.

The devil, as always, was in the details. No less than Schlieffen, Moltke was convinced the key to the swift, decisive victory Germany needed involved a massive sweep through Belgium, no matter what the French, Belgians, or even the British might do. If passage could be negotiated without a fight, so much the better. But when in 1914 German efforts in that quarter relied on threats and arm-twisting more than persuasion, Moltke did not even consider changing his strategic deployment plan, no matter that its implementation now involved overcoming the formidable fortress system of Liège: a tough and unpredictable nut to crack as a preliminary to a closely-timed campaign, and even if successful doing no more than creating a few-miles-wide bottleneck through which the entire right wing, over a half million strong, must pass.

As early as 1909, however, Moltke began to modify the plan. It began with his concern about even the short-term effect of an allied blockade of Germany. To secure the Netherlands as a neutral outlet, he abandoned any thought of incorporating them in his outflanking movement. In passing, it is worth considering that incorporating the Netherlands would have significantly weakened Germany's actual and projected force to space ratios: if France could not be taken out with a short right hook, a looping, underpowered swing might well prefigure an even more spectacular failure.

Even more significant for Moltke's revisions was the military resurgence of Russia. Combined with Austria's corresponding decline, it gave the tsarist Empire a far greater freedom of strategic action in much greater strength than anything previously projected. After 1905 the General Staff had maintained a contingency plan for a *Grosse Ostaufmarsch*, a Major Deployment East, but believed it impossible to implement except in the context of French—and after 1907 British—neutrality. This seemed so unlikely that in 1912 Moltke ordered the *Ostaufmarsch* not to be abandoned, as often asserted, but pigeonholed: no longer updated, but preserved for implementation should circumstances change.

The result was a complete focus on the French alternative, now more than ever an all or nothing proposition. What had begun in the military context of a quick, decisive victory had become a diplomatic and arguably a political/social imperative as well. Who knew what might be the domestic reaction if the bulk of the German Army was stymied in France while the Cossacks ravaged the eastern lands and rode towards Berlin? And what might be the consequences if the French actually broke through a southern sector held by only token forces? Italy had repeatedly promised to send a full army to the threatened sector. Well before 1914, however, its commitment to the Triple Alliance was essentially theoretical. As updated intelligence information indicated, the French were less likely to remain on the defensive than Schlieffen had projected in 1905, Moltke increased the number of troops available for the defenses of Alsace-Lorraine: for operational and political reasons the most probable site of a French offensive. By 1914 no fewer than eight corps were deployed in the southern sector. But their projected mission of holding the French in place, preventing their redeployment against the German pivot through Belgium and northern France, was designed to facilitate rather than complement the Great Wheel.

In no way was this a plan for a preventive war. It projected a preemptive war only in the sense of "do it to them before they do it to us." Given the relatively abstract, relatively ephemeral nature of the threats Germany faced, this was far more a *post facto* justification than a genuine preemptive operation like that initiated by Israel in 1967. And nor was the Schlieffen Plan—or the Schlieffen/Moltke Plan—a guaranteed formula for victory. It was closer to a gambler's gambit, requiring too many things to go impossibly right, and too many opponents to make obliging mistakes, to have anything but a gambler's chance of succeeding.

V

If the German Army emerges as more a facilitator than a designer of Germany's entry into World War I, the question remains: who *did* throw the switch?

The dominance of aristocratic elites and values at the foci of power, even in relatively open societies like Britain and France, is often described as a crucial cause of the Great War. Up-to-date types, businessmen, professionals, and administrators, are correspondingly assumed to have been relatively compromising and conciliatory. Genuine reactionaries, however, were as a type far less dangerous to peace than modern-minded men with cutting-edge views on power, race, history, politics, economics—even masculinity.

Germany was as up-to-date as any society in the world. The Empire's population was expanding. It was the leader in a broad spectrum of industrial and business activities. Its political system, with its synthesis of centralism and federalism, monarchy and populism, was seen as a work in progress, widely respected beyond German borders. Socially, culturally, intellectually, even sexually, Germany was a society of experimentation, a society seeking new forms. The consequence was instability. Dynamism was balanced by a sense of weakness, of vulnerable geographic and diplomatic positions, of ideas and practices subject to challenge by their very originality. Not for nothing has Imperial Germany been described as "the restless Reich:" a work in progress, never certain what it would become, or wished to become, when it grew up.[33] In that sense William II epitomized the country he governed, and believed he ruled.

Recent scholarship on the subject of the war's origins focuses less on culpability than contingency. Without denying the specific roles of ambition, belligerence, paranoia, and sheer incompetence, the emphasis is shifting to analysis of "chains of decisions" made by men who considered those decisions good ideas at the time. These were small groups, whose restrictively similar backgrounds made group dynamics more important than hierarchy or authority. In Germany there were enough of such groups that their interactions invited a low common denominator, what Stig Förster calls "polycratic chaos."[34] No preparations had been made, systematically over years or *ad hoc* at the beginning of the crisis, to determine supplies of raw materials, food, or basic military supplies. No serious negotiations with Austria-Hungary had been undertaken. Nothing like a council of state, not even an informal assemblage of "wise men" (or what might pass for such in the kaiser's Reich) discussed systematically the question of war and peace, the possible gains and the corresponding risks.

Nor were the shapers of German policy and opinion anything like united behind the postulated idea of a "fresh and decisive war" leading to results equivalent to those obtained in 1866 and 1871. Heinrich Class, long-time president of the Pan-German League and among the Reich's principal fire-eaters, nevertheless affirmed that a future war would be a heavy burden demanding the total energy of the German people and the willingness of every soldier to conquer or die. General Friedrich von Bernhardi, a leading spokesman for the uniformed war hawks, periodically described future conflict as a desperate exercise demanding a *Feldherr* with iron nerves.

Holger Herwig concludes that "a minuscule political and military elite" resorted to war as the best way of maintaining Germany as a great power.[35] It does not challenge that interpretation to amend it by suggesting that given the "almost critical lack of responsibility"[36] characterizing German decision-making in the summer of 1914, the army became a place of last resort, perhaps a refuge: the only institution in Germany that knew what it was doing and believed in itself—at least for public consumption. It was in the context of a Reich not merely restless but uncertain that the army accepted the task of preparing for a war that its own calculations suggested might well be unpredictable, uncontrollable, and ultimately unwinnable.

CHAPTER II

AUTUMN OF DECISION

War, especially at the beginning, is like a game of bridge. Bidding the contract is only a preliminary. The challenge lies in making it. And the German Army in August 1914 held a fistful of high cards. The kaiser announced a civic truce from the balcony of the imperial palace, declaring that henceforth he knew no parties, only Germans. The Socialist deputies in the Reichstag overwhelmingly voted for war credits. Newspapers from right to left underwrote and refined the trope of an unprovoked and justified war against a coalition taking advantage of a treacherous assassination to break up the Habsburg Empire, leaving Germany no choice from interest and honor except to intervene. Cheering crowds packed public spaces across the Reich, proclaiming support for a war that satisfied both interest and honor at no tangible cost—thus far.

I

Or so it seemed, on first impressions and in mythic retrospect. Contemporaries and historians alike have accepted until recently the German public's response to war as enthusiastic—indeed eager. The iconic photo of an unkempt Adolf Hitler cheering amid a jubilant throng in Munich has defined what is emerging as a far more complex, far more subdued response that most recollections of August 1914 were willing to recognize. The first crowds appeared in the streets on August 25, in major cities like Hamburg, Berlin, and Munich. If there was a dominant mood, it was to demonstrate support for Austria—seasoned by good-natured disorderliness on the part of young men out on the town. As the crowds grew in size day by day, the growing concern was for information—a concern driven by fear for the worst and hope that somehow this crisis, like all the others, would be averted, or at least localized.

The mood began to shift as lurid reports of Russian military preparations filled the newspapers. Rumors of mobilization circulated, especially in rural areas, confronting families with a grim prospect. It was one thing to seek the latest news as an interested bystander. It was another to face directly the near-universal certainty of sons, fathers, and husbands suddenly disappearing into uniform and boarding trains for who knew where. People began withdrawing savings and storing food. By July 30 shelves across Germany were emptying. Shops were refusing to take paper money. Banks stopped making loans and honoring withdrawals. Almost 300 antiwar rallies took place in Germany before July 30. Mostly Socialist in origin and presence, they nevertheless represented the kind of counterpoint that conservatives had feared ever since political socialism's emergence.

It is correspondingly significant that neither the civil nor the military authorities forbade or suppressed these meetings as long as they were not public. To a degree, that policy was motivated by inanition and distraction: there were enough administrative problems without seeking more. A calculated risk was involved as well. The popular mood was beginning to shift. Confirmation of Russia's general mobilization focused an original anxiety into affirmative solidarity, frequently manifested by street crowds singing hymns as well patriotic songs. There was cheering. There was enthusiasm. But much of this reflected relief from stress: the kind of relief one feels on finally entering the dentist's office! The second thoughts came that night—or next morning, as reservists of all categories began considering practicalities.[1]

For many young men, duty and patriotism outweighed even limited prudence. A quarter-million Germans volunteered for service in August 1914 alone. Over half were under twenty, the "conscription year." Over two-thirds were townsmen, representing a broad cross section of the small and middling bourgeoisie. The rest were workers—including almost eight hundred Socialist youth leaders.

In Britain, where until 1916 the army was raised entirely from volunteers, the rush came later, usually after significant self-questioning and discussion with family. In France the number of volunteers during the entire war was only 40,000, though it must be said that almost all Frenchmen were already on the rolls in August 1914. Germans simply signed on. In the war's first year the Potsdam Institute of Applied Psychology began collecting material for a psychographic study of "warriors." In answering the questions dealing with "war enthusiasm," one participant replied he had volunteered on the first day of mobilization, but from patriotism. Another stressed the national spirit he had imbibed in a student fraternity. A third declared himself unable to remain at home when family men were being called to arms. None spoke of hatred of Germany's enemies or anticipation of a "fresh and joyful" war. Most were at pains to express their preexisting awareness of modern war's brutal and tragic nature, despite ignorance of the details. But their country, the focal point of their experience and their identity, was under attack. A man had no choice but to take arms.[2]

These perceptions were only one subset of a quickly developing public understanding of Germany's war in quite precise terms as a defensive and existential conflict forced on a Germany unwilling to fight but prepared to do so—and win. That mindset informed a great majority of the 50,000 poems written in Germany during the war's first month. It also shaped the first days of a mobilization the pace of which might have been designed to leave no room for thought and recrimination. Twenty-four hours was not an unusual deadline for enlisted men to report—time to purchase a few non-regulation essentials, to reallocate one's domestic duties, to say goodbye, to say a prayer, perhaps to attend a church service for the men departing. The departures themselves were festive—at least for public purposes. The men were festooned with flowers, and given so many sweets that the soldiers were getting sick. And perhaps the cakes and candies were only an excuse. Beneath the cheers there were few illusions about the risks. Children picked up their parents' tension. There were more tears than cheers as the trains pulled out of the stations—and the cheers were likely to be in part anodyne, camouflage for less patriotic, less "manly" emotions.[3]

The transition from peace to war was greatly facilitated by the fact that the mobilization system functioned efficiently. In a sense it resembled a reunion, particularly for the men more recently discharged—and for the cadres, who rejoiced at some arrivals and regretted others: "Just don't assign Musketeer Schmidt and his two left feet to my platoon!" Both active and reserve regiments, organized in the same depots, were able to move out within the six to eight days normally authorized. The typical reserve regiment, which confronted far greater challenges than its active counterpart, began its existence on the second day of mobilization. The army had been able to lay in more or less full stocks of equipment. Boots and clothing were marked and sized to specific wearers. Every man had a rifle, and most were of modern pattern. In most battalions two or three of the company commanders and first sergeants were active soldiers, and able to keep confusion to a minimum. By the fourth day of mobilization the companies were up to strength, and reservists surplus to requirements in heavily populated districts—almost a hundred thousand from Westphalia's VII Corps alone—were on their way to corps less well endowed. As medical officers weeded out the less fit, the rest spent the next three days in fitting uniforms (especially boots), target practice, and route marches with full field equipment. No less important was accustoming new drivers to strange horses, and both to managing fully loaded wagons. But on August 9, the 15th Reserve Infantry Regiment, for example, was ready for the field: eighty officers, 3,230 enlisted men, and six machine guns.[4]

Germany's reservists took the field in 1914 with a boost unmatched in Europe's mass conscript armies. The smooth and rapid mobilization was more than an administrative *tour de force* and a strategic advantage. It contributed significantly to morale, and thereby effectiveness, by affirming the army's "culture of competence." The ability to provide boots that fit, deliver reasonably edible food, and have the troop trains run on time conveyed a sense that the system knew what it was doing that compensated for massive eventual levels of tactical ineffectiveness and strategic cluelessness.

The number of reservists who failed to report and failed to account for themselves was minuscule. In part that reflected willingness to accept the official justification for the war, in a lifetime context of participation in the state system—even committed socialists paid taxes and streetcar fares. In part reporting for duty reflected as well an absence of feasible alternatives. In a highly bureaucratized society, disappearing was difficult enough to be practically impossible without the kind of active/passive supporting networks that only developed after years of bloody stalemate.[5]

The army might have put "a nation in barracks," but the result in 1914 was less a people of warriors than a state of citizens in uniform. When the initial shakedowns and shakeouts were finished, there were over two million of them, active, reserve, and Landwehr. Almost a million Ersatz reservists remained unassigned, available to replace casualties and form new units: six divisions at the start. Most of the Landwehr was organized in brigades for rear security and lines of communications duty; there were also four divisions available for secondary missions. But the army's core, when account is taken of bits and pieces left scattered around the Reich, was its thirty-nine army corps: twenty-five active, fourteen reserve, and one hybrid, the Guard Reserve Corps.

It was a deck with a hole card in plain sight. Since 1875 German mobilization plans had incorporated "field reserve" divisions from reservists surplus to the active army's requirements. Initially considered rear-echelon formations, their status changed as debates on allocating the military budget and emphasis on a short decisive war found common ground in questioning the wisdom of holding back trained men who might provide decisive weight at the front. A decades-long process of trial and error on paper and in maneuvers resulted not only in organizing the reservists as full army corps, but in projecting their deployment alongside their active counterparts, with the same kinds of missions and expectations.

That was a major anomaly for a major military power. Most of Austria-Hungary's reservists were absorbed in a peacetime army whose active formations were kept at low strength by budget issues. Both France and Russia, however, incorporated reserves—divisions of them—into their mobilization plans. Russia did face real problems of deploying reservists expeditiously, given the remoteness of most mobilization centers and the limits of the rail system. France had no such excuses. Neither army, however, expected reservists, individually or collectively, to meet the demands of modern industrial warfare. Reserve formations were consistently stinted of cadres, equipment, and attention. They were kept as far from the front lines as reasonably possible. To borrow the American Civil War General James Longstreet's phrase, French and Russian generals chose to go into battle with one boot off. They would find themselves limping soon enough.

Providing cadres and equipment was not as easy as producing paperwork. In human terms, much depended on the officers and NCOs called up in the general mobilization. How much of their service did they remember? No less important, how much did they need to forget? In terms of equipment, the best the budget could fund and the factories deliver to the reserve corps was seventy-two flat-trajectory cannon: no howitzers of any kind, no air squadron, no bridging train. Twenty-five reserve regiments, almost a fourth of the total, took the field without a machine-gun company. But if all went according to plan, these shortfalls would make no difference.[6]

That was a big "if," and the railroad system did its part and more to bring it about—with more than a little assistance from the Railway Section of the General Staff and the hard-driving workaholic in charge of it. Lieutenant Colonel Wilhelm Gröner was one of the army's "new men." As a Württemberger and the son of an NCO he was twice an outsider by Old Prussian standards. He had made his way through the War Academy and the General Staff by talent, character, and industry. He ran second to a similar type, Colonel Erich Ludendorff, when Moltke the Younger had to select a chief of operations. But Gröner's eventual assignment was anything but a consolation prize. Operations depended on mobilization. Gröner was the mainspring of the mobilization's key institution. In 1912 he became its head. In 1914 he proved the right man for the right spot.[7]

A German military train was structured by capacity: 600 tons of men, horses, and equipment loaded into a mix of freight and passenger cars, usually around fifty, with the exact mix depending on the number of officers on board. "Forty and eight:" forty men or eight horses, a Great War universal, was the standard load. Speed was surprisingly slow. A maximum of around twenty miles an hour on a main line allowed for mechanical and administrative problems while enabling essential civilian traffic. Some trains moved men and supplies to the concentration zones. An active corps required around 140 of them. There were thirteen rail lines designated for deployment, and on average they carried a train every ten minutes. Other trains—many others, over 20,000 altogether—crisscrossed the Reich in all directions, carrying reservists to their depots, evacuating civilians from at-risk border areas, and not least relocating the East Prussian stud farms the horses of which provided the basis of the army's mobility once it disembarked.[8]

The rail deployment and its internal counterpoint worked with the kind of precision that led A. J. P. Taylor to talk of war by timetable. Trains crossed the Rhine at an average rate of 563 a day—one every ten minutes at Cologne's Hohenzollern Bridge. The mood on the trains was uniformly high, almost exuberant. Doggerel rhymes promised to teach Germany's enemies a badly needed lesson. Men sang the nostalgic, sentimental farewell songs associated with the *Wanderjahr* ("travel year") once associated with craft apprenticeship, and more recently with emigration. Songs like "The Watch on the Rhine" reechoed, especially as the men from the hinterlands saw the great river and its bustling war-themed activity. This was the first time most Germans had seen much of the land they would be fighting for. The weather was fine; the scenery tourist-worthy; and the crowds in the railway stations no less enthusiastic than at home. In many regiments crossing the Rhine itself was an emotional experience, confirming the combination of duty and patriotism increasingly infusing the ranks as groupthink replaced nostalgia.

Once off the trains, most of the men faced their first serious marching from the railheads to the forward concentration zones. It speaks arguably better for German training and planning than even the railroad deployment that over two million men and over a hundred thousand horses, none of them with any relevant experience, accomplished that task without collapsing into confusion. The administrators had done their jobs. Now it was the time of the soldiers.

Seven armies were strung out from Switzerland to the Belgian–German frontier, awaiting the starting gun. Their collective physical appearance may have been impressively uniform, but their human dynamics were kaleidoscopic. A persistent misunderstanding of the Second Reich's higher command system is that the generals were mostly either crowned figureheads or elderly excellencies doddering towards retirement. In this construction, real authority rested with the men with carmine stripes on their trousers: the general staff officers who pushed the buttons and pulled the strings. Reality was more complicated. Since its inception during the Wars of Liberation, the relationship between a corps or army commander and his chief of staff was intended to be symbiotic and synergistic. The commander provided experience, gravitas, example, and in a hierarchic society the status to secure respect. The *chef* focused on the technical aspects, broadly defined: march routes, troop dispositions, logistics, operational planning. His right of direct communication with the General Staff was no secret, but intended less as a safety valve or "second road" than a means of settling details quickly.

The relationship, in short, resembled a marriage—an arranged marriage. In a society where such arrangements remained familiar at all levels through the Nineteenth Century, the dynamics were neither unfamiliar nor necessarily uncongenial. The pairings, particularly at army levels, were considered with the same care that the army's stud farms took in matching mares and stallions. Successful interaction nevertheless depended heavily on behaviors seasoned with a strong dose of common sense.[9]

Those points made, there remained a good deal of politics behind the senior appointments. On the far left, the army was commanded by Josias von Heeringen. A former Prussian war minister, he had a solid record behind a desk and at sixty-four seemed a safe pair of hands for the limited assignment of acting as the base of the invasion. His four successive neighbors were a different matter. Crown Prince Rupprecht of Bavaria took his military career seriously, as the best way for a Bavarian ruler to stand out in a Prussian-dominated Reich. A qualified general staff officer, his career had primarily been spent as a troop commander, where he had earned solid respect as a commander and a leader. His chief of staff, Konrad Krafft von Dellmensingen, had since 1912 held that post in the Bavarian Army, which had its own general staff linked closely to its imperial counterpart. He was widely and legitimately recognized as the pick of Bavaria's stable, disqualified only by his unfortunate place of birth from moving higher. Their Sixth Army included four Bavarian corps, and had the mission of anvil, enabling the movement of the right flank while fending off any serious French offensive against the hinge.

Rupprecht's right-flank neighbor would become the most controversial of Germany's wartime appointments. Imperial Crown Prince William got his job literally by accident. The Fifth Army's designated commander, Hermann von Eichhorn, who had commanded an army inspection before the war and was altogether an appropriate choice, had been injured earlier in a riding accident. His replacement almost immediately became a figure of fun to Allied propagandists: "Little Willie," commanding by virtue of birth and making a consistent botch of it, by his father's orders the stooge of his *chef,* Konstantin Schmidt von Knobelsdorf. "Whatever he says you must do," the kaiser allegedly told his heir. Knobelsdorf had just finished supervising the Crown Prince's brief period of training with the General Staff, and the ambivalence of that student–teacher relationship was never quite resolved. But Knobelsdorf had thirty years of experience, was considered a candidate to succeed Moltke, and was assigned first-rate subordinates. Nor was William one to overrate his own military capacities, and he would show better judgment than expected as the war progressed.

William's neighbor made the royalty list three in a row. Duke Albrecht of Württemberg was closer to Rupprecht than William in experience and ability. His chief of staff Walther von Lüttwitz had a reputation for unspectacular competence. His Fourth Army included Württemberg's two corps, and was the first in the sequence to have a really challenging mission: functioning as the pivot for the right wing as it swept across Belgium.

Rupprecht, William, and Albrecht exemplified the enduring federal nature of the Second Reich. The non-Prussian contingents, Bavaria, Württemberg, and Saxony, retained and sustained significant rights, guaranteeing various degrees of autonomy and not to be ignored even in a war for the empire's survival.[10] Saxony might perhaps have been better served had it too had a prince with similar military qualifications. The Third Army, part of the right wing, was overwhelmingly Saxon: three of its four corps. Its commander, Max von Hausen, had been Saxony's war minister from 1902 to 1914 and was summoned from a brief retirement to command Third Army. He seems to have dominated his chief of staff, Ernst von Höppner, but would prove not so much cautious as indecisive at too many points in the coming weeks.

The consistent problem of selecting higher commanders was "who might do a better job?" Obvious candidates were thin on the ground, and no better proof existed than Karl von Bülow. He was not an incompetent—anything but. He had served in the War Ministry, been deputy chief of the General Staff, and commanded a peacetime army inspection—the latter an administrative job, but the highest troop assignment available. At sixty-eight, he was reasonably vigorous and his health seemed fairly good. Moltke regarded him as the best of Germany's army commanders: systematic, precise, with a reputation as a drillmaster, he was a clear choice to command the right wing's pivot and keep a weather eye on Hausen and the Saxons. On the other side of the equation, Bülow had never displayed any qualities beyond those of what British military shorthand calls "a good plain cook:" certainly no signs of the *coup d'oeil* to command six army corps, or the energy to force the pace of an advance that could afford no delays, whether from enemy action or internal fog and friction.

Those latter qualities were more obviously present in Alexander von Kluck, who commanded the Schlieffen Plan's sledgehammer. The First Army had no fewer than seven corps plus cavalry and Landwehr: a challenging assignment for the most talented subordinates of Napoleon Bonaparte or Robert E. Lee. Kluck at least looked the part: grim-faced and bullet-headed, with jowls still in place and a stomach still resting mostly above his belt line. Middle-class by birth and Westphalian by heritage, he had risen by merit, making his reputation in East Prussia as an aggressive, risk-taking opponent in maneuvers, a good trainer, a solid administrator, popular and respected among his subordinates. Raised to the nobility in 1909, he commanded the Eighth Army Inspectorate before taking charge of the First Army. Surveying the list of eligibles, Kluck was as good a choice as any for the invasion's key field command, and most probably better than most. His chief of staff Hermann von Kuhl was widely respected in general staff circles as a historian and an intellectual, a protégé of Schlieffen's insofar as any existed, as aggressive and decisive as Kluck himself.

Any armed force going to war after an extended period of peace, or even of irrelevant combat, takes gamblers' chances with its senior command structure. But even allowing for inexperience, comparing the mobilization/concentration performance with its initial command experience strongly supports an argument that the German Army had spent far more time preparing for war than thinking about it. The senior generals as a group were the system's creations and servants, and consequently were unlikely to act outside the box should anything go significantly wrong. That in turn meant the responsibility for fixing their system would have to devolve downward to the field soldiers—thereby reinforcing the operational/tactical orientation generally fostered in the Imperial Army since the Franco-Prussian War.

II

The virgin soldiers who disembarked, stretched boxcar-cramped limbs, and started for the frontier under the August sun, gave the near-universal impression of a drab, anonymous flood. In 1910 the Imperial Army had introduced a field uniform, grey with a greenish tint: with a bit of wear the color blended well with smoke, mud, and central Europe's late-fall foliage. Tradition, however, was served at the feet and head. In contrast to the heavy shoes and puttees favored in most armies, Germany clung to calf-high leather boots as providing better protection and support on the march and less likely to impede circulation. The headgear, however, was vestigial. The leather spiked helmet, the *Pickelhaube*, would provide Allied troops with the war's most prized souvenir. For its wearers it was a literal pain in the neck, offering no protection from rain or sun, and its gray cloth field cover only enhanced its qualities as a heat conductor.

To the average soldier, what he carried was more important than what he wore. He carried as much as seventy pounds, most of it in a knapsack nicknamed *Affe*, "monkey:" the eventual source of the English-language trope of someone with an addiction or a problem carrying "a monkey on their back." Six ammunition pouches, bayonet and entrenching tool, mess kit and haversack, were suspended from a harness of belts and straps designed to distribute weight evenly over the upper body with a minimum of movement-impeding handles and straps dangling below the waist. Sometimes it even worked as designed.[11]

Not even Teutonic artifice could keep a fully equipped infantry private from resembling the proverbial Christmas tree. The German soldier was, however, fortunate in that his superiors did not emphasize spit and polish for its own sake in the field. If lacking the freedom of their French opposite numbers to leave everything unbuckled and unbuttoned except their flies, as time passed German privates nevertheless tended to look positively scruffy in the field and on the march.

In the 1870s army doctors had evaluated the merits of the coca leaf as a source of quick energy on the march, a possible cure for colic, constipation, and hypochondria.[12] In 1914 soldiers still depended on tobacco, alcohol—officially available only when authorized—and above all hot, high-caloric food and strong coffee. The German soldier's haversack contained only emergency rations, to be touched only on an officer's authorization. The dietary basics were bread baked in more or less stationary field bakeries, meat provided by similar butcheries, and vegetables and seasonings shipped from Germany or obtained locally by purchase or requisition. Just before the war, the army had introduced kitchens on wheels, able to boil coffee and cook stew on the move—thus the nickname *Gulaschkanonen*—and issue them at any convenient halt. This was particularly important for men likely to end a day too weary to take any pains with anything, and the initial inability to supply all the reserve regiments with the regulation number of kitchens was arguably no less significant in the war's initial stages than the corresponding absence of howitzers.

The army moved by corps, acted as corps, and thought in terms of corps. These were territorially recruited for the purpose of facilitating mobilization. For morale purposes, corps districts coincided whenever possible with provincial boundaries or historic regions. All boasted their own traditions, their own heroes, their own dialects: prefabricated cohesion. The strength of a corps had originally been calculated as the number of men able to come into action in a single day from a single line of march: during the Wars of Unification this was about 30,000 men. Additions, particularly of more guns and the ammunition trains to feed them, had brought the numbers of an active corps to around 40,000, with reserve corps a few thousand less. A force that size usually needed more than one road, which meant utilizing local, unimproved routes and even country tracks.

Fog and friction was further exacerbated by organization. The German corps of 1914 was a binary system: two divisions, each of two brigades with two regiments. Operationally the brigade was an extra link. The telephone and the automobile enabled a division commander to control his regiments directly, and a division with four regiments had a flexibility that could prove welcome in the maneuver warfare projected and planned for: executing a primary and a secondary tactical mission while retaining a strong reserve to exploit success. Institutionally, the German structure was a legacy of Prussia's Napoleonic-era military reform movement, reflexively copied in the intervening years across continental Europe. *Sub rosa*, the brigade system also provided an additional layer of higher commands in an army increasingly concerned about the limited promotion opportunities for senior officers.

The German corps commander was nevertheless expected to fight his corps as an entity. His major supporting arms, the heavy howitzer battalion for firepower, an air squadron for reconnaissance, and a bridging train for emergencies, were under his direct command. He expected, and was expected, to be known and recognized throughout his formation. Corps command was the accepted capstone of an ambitious officer's successful career. Beyond lay only the ephemera of army inspections, which might seem mere baubles compared to the power and status a corps commander enjoyed in his own district.

Absent a detailed prosographic analysis, particularly when compared to their immediate superiors, German corps commanders in 1914 could legitimately be described as the pick of the litter, the best of the best insofar as that could be determined without the ultimate test. Their counterparts in the reserve corps were usually a few years older, with the corresponding issues of health and energy, but their service records were not inferior in any distinguishable way. A good few seem to have been retired because of there being "more generals than slots," denied corps command for the same reasons obtaining in any peacetime system: irritating the wrong people, making the wrong enemies, or just becoming eligible for promotion at the wrong time.

So another element was added to the German Army's operational–tactical orientation downward focus in August 1914. This point has so often been made and repeated—including in the present text—that it is easy to overlook the synergy among war's "four levels:" policy, strategy, operations, and tactics. The perceptive policy, or a coherent strategy, does not guarantee victory. Wars can be and are decided at their sharp end. Armed forces unable to execute in the field can compensate for shortcomings and frustrations at higher levels of planning and preparation. *That* was the challenge Germany faced. How well would the army respond?

Initial experiences were disconcerting. On the right wing, the First and Second armies, almost 600,000 men and over 400 battalions, were stacking up on each other in the few square miles in front of Liège. The crucial point was in danger of becoming a sticking point. If the Liège bottleneck could not be cleared promptly, the odds were that none of the rest of the German strategic plan was going to matter. This would be a case study in a pattern of soon-to-be-familiar devolution of German war-making's focus downward, from policy and strategy to the level of specific tactical problems. A major strategic and industrial center, Liège was defended by a system of detached steel-and-concrete forts begun in the 1880s, regularly and recently updated, and regarded as being as formidable as anything on the continent. Their overcoming was the responsibility of a task force formed from six brigades on a peace footing. Seriously underestimating Belgian skill and will, expecting sufficiently limited resistance to enable carrying the position by *coup de main*, the Germans instead initially suffered heavy casualties—heavy at least by peacetime standards—against a determined defense the effectiveness of which was enhanced by German inexperience. By the end of August 8, after five blazing days, Liège still held out and the German invasion plan hung by a thread, at least psychologically. The German deployment was admittedly still in progress, not to be fully completed until August 17, though the First Army was in place by the 14th. Trains were arriving and unloading on schedule, but Liège was a bottleneck unprovided for in prewar plans—an anxiety-generating wild card challenging methods, preparations, and scheduling.[13]

Meanwhile the "real" war had begun in the location arguably considered least likely by the German General Staff. France's Plan XVII was significantly more contingent than its German counterpart. It was a concentration plan, designed to bring maximum force to the northeast frontier in case of war. Its intention was to deliver, with those forces, an all-out attack against the German armies—an attack delivered in response to whatever moves the Germans made. Plan XVII, in other words, was not a blueprint for specific operations. As the German intention of driving through Belgium became clear, French commanding general Joseph Joffre proposed a two-pronged riposte. The main blow would be on his left, against the German center: the hinge of their advance into Belgium. It would be preceded by a jab, initially almost a feint, into Alsace-Lorraine, to attract German attention and German reserves, boost French domestic morale, and convince Russia that its ally took its obligations seriously. On June 7, French vanguards entered Alsace.[14]

A day earlier, Krafft had informed Moltke that Sixth and Seventh Armies would fight an initial delaying action, then counterattack once their full strength was deployed. Moltke approved. There was, however, a significant drawback. Heeringen had an extreme and well-known dislike for Bavarians, a legacy of his time as Prussia's war minister. He had no intention of deferring to the *Weissblauen*, despite mobilization orders putting him under Sixth Army's control. When the French took Mulhouse on August 8, Heeringen contacted Moltke directly and requested authorization to counterattack. Moltke approved; Rupprecht and Krafft pouted. Heeringen's attack succeeded with heavy casualties, unexpectedly heavy expenditure of ammunition, and at the price of weakening the link between the two armies. Moltke responded by confirming Rupprecht's command of an informal army group, and by ordering him to undertake no more than local offensives under favorable conditions. On August 14 the French First and Second Armies began a full scale invasion of Alsace-Lorraine.

Meanwhile Rupprecht and Krafft were turning the situation in the south to their tactical advantage. Joffre timed his full-scale offensive in this sector for policy reasons: to coincide with the projected date of Russia's attack in the east. Seven corps and a corps-sized group of reserve divisions advanced into France's lost provinces, increasingly slowed by rain, and taking increasingly heavy casualties from well-handled German artillery and determined German rear guards often built around machine guns. Krafft suggested using the retreat as a preliminary to luring the French into a pocket, perhaps even letting them cross into Germany, then counterattacking in force. Initially Moltke was interested. But the determined resistance of Sixth Army's Bavarians slowed the French advance, and Moltke was unwilling to sacrifice German soil even for a possible Cannae *manqué*. His directive: adhere to the original plan.

The Bavarian command team was frustrated by what it called Moltke's vagueness, by Heeringen's unwillingness to cooperate, and by what Krafft complained was a passivity that would weaken the Bavarians' offensive spirit. More than simple dynastic vanity underwrote that last concern. In the Franco-German War* the Bavarian Army had been the German weak link. Too large to be sidetracked, its training, its leadership, and its replacement system were consistently overstressed.[15] There were enough embarrassing checks and lapses to make the Bavarians something of a joke among the Prussians, and for the next forty years the Royal Bavarian Army had sought assiduously to shed the tag of second best. Bavaria's official historian of the campaign calls it a mistake to have deployed the high-quality army of Germany's second-largest state in a secondary theater. If mistake it was, the driving force was not political rivalry but railway scheduling: Lorraine was the shortest distance from Bavaria in a situation where time was everything.[16]

In any case, Krafft and Rupprecht badly wanted the war's first major battle to be a Bavarian show. On August 17 they ordered Heeringen to close up for a counterattack on the 19th. The same day the High Command despatched an ambassador to Sixth Army's headquarters. By no coincidence, the officer was head of the General Staff's Political Section. Lieutenant Colonel Wilhelm von Dommies diplomatically repeated Moltke's intention that Sixth and Seventh Armies continue their fighting withdrawal and stand firm: there were to be no adventures, and they must secure the invasion's left flank. Rupprecht's response was "give me a free hand or specific orders." Dommies brought no written order of any kind, and was sufficiently intimidated by the meeting that according to Rupprecht he left behind his helmet and sword: a rough Prussian equivalent of forgetting one's trousers.[17]

Krafft was nevertheless sufficiently concerned to phone headquarters with his intention to attack. The response, delivered by Moltke's deputy, Quartermaster-General Hermann von Stein, was "it is your responsibility." It is worth noting that Stein's responsibilities were on the logistical side, not the operational. It is worth noting as well that the prevailing attitude in Oberste Heeresleitung (OHL) was that Rupprecht would manage simultaneously to

---

* The final War of German Unification goes by two names in the history books. It began as a Franco-Prussian War, with Prussia having several allied German states. By the end it was a Franco-German War—not merely because the German Empire had been officially proclaimed, but because men from all over Germany had paid a common blood price for victory and unity.

lead the French on and defeat them by an offensive. This casting of fate to the winds boded ill for systematic execution of any general plan of campaign.

Sixth Army's forward units crossed their start lines at 3:30 am on August 20. Almost immediately they ran into a French advance that began about the same time. The result was a confused grapple over eighty miles of broken terrain, decided—as much as the word can be applied—by relative German fire superiority and relative German skill in minor tactics. The Bavarians kept the initiative; by day's end the French Second Army was streaming back in disorder amounting in too many cases to downright panic. Its commander, General Edouard-de Castelnau, ordered a retreat to his original start lines. Second Army's collapse opened the flank of First Army on Castelnau's left. It fell back in turn, in one case at least with bands defiantly playing.

The Bavarians followed up their victory the next day with a flank movement supported by what seemed to the French to be all the guns in the world. Resistance collapsed almost immediately and Castelnau ordered a further retrograde movement. Regiments that were already shaken disintegrated. Stragglers spread alarm and despondency far and wide. Civilians joined the western-bound uniformed throng, setting at defiance an already clueless traffic-control system. The retreat only stopped around the fortress of Nancy.

French casualties were never accurately calculated, nor did the war diaries provide much useful information on specifics. Between them, First and Second Armies had lost probably around 10,000 men on August 20 alone, and at least that many again in the succeeding days. In Munich they displayed flags and cheered Bavaria's king, Ludwig III. Kaiser William spoke of the greatest victory in the history of war. But the Bavarians were so shaken and disorganized by that victory that it took three days to develop anything resembling a pursuit—days the French used to replace their casualties and recover their equilibrium. The Battle of Lorraine was the first case study of what became a Great War cliché: there can be a great deal of ruin in a modern army.

Heeringen, no more cooperative than ever, had fought his own separate but similar battle in the Vosges and across the plain of Alsace. The Seventh Army was in no better state of organization than the Sixth: the staffs of both were reacting with shock to the intensity and the destructiveness of modern high-tech war. Landwehr and Ersatz formations, intended for rear-echelon duty, had been almost immediately committed to the front line as reinforcements. Blood was the price of their improvised character and the limited training of many of their personnel. Stalemate was the immediate result.

Initially Rupprecht and Krafft intended to shift their axis north to support the Fifth Army, which was more heavily engaged than had been expected. Eventually, however, the High Command informed them that the railway network could bring their troops no further than Aachen. By the time they marched the rest of the way to the combat zone, the issue would be settled. To the north, the German Fourth and Fifth Armies had begun advancing northwest into the Ardennes on August 18, screened by a cavalry corps and initially meeting limited resistance. The advance began on August 18, but its pace was limited by a thin road network, broken terrain, and high humidity. Three days later, Joseph Joffre sent his Third and Fourth Armies into the Ardennes from the other direction. The French generalissimo, by now aware of the massive German concentration in Belgium and the probable scope of its advance, reckoned with relatively weaker opposition in the center, and expected to disrupt the enemy offensive by dislocating its hinge.[18]

Heat, haze, and thunderstorms handicapped aerial reconnaissance, but the German cavalry outperformed its French counterparts by discovering and reporting that the French were on the move in force. The Fifth Army responded by proposing an attack. Moltke refused; Knobelsdorf proceeded anyway, perhaps from conviction that this was how a German field army should confront its foe, perhaps from ambition. The movement, however, would leave the Fifth Army's right exposed and open. A staff officer passed that information north, and the Fourth Army's left flank corps requested permission to turn south and take the cover slot. Albrecht agreed, despite the fact that two of his three corps were a day's march in the rear.

The result was a misbegotten, murderous, and until recently almost forgotten encounter battle in the Ardennes.[19] Better expressed, it was a series of separate battles, head to head and corps against corps. The signature combat took place around Rossignol, where the French Colonial Corps was outflanked and broken, taking almost 12,000 casualties. Another French corps disintegrated. A third was defeated by a single German brigade—itself initially outflanked. Overall the Germans dominated the battlefield tactically, employing improvised entrenchments effectively, deploying more quickly, making better use of ground, and understanding that the rifle was more than something on which to fix a bayonet. German artillerymen demonstrated that it was the men who mattered more than the guns, consistently neutralizing the technically superior French 75s, leaving the infantry to demonstrate their dash and valor without effective fire support. French tactics did not, as so often asserted, depend entirely on heedless bayonet charges. Inadequate training, limited flexibility, and not less, inferior marksmanship left the men in the ranks to be ground down by an enemy who understood and applied war's minutiae.

The consequences were predictable. Across the battlefront the French suffered three or four times the casualties they inflicted. Arguably even more significant than the imbalance in losses was the fact that the German reserve regiments proved at least equal to their active-service opponents—an unexpected shock to a French Army that considered its reserve formations useful at best for secondary missions. Another set of consequences was no less predictable, but a deal less obvious. German losses had not been light, particularly among junior officers and NCOs. German flexibility had resulted in disrupted chains of command, with companies dispersed almost at random to plug holes or exploit opportunities in the terrain. Marching and digging had tired garrison- and civilian-soft soldiers; their first day of combat had been even more exhausting, emotionally no less than physically. All of these would become hallmarks at the sharp end of Great War battles, though there was nothing new about any of them. The differences were of degree—not only degree of intensity but degree of reach. The Fifth Army's headquarters, GHQ and corps alike, were suffering their own versions of traumatic stress. Nervous systems, institutional and emotional, had been strained to the limit. From army headquarters forward, electronic communications were random at best. Runners and messengers were killed, got lost, or presented outdated information. Unable to acquire or process information on the state of the French, all too conscious of their own randomized situation, William and Knobelsdorf initially decided to stand in place the next day. Optimistic reports of victory from the combat zones and a free hand from the high command were not enough to overcome the inertia of victory. The Fourth Army occupied some vacated terrain, but no more than that.

Had Joffre's intentions for August 23 been fulfilled, the Germans might have turned a tactical victory to an operational one just by remaining in position and on the defensive. The French generalissimo, ignorant of the real state of affairs, ordered the attack to be continued. Chances of success depended on sequential changes of fortune unlikely to be forthcoming in a sphere of activity where luck is almost always the residue of design. His army commanders, initially no less confused as to what had happened forward of their headquarters, then responded to an unfolding reality by a general retreat. Within two days the French central armies were back in their starting positions, seriously bloodied and badly shaken, with over 40,000 dead plus those wounded and taken prisoner.

Joffre reacted by preparing proscription lists of failed subordinates. By September 6 he would relieve two armies, ten corps, and thirty-eight division commanders: a "hecatomb of generals," a modern counterpart of the French revolution's "red widow," *Madame la Guillotine,* and like her intended "to encourage the rest." Armies, like fish, can rot from the head.[20]

The Germans were facing the same situation—only geographic instead of human. Their "head" was at Liège, where the single bright spot had been a General Staff colonel making his way into the city, demanding and securing the surrender of its citadel single-handed. Erich Ludendorff would be heard from again. But his "hussar's trick," in German military parlance, did nothing to change the situation, although the citadel's capture made headlines throughout Germany. It led the kaiser to shower kisses on Moltke, who one hopes was suitably disconcerted. But Liège's forts continued to hold out, and to block the German advance.

William reacted to that news like a frustrated lover, excoriating Moltke for bringing Britain into the war by invading Belgium. The badly-strained chief of staff responded with an outburst of tears. At the cutting edge, however, the army found its feet—and discovered Liège's weaknesses. The forts, state of the art at their construction, had never been systematically updated. There was no internal communications network, no systematic integration of machine guns into the fire plans. Ventilation systems were rudimentary. Sanitary arrangements ranged from primitive to nonexistent. In 1910 the German Army had introduced an updated 21-cm mortar, designed to crack open Liège-style concrete. The Second Army had four battalions of them. When the *coup de main* failed, they began moving into position. They were to do the heavy work of disabling the forts one by one, destroying guns, blowing up magazines, knocking out power. The combined stench of fumes and excrement further demoralized garrisons still getting used to their uniforms. The vaunted 42-cm "Big Berthas" arrived in time to complete the process and garner the publicity. Between August 13 and August 15 a half-dozen forts were more or less spectacularly disabled. The remaining two surrendered on the 17th.

The way to France was open. How much time had the Belgians bought? The French said ten days, the British four or five, the Germans said none at all. Gröner's railway men did their part by repairing the Aachen–Liège lines. The real damage, however, was psychological. Moltke never quite recovered from the Imperial tongue-lashing, and spent as much of his remaining tenure looking over his shoulder as focusing on the Great Advance. And that situation was becoming increasingly uncertain.

Whatever potential the cavalry might have had to contribute to a quick, decisive victory, it was dissipated literally in a matter of days. The often-cited overemphasis on mounted tactics had less to do with that development than prewar issues of structure and deployment. Ten of Germany's eleven cavalry divisions were created on mobilization, so their subordinate units were correspondingly unused to working together except occasionally and *ad hoc* during maneuvers. Their staffs were too small—fewer than eighty men including grooms and orderlies—to provide effective control. The radio sets intended to facilitate communication were so heavy and unreliable that they tended to be left in the rear echelons. Logistics were an ill-considered compromise between mobility and supply, with trains kept to a minimum. Cavalry regiments, correspondingly short of food, ammunition, and above all forage, were expected to make up the difference by living off the country as they advanced, or by relying on the nearest army corps. The results were predictable: delay, confusion, empty stomachs and above all empty nosebags.

Matters were worse at higher levels. The "Higher Cavalry Commands" (Höheres Kavallerie-Kommando), though usually Anglicized as "cavalry corps," were also improvised, with small staffs and no logistical structure. Intended as much to coordinate mounted operations as to command them, the HKKs reflected the General Staff's uncertainty of exactly how best to use its cavalry. The principal missions, somewhat by default, were close reconnaissance, the purview of the divisional cavalry, and screening—the implementation of which involved spreading out the HKKs ahead of the armies along the entire front like beads on a string. The decision was hardly a complete waste; the German advance as a whole benefitted from the cavalry's success in keeping its French opponents—and its British ones as well—essentially in the dark regarding troop movements. The drawback was that the crucial right flank, intended to strike the decisive blow, had a single HKK of three divisions—around 15,000 men all told. These were expected simultaneously to cover the German advance, keep the Belgian Army from making an organized retreat towards the fortress of Antwerp, and track the arrival and deployment of the BEF (British Expeditionary Force). And fewer than two weeks into the war, on August 12, while Liège was still under attack, the HKK suffered a check that threw it off balance for the rest of the campaign. Two of its brigades were shot up making a series of mounted attacks in squadron strength at the town of Halen. The loss of horses in the field and the loss of grip in the command had much to do with the cavalry's failure to discover the BEF, and would have more to do with its employment during the September–October Race to the Sea as a flank guard, as opposed to a last-ditch instrument of exploitation. Were these decisive to the invasion's outcome? Individually, even together, certainly not—but nevertheless these were contributions to the German Army's acceptance of the kind of situation, in the war's crucial sector, which prewar thinking considered fatal: a static front.[21]

The delay in front of Liège and the cavalry's shortcomings made Germany's war in its crucial sector almost by default a footsloggers' war. Bülow and Kluck correspondingly forced the pace, pushing to the limit the unseasoned reservists who formed the majority of their armies. Kluck's foot soldiers logged up to twenty-five miles a day, day after day, in August heat and August humidity. Forty percent of the heatstroke casualties suffered during the whole war came in its first months. March discipline suffered as well. Straggling was endemic. Passing through towns and villages men fell out, initially looking for something to drink or eat, then escalating to looting, arson, and sometimes worse.

The German Army was at bottom a citizen army but in an authoritarian context. It could not count on the "republican virtue" that underwrote the drumhead courts-martial and improvised executions that did much to hold its French opponents together in the war's early days.[22] "Never give an order you know will be disobeyed" remains a useful rule of thumb. Nor were officers and NCOs immune to blisters, thirst, and fatigue. A chunk of bread or a bottle of wine handed over by a grinning private did much to mollify the most authoritarian superior.

Retail-level foraging was a marginal issue compared to the systematic violence against civilians all along the German front of advance. Even in the *Reichsland* of Alsace-Lorraine 1,500 people were arrested, a half-dozen shot, and over 15,000 reservists called up, sent to Germany, and scattered throughout the army. Elsewhere exact numbers vary, but the accepted figures are around 900 French and over 5,500 Belgian civilians killed in the war's first four months, and around 20,000 buildings deliberately destroyed as reprisals. Reprisals for what, precisely? The Germans insisted they preferred for obvious practical reasons to establish at least "correct" relations with civilians, especially in Belgium, where speed was of the essence. German cavalry vanguards posted warnings against civilian belligerence. Initially, though not always, they paid for requisitioned goods in hard cash. When conciliation was insufficient, the invaders reacted decisively to prevent reemergence of the low-intensity guerrilla war that had cost over a thousand soldiers' lives and significantly disrupted lines of communication during the Franco-German War. The operative words were "if necessary;" in a matter of days they became "when necessary."

The question of motivation for the atrocities committed in these early days remains correspondingly controversial, even to the nouns used to describe it. "Executions," "incidents," and even "reprisals" still find places in the narrative, but "murder" and "killings" now dominate literature on the subject. At one extreme is the thesis that the Germans, in Belgium at least, sought to show they were masters by a deliberate campaign of terror based on *provocateurs*. At the other is the contention that French and Belgian stragglers, sometimes changing into civilian clothes, along with members of the Belgian "inactive Civic Guard" mobilized only on August 5 and without either training, organization, or uniforms, took usually unsystematic and occasional pot-shots at German troops that started a race to the bottom. In the middle stands a "perfect storm" approach, describing a "Great Fear" of large-scale civilian resistance sweeping through ranks of hungry, tired, stressed, and frightened civilians in uniform, reinforced by being in a land of "others," fostered as well by collective ignorance of the ricochet effect and penetrative power of a modern rifle round. Especially in built-up areas a stray shot, even if fired by a nervous or careless German, might well seem to come from anywhere and from any hand.

Anxiety was sustained by waves of lurid rumors involving the mutilation of the wounded and the killing of prisoners. It was further underpinned, for Protestants at least, by anti-Catholicism that focused on priests and churches. The civilian-sustained internal security measures such as roadblocks and bridge guards that the soldiers had had ample opportunity to observe as they crossed the Reich further conditioned them to expect the same as they entered enemy territory. Alcohol, especially the raw high-proof distillate common in villages and devastating even in small amounts, frequently added to the mix by blurring judgment.

There is no question of the officer corps' principled hostility to civilian involvement in war making. This was understood as a harbinger of social revolution, aside from any operational considerations. Nor is there any question that the High Command and its senior generals warned subordinates to expect civilian resistance and authorized "the most drastic measures:" taking hostages, burning buildings, and executing civilians if necessary.

Those kinds of collective punishment clearly defied the 1907 Hague Convention on Land Warfare, which Germany had signed. Implementing these gave pause even to officers steeped in the concepts of mission performance and military necessity. A familiar, if not general, pattern involved juniors initially referring upwards reports of *franc-tireur* activity until someone from a higher headquarters replied "you know what to do." The results of this back-and-forth were arguably worse than they might have been with an initial firm decision at either end of the command system. As it was, no one wished to appear a slacker.

The results were sufficiently drastic that one corps commander intervened directly to stop the process he had himself initiated. "We are not Huns," one general wrote his wife, "and do not want to sully the honor of the German name." The letter was dated August 26. By the end of the first week in September the violence was essentially finished. In practical terms, pillaging and violence were bad for discipline. There is some point as well to the suggestion that in occupied territory, tales of German brutality spread rapidly, lost nothing in the telling, and contributed to a persuasive pattern of overtly submissive behavior. Culturally, the concept of an officer's honor acted to some degree as a check on systematizing and expanding reprisals, especially in the absence of events that could be processed as provocations.[23]

III

General Headquarters had remained in Berlin until August 16, when it decamped for the developing front in eleven trains the occupants of which included the emperor himself. The destination was Koblenz.

Five hundred miles from Berlin, it was psychologically no closer to the sear of war. It was also arguably the worst possible place for William. At his best he was the kind of man who wore better at a distance and in limited contact. He belonged in Berlin, pointing with pride, occasionally viewing with alarm, and in position to be sidetracked when necessary, rather than replicating Frederick the Great and William I by more or less taking the field in person. In Koblenz he was an inescapable presence, but had literally nothing to do and no one had time to entertain him.[24]

His relegation to figurehead status was obvious enough that William himself was well aware of it. But did it matter? The answer is a clear affirmative. The Second Reich was not exactly authoritarian, but it was an executive state—one in which during the previous quarter-century political government and administrative government had been increasingly overshadowed by William's "personal government."

In such a situation the executive can be a figurehead, but must function effectively as such. Of all Germany's institutions of governance the army, as previously described, had the least respect for the kaiser because it had more chances to see him up close and personally. As the war progressed, the High

Command could not avoid observing William's decline into an object of pity and ridicule: a pricked balloon. The logical result was for the military to fill the vacuum—not, it must be emphasized, a very large one—left by the emperor's deflation and eclipse and take over running the war itself.

But there is a difference between making decisions behind the scenes and taking center stage. The great danger at war's higher levels is not that commanders collapse from fear of responsibility. The real danger is that they become unable to think clearly. Their brains freeze. They exude uncertainty, whether through hesitation or pretension. That begins to create doubt in their subordinates—and that is when battles, campaigns and wars can begin to unravel.

Center stage in Germany's war now belonged to Helmuth von Moltke. Nephew and namesake of the iconic victor of the Wars of Unification, his familiar cognomen was, inevitably, "Moltke the Younger." But he had another nickname in the higher circles of the General Staff: "Gloomy Julius" (*der traurige Julius*). Reflecting Moltke's characteristic pessimism, it was hardly a tag to inspire confidence. Moltke himself, on being offered the post of chief of staff, asked William if he expected to win twice in the same lottery. Nor was Schlieffen, with his plethora of personal and professional quirks, an easy man to follow. As a peacetime *chef*, however, Moltke had demonstrated reasonable synergies of flexibility and firmness, original insight and situational awareness. He had handled the military aspects of the July crisis with reasonable aplomb. On August 1, 1914, Moltke the Younger was not seriously regarded as either a weak link or a disaster waiting to happen.

A possible straw in the wind might have been Moltke's insistence that his wife accompany him to Koblenz. Eliza von Moltke was a formidable person in her own right, independent-minded, deeply interested in the occult—not a "soldier's woman" in any of the usual senses. Nevertheless, Moltke was making war with all the comforts of home, albeit after a fashion. But much is forgiven a victorious general, and by the time General Headquarters was unpacked and settled, the future was looking positive—especially on the vital right flank.

The Belgians were obligingly retreating. The First Army was driving south of Brussels, the Second was closing on the fortress of Namur, and the Third was keeping pace towards Dinant. Initially Moltke put Bülow in operational control of his neighbors on the flank. It was an arrangement similar to that of Rupprecht and Heeringen. It would prove no more successful, and not merely because of personal rivalries. Each army faced a full operational plate that left little energy for worrying about its neighbors. Hindsight suggests the wisdom of organizing the German front in three army groups: left, center, and right, each commanded by the relevant royal prince, with William on the right under Moltke's direct eye. The notion never emerged in prewar considerations. Perhaps it involved finding three more competent army commanders. More likely Moltke was concerned with not inhibiting his subordinates' initiative.

All European armies in 1914 placed great and unwarranted faith in electronics to enable centralized control of even a continent-scale campaign. Moltke carried it to extremes. He insisted on remaining in Koblenz, partly to keep an eye on the emperor, partly to keep in touch with the eastern theater of operations. For security reasons, he established his telegraph service in the relatively remote valley of Bad Ems, accepting the increased complexity of communications. Telephone and radio connections were insecure, unreliable, and not least still outside the comfort zones of generals whose formative years antedated the eras of Bell and Marconi.[25] As for the internal-combustion engine, Joffre, otherwise a product of the Nineteenth Century if anyone was, increasingly relied on a high-powered car driven by a former Grand Prix champion to connect with his subordinates. Such an idea was unlikely to have crossed Moltke's mind.

His right-wing commanders, moreover, seemed to be doing quite well enough on their own—with a little help from Joffre. The French generalissimo had consistently underestimated the scope of the German sweep through Belgium, expecting its flank to be somewhere around Namur. He had correspondingly ordered his right-flank Fifth Army to remain concentrated against that projected advance. Fifth Army's commander General Charles Lanrezac was convinced the Germans in fact proposed to cross the Meuse River north of Namur in force—no fewer than eight corps' worth of force.

While the French generals argued, the Germans occupied Brussels without a fight on August 20. Namur went under on August 23, owing largely to German Big Berthas and two batteries of Austrian 305 howitzers. The advance was characterized, as mentioned, by an increasing number of "reprisals" for alleged guerilla activity. The largest and most notorious came in Louvain. Beginning on August 25, the university city was subjected to three days of arson, executions, and pillaging, culminating in the burning of the world-renowned university library and the deportation to Germany of over 40,000 civilians. Kluck, whose troops were responsible, spoke of stern and necessary reprisals. Breakdown of discipline at company level is a more accurate explanation.[26] As an arguable counterpoint, Namur was spared what might have become a similar catastrophe through the common-sense cooperation of the local bishop and the German commandant. But Louvain became the enduring centerpiece of a court of international judgment branding the Germans as Huns: beasts beyond the civilized pale, bearers of a degenerate *Kultur* determined to crush Europe under its jackboots. Neutrals, the US in particular, were bombarded by an "if it bleeds it leads" journalism competing for circulation by distributing horror stories. The realities were bad enough, and the Second Reich's image has never recovered from them.

Kluck's eyes, and Bülow's, were on other prizes. The French Fifth Army was isolated, awaiting the delayed arrival of the British Expeditionary Force on its right flank. On August 21 Bülow's vanguards pushed ahead across the Sambre, and held their bridgeheads against French counterattacks more characterized by élan than preparation. The next day a full-fledged encounter battle developed between the Second and Fifth Armies. By evening the three corps of Lanrezac's center and right had been forced back away from the river with swingeing casualties. One regiment left almost half its men in a single small copse. An Algerian regiment counted 1,200 casualties, including 33 officers—a crippling loss for a unit where French was very much a second language.

Had the Third Army forced its pace, Lanrezac might well have suffered the kind of operational-level envelopment the German plan was evolving towards as a "best probable" option. But the weather was hot and the civilian population uncivil. Hausen was cautious, Moltke's intervention dilatory, and Bülow's urging ambiguous. The result was less "order-counterorder-disorder" than a casserole of communications that left Hausen to his own indecisive devices. Not until early on August 23 did Moltke unmistakably instruct him to get across the Meuse River. By that time the French were in position to make a day-long fight that blocked the Third Army's advance and inflicted enough casualties for one melodramatic corps commander to report his command "shattered." The Germans responded by sacking the town of Dinant with an enthusiasm not always seen in these "reprisals."

Lanrezac, like his counterparts, in principle regarded defense as a mere preliminary to an offensive. Initially he planned another attack for the 23rd. Reports of his own casualties and of the successful German crossing to the south combined with word of Kluck's encounter with the finally-arrived BEF at Mons to change his mind. Accordingly at 9 am on the 24th he informed Joffre of the Fifth Army's "retrograde movement" in the general direction of Paris.

The Japanese Army's mantra was "in the hour of victory, tighten your helmet straps." The Germans chose to loosen their belts. OHL was deluged with reports of enemy retreats in every sector; of thousands of prisoners and hundreds of guns captured; French armies shattered and the BEF in full retreat; the Belgians shut up in Antwerp. Wilhelm Gröner, anything but a front-runner, proclaimed German victory on August 25. Gerhard Tappen, OHL Chief of Operations, with a presumed finger on the pulse of events, predicted it would be all over in six weeks. Baden's military representative in Koblenz informed his government that the campaign was decided; future questions would involve the occupation.[27]

These reactions cannot be entirely dismissed as a toxic cross between hubris and euphoria. The German Army had broken through the Belgian fortresses. It had emerged as victor in the Battles of the Frontiers. Even its initial encounters with the British at Mons and Le Cateau did not develop quite along the lines of BEF mythology. British staff work, British planning, and British tactics all bore the stamp of a small army still hobbled by its colonial legacies. The ostensible regulars filling its ranks were often a mixture of teenaged recruits who had much to learn and resummoned reservists who had forgotten even more, and who often had not exactly lived civilian lives of moderate drinking and healthy exercise. Since the Boer War the British Army had seen almost no fighting. Combat experience of any kind was correspondingly limited, usually to relative seniors: captains and sergeants. Even Tommy's vaunted marksmanship was in good part a construction of wishful thinking of the kind common to any inexperienced troops in their first actions. Certainly no German records confused it—as yet—with machine-gun fire.[28]

In the BEF of August 1914, courage and good will were present in plenty. Skill was another story. This does not denigrate the officers and men who paid in blood their tuition in high-tech war—and who within weeks may well have "saved the sum of things for pay" in the trenches around Ypres. But their defining initial challenge was having to retreat faster than the Germans could pursue them.

And that pursuit opened a door to a zone of fog and friction the Germans had not expected. Heat, fatigue, and—surprisingly—hunger were thinning the front-line ranks at a time when enthusiasm and pride could keep the softest of uniformed civilians in ranks as long as they could move and stand.

IV

The Imperial German Army had never ignored logistics. Operations, however, took pride of place. Planning revolved around operational factors—a pattern that became increasingly pronounced as pace, speed, and initiative came to define the German approach to war. Not until 1900 did logistical officers begin the equivalent of staff rides. The quartermasters were expected to serve the operational concept. That was well enough in principle, particularly since Germany's enemies were also its near neighbors. Practice, however, generated problems.

They began with the railroads that made possible the mobilization and concentration of the unprecedented numbers deployed. Railheads were expected to be a maximum of a hundred kilometers, a little over sixty-two miles, from the combat zone. Any further and the horse-drawn supply columns could not keep in touch. As early as August 22, however, the First Army in particular was advancing faster than the railway troops were able to repair demolitions and replace rolling stock. By the 28th the gap was almost double the projected maximum. Motor transport was improvised as a stopgap. Since 1907 government subsidies had been available to civilian buyers of suitable trucks. By 1914 there were over 3,700 of them, over half mobilized from the beer industry. Now they mostly hauled shells, but they were still fundamentally designed for short hauls on city streets. Given adequate roads, an army truck column could make about sixty miles a day. But that was predicated on the kind of regular servicing obviated by the pace of the German advance. The problem of skimped maintenance was exacerbated by the shortage of experienced drivers. Even in Belgium and northern France, moreover, paved and graded roads were not the rule. By the Battle of the Marne well over half the army's motor vehicles were out of service.

That threw an additional burden on the horses. First Army alone had 84,000 of them. They required almost two million tons of fodder a day: grain and hay, not mouthfuls of grass cropped during temporary halts. Back-of-the-envelope calculation can provide the point at which horse-drawn supply trains were primarily sustaining themselves rather than the combat units. These horses, conscripted from farms and stables, were as a rule accustomed to regular rest and good treatment; many were almost family pets back home. They were also accustomed to men who knew how to care for them—often in short supply in urban units. An overworked man will try to keep going. An overworked horse will lie down and wait to die. The roadsides of Belgium and northern France were littered with their cadavers.

The third problem confronting the logistical services involved ammunition supply. It soon became obvious that the use of ammunition, artillery ammunition in particular, was exponentially greater than prewar calculations had expected or allowed. In October Krafft von Dellmensingen summarized the problem: without the guns, the best infantry was hung out to dry. That meant the barrels had to be fed. *That* meant prioritizing ammunition resupply above all else. That meant other items ran short: food in general and bread—bulky and easily becoming inedible—in particular. In 1870 it had been possible—just—for the Germans episodically to live off the countryside. Now the force-to-space ratios of the right wing made that impossible. It was "first come, first served." Too often foraging generated high levels of wastage and produced too much half-ripe fruit and unripe grain. Water was an even greater problem. Wells quickly ran dry. Free water sources were polluted by boots, hooves, and manure. As a result dysentery and diarrhea contributed to increasing levels of straggling. In the last ten days of August, the First Army reported 7,500 battle casualties and over 2,500 sick; the respective figures for the Second Army were 11,500 and over 4,000. Both ratios were unexpected throwbacks to the Eighteenth Century. The German Army was stumbling towards the Marne with its trousers down—often literally and certainly metaphorically.[29]

The optimism that nevertheless infused OHL inspired Moltke's first comprehensive command initiative. On August 27 he issued a General Directive stating that the Belgians and British were finished; the French were in full retreat towards Paris, and it was time for the kill stroke, or for Moltke's version of it. The First Army would continue southwest of Paris; the Second would advance on the city itself and the Third on Château-Thierry, the Fourth and Fifth would press forward in the center; the Sixth and Seventh in the left would take Nancy, then advance between Toul and Épinal. Each army was to press forward energetically while covering the flank of its neighbor, a counsel of perfection to date lamentably unachieved.

Depending upon perspective, Moltke's developing reconfiguration reflected legitimate situational awareness or culpable loss of focus. The geographic and operational logic of this general advance was to pull the German axis from southwest to south, a fact Moltke acknowledged. On the other hand, however serious had been the Schlieffenesque rhetoric of a comprehensively coordinated operation with "the last man on the right touching the English Channel with his sleeve," the invasion had devolved into series of individual operations by single armies. Their commanders were not amenable to any but the most urgent forms of cooperation. They were also winning victories. How best to maximize the results?

Well before the war, Moltke had considered the obvious and often-generated possibility of the grand strategic flank movement being operationally countered effectively enough to cause a frontal battle.[30] Breakthroughs had been correspondingly practiced in the 1912 and 1913 maneuvers. From Moltke's perspective in the waning days of August, a broad-front strategy along the lines of Dwight Eisenhower's three decades later might not be optimal, but it was situationally promising. Moreover, the casualty rates on both sides and the German logistical situation suggested that a war, not of attrition as commonly understood, but of exhaustion, might be unfolding. In that case, given the operational situation and the discrepancy in resources, the French *had* to crack somewhere. And that might create the opportunity for a decisive battle of the kind German planners had been considering as a model for forty years: a double envelopment not on a strategic but on a tactical/operational scale, Cannae in a modern context with the Sixth and Seventh Armies driving the French in front of them northwest onto the Fifth Army's guns.[31]

Optimism also informed Moltke's reinforcing an eastern theater shaken by an unexpectedly successful Russian invasion. This was not a hasty measure. Moltke had a week to make up his mind. His decision on August 26 to send troops from the right wing was contingent on the fall of Namur. Two corps of the Second Army were now free for other duties, but Bülow expressed no need for them. Moltke's developing intention to tighten the German envelopment by swinging east of Paris would contract the front to a point where the corps could not be immediately readily deployed. The two additional corps investing Antwerp and the French fortress of Maubeuge could be made available in a matter of days. The transfer to the east might be a risk, but hardly seemed a gamble—as long as the cards continued to fall favorably.[32]

Joffre's response to his strategic situation was to do his best to reassure the politicians, continue retreating in the north, and begin forming and organizing a new army around Paris. Composed of local units and troops drawn from Alsace-Lorraine, it would deploy west of the Germans and strike Kluck's flank. And if Moltke's revised plan, unknown at this stage to Joffre, were followed, that flank would be increasingly vulnerable: a case study in the principle of the obliging enemy. Joffre's second stage involved using the Fourth and Fifth Armies and the BEF to transform the counterattack into an offensive: this time the real offensive, as it should have been delivered.

The Germans for their part continued to suffer electronically from low-tech high tech, a circumstance largely self-inflicted. Moltke, under pressure to bring OHL closer to the emerging decision point, shifted to Luxembourg on August 30. He initially wound up in a schoolhouse with neither gas nor electricity. His communications system was one—just one—radio transmitter with no priority system, and a single telegraph transmitter with a range of under two hundred miles: it required four relays for OHL to reach Kluck's headquarters. Twenty-hour delays were common. Nor was this situation anomalous. The First and Second Armies lacked radio connections with their corps and with each other.[33]

It was in this context of a brontosaurian gap between musculature and nervous system that the final German moves began. Lanrezac's counterattack at Guise on the 29th and 30th gave Bülow a nose bloody enough that before continuing the retreat on the 31st he rested the entire Second Army. The delay seemed amply justified. The virgin soldiers of the Second Army had experienced weeks of hard marching, hard fighting, and short rations. A day's breather allowed the field kitchens to catch up and feed hungry, tired foot soldiers and for Bülow to report total victory, with the French completely defeated. His chief of staff described French "moral capacity" as broken. The next few days, army headquarters was convinced, should see the final drive on Paris.

Joffre for his part took advantage of the time thus gained to order a further hundred-kilometer retreat. The government collapsed; the new government retired to Bordeaux. But this final retreat set the stage for victory on the Marne. Before becoming chief of staff Joffre had been an engineer and a logistician. He understood the craft of using the rails for strategic movement—understood it better than his opponents. There is a supreme irony in the fact that the Germans, still generally presented as the masters of railway war, were outperformed at the Great War's decisive point by the bumbling amateurs of 1870. Truly, in Napoleon's words, "the animals had learned something." The French rail network performed brilliantly in moving men and equipment laterally. As for spirit, the *poilus*' morale proved stronger than the politicians'. The infantry in particular was holding together, with straggling on the march and "getting lost" on the railroads at a minimum. The élan of mobilization was giving way to teeth-gritting determination, at least for public consumption. The doubts inculcated by defeat were being kept to oneself. The French after all might not be ready to crack.

That did not mean they could not be broken. The question was how best to do it. Bülow had been pressuring Kluck for several days to swing south and cover the Second Army's open left flank directly. Never quite certain of his exact authority, Bülow relied on collegiality, reasoning with and persuading his colleague. Kluck and Kuhl took no pains to reply, let alone comply. In the aftermath of Mons/Le Cateau, they saw unshared laurels and a clear chance to destroy the BEF. Nor was this mere glory-hunting. Following Bülow's intention seemed at First Army HQ at best an opportunity to execute a limited envelopment of a single French Army. If Schlieffen had possessed a guiding operational principle, it was the high risk of short hooks. It was in that context that First Army's commander formally and successfully requested Moltke to free him from Bülow's control, nominal as that had been. The request was granted on the 27th, and the First Army continued advancing southwest, accepting the risks of increasing the distance from Bülow's open flank.

On August 31, Kluck grandiloquently informed Moltke that he had swept the enemy in front of him from the field. Reality was more pedestrian. The British by then in fact had successfully, and barely, retreated just far enough beyond the First Army's tactical range, and bloodied the increasingly weary German cavalry just sufficiently that Kluck and Kuhl declined to continue a direct pursuit that invited a wild-goose chase to nowhere in particular. Nor was it exactly a resumé-enhancer that the First Army could show no bags of exhausted prisoners and abandoned guns to back its boast of sweeping the field. Acting on their own initiative, Kluck and Kuhl decided to strike a more accessible target, and turn southeast against the French. It is ironic that one of the few times in four years that a senior German general made a decision on the operational as opposed to the tactical level, that the decision was seriously questionable. Terence Zuber deconstructs the British-constructed myth of a heroic and successful stand at Le Cateau sufficiently to make a case that Kluck could readily have overhauled and destroyed at least the BEF's II Corps, had he not chosen to change direction in mid-advance.[34]

"Could have, should have, would have." Average minds can run in the same channels. On September 2 Moltke replicated Kluck with a General Directive definitely changing the right wing's axis of advance to the southeast, with the stated intention of driving the French away from Paris. The decisive blow would now be struck by the Second Army, supported by the Third. The First Army would follow the Second Army and cover its right flank. Kluck was both confused and contumacious. He was a day's march ahead of Bülow, and in a time-driven campaign correspondingly unwilling to halt in place for the Second Army to catch up. Nor was he intimidated by reports of a new French strike force somewhere around Paris. Instead he detailed a single corps to cover his now wide-open right and sent the rest of the army towards the Marne and what he believed was the left flank of Joffre's Fifth Army and the whole French front, with the intention of achieving—finally—the envelopment that the First Army had been created to execute.

Far from Kluck discussing the decision with Moltke, the chief of staff learned of it only through the First Army's belated communication of its orders and objectives on September 4. The tone was arrogant, demanding to be kept informed of the movements of the other six armies and suggesting Bülow lacked a true *Feldherr*'s nerve. Its composition and delivery required no fewer than sixteen hours.[35]

The High Command's section heads responded by advocating Kluck's relief for insubordination. Moltke demurred, probably recognizing the risks of designating and integrating a replacement at what was becoming the campaign's critical juncture. Instead, on August 4 the chief of staff issued orders, developing from the directive of the 2nd, for what amounted to an entirely new operational plan. Now Kluck would stand in place and Bülow was to join him, guarding the flank against an attack from Paris. The Third, Fourth and Fifth Armies would continue their respective advances south/southeast, coordinating with Rupprecht's projected offensive from Lorraine.

The revision reflected Moltke's growing conviction that continuing to attempt a Schlieffenesque outflanking of both Paris and the British and French forces in the region was futile, given the Allies' successful retreat and the improved concentration that had resulted. Deploying as a flank guard, the two armies originally conceived as the decisive striking force owed something to Moltke's growing concern with the projected threat from Paris. It owed even more—depending on one's perspective—to the chief of staff's recognizing operational realities and taking corresponding counsel of his judgment, which was anything but sanguine. Not for nothing was Moltke called "Gloomy Julius." In a conversation with the banker Karl Helfferich—whose presence at OHL was as much a symptom of its problems as a contribution to the war effort—he said that Germany had enjoyed successes but had not won victory. There were too few prisoners, too few captured guns. And that meant the hardest tasks were still ahead.[36]

That perception had, as indicated, earlier encouraged Moltke to look to his left flank. The Sixth and Seventh Armies, still in their arm's-length command relationship, had begun their attack on August 24, reinforced, more or less, by a half-dozen newly created Ersatz divisions. But these untrained and half-trained men could not replace the casualties of almost three weeks' sustained combat. The offensive stalled for a week as OHL bounced between pursuing the design of the August 27 directive and deemphasizing operations on the left while the war was won around Paris. Then Rupprecht decided on his own initiative, as a matter of honor as much as operations, to go ahead. Rupprecht appealed to Moltke in person. Moltke replied that the offensive could continue—but the heavy guns made available for its support must be returned, and the Sixth Army's gunners must understand that supplies of ammunition were now limited.

Rupprecht might be pardoned for anger at Prussian arrogance. Less excusable was his decision on his own initiative to go ahead towards Nancy—across the plateau of the Grand Couronne, some of the best defensive ground in eastern France, and some of the best fortified. Beginning on September 3, the Sixth Army mounted a series of attacks that began with bayonets fixed, bands playing and colors unfurled, but stalled in a maze of trenches and recoiled under French counterattacks. The price of that initiative was paid by his subjects. His chief of staff, Krafft, and the prince were violently hostile to abandoning the attack because of its negative effect on troop morale. The assumption was that enough men remained standing to be inspired. Bavarian casualty reports for the war's first six weeks were incomplete and inaccurate. The best estimate is that 300,000 men bore arms under the blue and white. Over 80,000 became casualties, including 17,000 dead—nearly 25 percent. In the infantry regiments the figure was around 60 percent.[37] And that was in a secondary theater, for what turned out to be nothing in particular.

In the German center the Fourth and Fifth Armies were continuing to advance: slowly, at heavy cost, enduring determined counterattacks, pushing back the French in front of them, but with no clear signs of a breakthrough in either sector. Cooperation between Albrecht and William ranged from episodic to nonexistent. The offensive's last gasp came on September 10, when the Crown Prince and Knobelsdorf sent three corps into a nighttime attack with rifles unloaded and bayonets fixed against ranged-in 75s that benefitted for one of the first times in the campaign from systematic aerial observation. The resulting massacre indicated that refocusing the invasion's decisive point to the center was a chimera. The High Command ordered a withdrawal to more defensible positions, and by mid-September the central sector of the Western Front was beginning to settle into place.

Without clear, coherent frameworks, mission-type operations invited melting into entropy. Moltke's significant alteration of the campaign's orientation called for an explanation, especially given the confidence of the commanders and *chefs* of First through Fifth Armies that they were on the edge of victory in their respective sectors. Conference calls were far in the future. Summoning the command teams to OHL was impractical given the crowded condition of the roads. Moltke had neither the temperament nor the tools to imitate Joffre and go forward in person. His only reasonable option was to send a staff officer to each army. The problem was making sure OHL's changed intentions were understood.

Briefly stated, none of the army command teams did anything but temporize. Kluck in particular balked. Kuhl had war-gamed this kind of move as a junior staff officer under Schlieffen's auspices in 1905. Both generals remained unworried about the prospects of a sortie from Paris and were indifferent to aerial reconnaissance reports of significant French troop movements in the area. The first installment of the bill came due on September 4. The French Sixth Army struck the reserve corps covering Kluck's right flank. The BEF, its commander Field Marshal Sir John French energized by Joffre's tearful urging, hit Kluck frontally. The Fifth Army under a new commander engaged Bülow; another newly organized army, the Ninth, its corps transferred from the Fourth Army, confronted Hausen. Moltke remained in Luxembourg, around 280 miles from both First and Second Army headquarters, later justifying his decision on the grounds that he had to protect the emperor. Holger Herwig notes that the distances by air were half that, but the image of Moltke in a Taube is difficult to conjure up.[38] As a consequence, the Germans fought three separate army-level battles. Hausen's Saxons defeated the Ninth Army, the principal feature being an admirably executed surprise, which was a predawn bayonet attack unsupported by artillery. But the French commander, another new face named Ferdinand Foch, refused to accept the consequences; his lines held. The worn-out men of the Third Army were unable to develop their initial advantage and Hausen, suffering from a severe case of dysentery that developed into typhus, was not the man to galvanize it.

On the other wing of the Great Advance, Kluck was pressed so hard on his right that he redeployed two corps to restore the imperiled sector. That in turn opened a thirty-mile gap between Bülow and Hausen. Into it advanced, carefully but steadily, the BEF. Bülow responded by pulling back his own right flank. Kluck doubled down, putting everything the First Army had left into defeating the Sixth Army before the British could close up and close in. As the distance between them increased, neither German general bothered to keep OHL abreast of the changing situation. Out of contact for two days—almost unbelievably, there would be no radio links between OHL and its army headquarters until September 9—Moltke was desperate for information. He responded by sending a staff officer north by car.[39]

Lieutenant Colonel Richard Hentsch was OHL's chief intelligence officer, one of Moltke's inner circle. He had a reputation for clear thinking and perceptive analysis. And he had already visited Kluck's and Bülow's headquarters. His mission might even be called Napoleonic. As battlefields grew beyond the direct control of commanding generals, it increasingly became the emperor's practice to despatch aides-de camp, selected middle-ranking officers, to trouble spots, serving as his eyes and speaking with his authority. The pattern had been familiar for a century. Moltke gave Hentsch no written orders. Exactly what he authorized Hentsch to do remains a conundrum—a fact speaking volumes for the lack of grip at OHL's highest levels. But there is no doubt, based on their preliminary discussion, that Hentsch assumed—legitimately, given a century's worth of precedent— that he could act in Moltke's name to sort out the situation on the army's right.

Hentsch was often subsequently described as "pessimistic" during his mission. In fact Hentsch seems to have been in top emotional form, and with no outward signs of the gall bladder trouble that killed him later in the war. In contrast, when he arrived at Second Army headquarters, Bülow described his men as burned out and called his situation extremely serious. When interrupted by a dramatic phone call describing a local French victory, Bülow's response was to warn even more strongly that the gap opened by Kluck invited a full-scale Allied breakthrough. Hentsch agreed the First Army was in trouble and asserted that he had authority to order Kluck to retreat. Was this merely fustian to stiffen Bülow's spine? That night Hentsch wrote Moltke that Bülow's situation was "serious but not desperate." At 6 am on September 9 he left for Kluck's headquarters to see for himself.

Hentsch required over five hours to get through tangles of wagons and crowds of stragglers, once being shot at by mistake. After experiencing the rear-echelon chaos he seems to have encountered, he was surprised at the optimism he met at First Army HQ. He responded by describing the great offensive as stalled from Lorraine northwards, the Allies as on the move, and the Second Army as reduced to remnants. He insisted retreat was temporarily necessary as the best way of reordering a situation drifting out of control.

The First Army's fighting cocks initially demurred, arguing a decisive victory was within reach on their front. Kuhl remained convinced that a complete victory beckoned and had been thrown away. But when Hentsch asserted he spoke with Moltke's authority—*Vollmacht* in General Staff-speak—neither Kuhl nor Kluck seriously challenged the decision. Preliminary orders for a withdrawal toward Soissons went out in a matter of minutes. Kluck and Kuhl have been widely criticized for suddenly becoming so amenable to orders. Their behavior has been described as reflexive submission to the authority of the General Staff, even when asserted by junior officer proxy. It has been attributed to a lapse of nerve at the campaign's critical point: battle captains would have sought to turn the tide by fighting it out, all or nothing. Kluck and Kuhl have also been faulted for not checking directly with Moltke, even by air, since the First Army still had no phone connections with Luxembourg. Each point has its merits. But one factor usually overlooked was the phone connection to the Second Army that by now did exist. After Hentsch's departure, Bülow received a report from the air squadron attached to his headquarters. It described massive enemy forces advancing into the gap between the Second and First Armies. This confirmed Bülow's belief that there was no more time: at 9:02 am he informed Kluck and Hausen that the Second Army was beginning a general retreat.

If Bülow was not simply taking counsel of his fears, he was putting unusual faith in an untested cutting-edge technology. Aerial reconnaissance was still far more a matter of perception than photography. The Allied advance was anything but dynamic; the Second Army was far from a broken reed. The problem was that if Bülow were to make a stand, he would have to depend on Kluck and Hausen to retrieve the situation—an act of faith as contrary to fact as any manifested in the German high command during the whole war.

Bülow's message took Kluck between wind and water. Kluck's ranks were thin, his men beyond tired. To go forward as Bülow went back was to thrust the First Army into a high-risk tactical situation. He might well have seriously considered, if not decided on, pulling back while Hentsch was still stuck in traffic. Certainly nothing the OHL representative said was likely to encourage Kluck to pursue his offensive because of developments elsewhere.

If Moltke's subordinates were focused on making immediate decisions, the chief of staff had had more time to reflect than he needed. His subordinates had noted a rapid decline in everyday energy, an unwillingness to act even in routine matters. The chief of the Military Cabinet, responsible to the kaiser for personnel matters and a correspondingly powerful figure, declared Moltke's nerves were not equal to the situation. On September 7, the chief of staff had written his wife expressing his horror at the "countless" homes and lives destroyed at his hands. On the 9th, reacting to an intercepted report of a BEF advance between the First and Second Armies, he recommended a general retreat to William, and received a colorful rejection. Moltke's health was by now as dubious as his morale: the recurrence of a long-standing arteriosclerosis was complicated by a gall bladder infection. Hentsch returned to Luxembourg on the afternoon of the 10th and urged Moltke to see for himself how the situation was developing. Moltke set off next morning—finally—for his field headquarters, starting with the Fifth Army where things were least urgent. In the middle of the exercise he was informed of a radio message from Bülow to OHL describing a French attack developing in force against the Third Army. Moltke drove to Hausen's headquarters, confirmed the operational situation, and then received an intercepted message from Albrecht to OHL reporting similar movements in his sector. The German right was stymied and the left held in play. Now the center seemed at risk. Helmuth von Moltke made his first either/or decision: he ordered a general retreat. Three days later he was gone: ordered by William to resign on the grounds of ill health, which was neither an inaccurate nor an inappropriate diagnosis. With him went what chances ever existed for a German military victory in a short, decisive war.

V

It is a familiar cliché that victory has many fathers while defeat is an orphan. The German defeat in the August 1914 campaign is an exception. There are enough explanations, and variant explanations, to provide material for a separate monograph. Setting aside the obvious one that the French Army and the BEF had a good deal to do with the campaign's outcome, focusing just on the German experience suggests three sets of general explanations.

One asserts the German Army was the wrong tool for the job. The German Army of 1914 was a heavy, blunt instrument—and arguably an instrument not heavy enough for its purposes. A defensible proof of the Schlieffen Plan's theoretical nature is its inclusion of corps that did not exist, and which for institutional and political reasons remained uncreated. In turn those missing pieces created in 1914 a strategic/operational matrix characterized by shimming and shoring up. German troop movements increasingly reacted to situations as opposed to creating them. And how many times in retrospect do the Germans seem short a corps or two at a key point?

The German Army fell short as a mass instrument in another way as well. It was constructed around a conscription system universal in theory but almost haphazard in practice, providing mediocre training and diluted by reservists whose already limited skills had eroded from disuse. It was commanded by an officer corps whose preparation was geared to developing solid, above-average competence. There was little or no room for the unconventionality that might confuse its own side as much as bewilder an enemy. The German Army was infused with an ethos of administration that encouraged the devolution of focus into tunnel vision. Men were cogs, a mentality arguably reflected in the lack of concern for basic health in senior command and staff appointments. Bülow's catalytic decision to retreat on September 9, for example, was made by a man suffering from severe arteriosclerosis. His chief of staff was afflicted by cardiac problems, exacerbated by a month of unremitting, unprecedented stress, which would kill him in 1916 and the symptoms of which he was self-medicating with alcohol.

It is ironic to consider the prospect that the German Army of 1914 failed because it was insufficiently militarized. It was a machine to be sure—but a machine resembling nothing so much as a Nineteenth-Century steam turbine, producing energy with limited efficiency and requiring a high input of fuel. Predictably it seized up under the high stresses of the August campaign.

The second set of general explanations for the army's failure asserts the impossibility of the task assumed relative to the tools available. It stems from the premise that the short, decisive war on which German policy and strategy were predicated depended on an institutional katana, a finely tempered blade wielded by a master. To extend the metaphor, creating such an instrument was beyond the capacity of Europe's swordsmiths in the autumn of 1914. This fact is highlighted in three contexts: firepower, mobility, and communications. Most frequently the discussion focuses on firepower. Modern artillery, rifles, and machine guns created a literal "perfect storm" that gridlocked combat, setting both skill and courage at naught. The prewar army understood and took seriously, if not always perceptively, the complex physical and emotional problems of mastering high-tech battlefields in a context of mass armies with low-average skills. And like their counterparts elsewhere in Europe, the Germans were able to do little more than nibble around the edges of a situation that was far from resolved as late as 1945.

Since the beginning of organized war, combat has involved the interaction of fire, protection, and mobility. Think of these three as a triangle with variable angles. By 1914 the triangle had become acutely obtuse. Protection was a fraction of an inch of uniform cloth. Mobility was determined by muscles, human or equine. The angles would eventually be adjusted by the internal combustion engine, which was still at such an embryonic stage of development that it could neither provide mobility nor carry protection to any significant degree.

That meant the normal advantage of the defense metastasized to a degree than none of the combatants were really able to understand or institutionalize in the war's first weeks. Casualty rates were not merely higher than at almost any time in the war's later years. At this stage the heavy losses tended not to be considered as requiring systematic attention. Rather, they were perceived as the price of a short, victorious war.

Given that in combats between similarly configured forces the attacker suffers significantly higher casualties, and given the rough initial numerical equality in the western theater, then the Germans were mathematically certain to find themselves increasingly on the wrong side of the balance sheet. Compensating for the missing numbers would require institutional and technical force multipliers that did not exist. Even away from the combat zone, motor vehicles were far too few and far too unreliable to keep up with logistical demands, let alone moving men and guns at rates high enough to increase operational mobility on any meaningful scale beyond the pace of feet and hooves.

If the internal combustion engine was at too early a stage of development to compensate for firepower and enhance mobility, electronics were in a similar state relative to communications. The telegraph, the telephone, and the radio alike required stable environments to make systematic contributions. Keeping even higher headquarters reliably connected in circumstances of relatively slow movement proved a greater challenge than the German signal services could meet, especially given the relative indifference of command authority to the problem. Wires were constantly being cut or broken. Radio service was unreliable. More seriously, electronic communications were erratic. The sender–recipient connection was insecure; messages were readily overheard or intercepted by other headquarters. The German invasion was under massive time pressure. Episodic information was often correspondingly seized upon as a guide to decision-making on the grounds that it was better than tapping in the dark. The result, as regularly demonstrated earlier in this chapter, was an electronic version of order-counterorder-disorder. Sometimes innovations can have effects opposite to those intended, and sometimes less can indeed be more.

The third category of explanation for the German Army's failure in the war's initial stage is that it existed in the context of a society structurally unprepared for the war it accepted. An essay in an anthology *Sexualmoral und*

Zeitgeist im 19. und 20. Jahrhundert perceptively, if cynically, observes that in the decade before 1914, German attitudes toward sex and war were essentially similar. Both were based on a deep, comprehensive curiosity that receded whenever action seemed possible.[40] In that sense the German Army of 1914 epitomized the society it served and reflected. Internally, the tension between maintaining the domestic status quo and developing as an instrument of *Weltmacht*, Stig Förster's "dual militarism," and the related issue of quantity *vis à vis* quality had a polarizing effect. Externally, the army's ambivalently subaltern relationship to political authority was juxtaposed to its relatively synergistic connection with civil society. The result in 1914 was a people that did not submit blindly to military authority, but were willing to accept it. Would that prove sufficient to overcome the consequences of the marginal victory achieved at such cost in six weeks?

CHAPTER III

REEVALUATING

Moltke's successor, in good part as much from a shortage of candidates and by proximity as by positive choice, was War Minister Erich von Falkenhayn. He had accompanied OHL to Luxembourg when his proper place was in Berlin, and had since devoted most of his energy to carping at Moltke. On September 9 Falkenhayn had informed his diary that when Schlieffen's notes had come to an end, so had Moltke's brain. Now he was in charge, and the first thing he discovered was that Moltke had not completely fallen apart when unable to rely on his predecessor.

---------- I ----------

On September 6, increasingly concerned with the extension and attenuation of the right wing, Moltke had ordered Seventh Army headquarters and a corps each from the Sixth and Seventh Army to entrain for Brussels. His original intention was to support and extend Kluck's enveloping movement. Instead he had been constrained to deploy Heeringen's contingent to bridge the gap between the First and Second Armies, and the advance units were moving smoothly into position. Kluck and Hausen had also successfully disengaged with minimal difficulty. Indeed the complaints recorded from the rank and file at abandoning what they saw as a victory, even if largely reported by officers, indicated that there was a good deal of spirit left on the front lines. An unarguable demonstration of frustration was the chaos the retreating troops left behind them: broken windows, smashed furniture, ruined clothing—and ubiquitous piles of excrement. BEF accounts in particular make much of this as proof of intractable Hunnishness; German records are predictably silent. The principal common denominator appears to be neither a breakdown in discipline nor the kind of requisition-cum-looting that characterized the advance, but anger and frustration expressed in otherwise pointless vindictiveness.

The retreating troops had time to indulge their spite. Allied pursuit was systematic—that is to say, slow. The British acted from caution, the French from exhaustion. Falkenhayn believed a quick decision was still possible. His initial intention was to continue the retreat until the First Army's still-open flank was secure, move the Sixth Army from Lorraine onto Kluck's flank, and resume the offensive on September 18, with the Bavarians executing the envelopment. The Allies moved just a little faster, and were a little faster when the Germans shifted north and tried again—and again. The "race to the sea" convincingly demonstrated that corps-scale attacks improvised from the line of march and logistically dependent on French and Belgian railway systems not yet fully operational did nothing but use ammunition already disturbingly scarce and increase a casualty rate that finally was causing concern. By early September the replacement depots were almost empty of men with any serious training. Everything had been put in the proverbial shop window, and too many front-line companies were beginning to resemble platoons.

Falkenhayn sought to compensate by sending three cavalry corps northwest as a strike and exploitation force against the Allied left. This was the first time German cavalry had been used in significant strength for combat as opposed to serving as a screening force. It was also a month and more too late. The loss in horses and the exhaustion of those that remained did as much as Allied firepower to keep the troopers' movement limited and their operations inconclusive.

Falkenhayn's response was to order Fourth Army headquarters transferred to Belgium to coordinate an advance along the Flanders coast. Strategically this would give Germany a base area for an expanded naval war against Britain, which Falkenhayn from the war's first days considered the Second Reich's most dangerous enemy.[1] Operationally the Fourth Army would then swing south, and in effect cross the Allies' "T" in a land version of the naval maneuver. The Sixth Army would hold on the Fourth's left and support its attack as opportunity offered. Albrecht of Württemberg had emerged, albeit somewhat by default, as the best to date of the army commanders, and the core of his army was the first real wartime addition to German fighting power. Beginning in mid-August thirteen new divisions began their organization. They would enter German military mythology as the "innocents" driven to slaughter in the First Battle of Ypres.

Contrary to legend, these divisions were not composed primarily of adolescents from the universities and the bourgeoisie. As many as a third of the quarter-million or so "war volunteers" (*Kriegsfreiwilligen*) accepted in August 1914 may have been workers or craftsmen. Their distinguishing demographic characteristic was youth. Over half were under twenty. Their distinguishing military feature was random distribution. In one regiment the youngest was fourteen; the oldest a veteran of the Franco-German War well into his sixties. Volunteers made up three-quarters of the 201st Reserve Infantry Regiment, organized in Berlin. Detmold's 219th had fewer than 20 percent. No matter the balance of volunteers, each regiment was completed by Landwehr and Ersatz reservists left in the depots by reverse selection. The Landwehr were mostly older, their training long behind them. The Ersatz men were likely to be ones with no training at all. Between them and the volunteers, that was the condition of about 60 percent of the rank and file.

Giving this mixed bag, less than two months to be ready for combat was an irresponsible response to an unexpected situation. It is worth noting that the British New Army divisions, universally cited as the norm for inadequate preparation, usually had at least six months' training before entering the front line. Their German counterpart lacked everything from maps to lieutenants. Meals tasted as though the cooks had taken special courses on preparing inedible food. Material shortages resulted in officers and NCOs keeping men busy with saluting drills and exercises in foot care and oral hygiene, not from desiccated pedantry but because of the lack of any reasonable alternatives.

Nevertheless, by the end of September the new divisions were passed as fit for active service. By October 8, four corps were under way to Flanders.

The railways delivered them efficiently, but once in the field the regimental officers in particular were unable to convey that sense of competence—not to say basic situational awareness—that is a major element of compensating for fear and confusion among inexperienced soldiers.[2]

Those formations were Falkenhayn's war babies, created by his authority as war minister. His orders to Albrecht were to attack without regard for casualties. His underlying principle was a need for speed no less intense than on August 1. The most favorable interpretation of Falkenhayn's decision is a belief that enthusiasm and mass would carry the day against the presumably limited force the Allies would be able to deploy. Or perhaps, like Moltke and Schlieffen before him, the new chief of staff had been half-unwittingly swept up by the force of destiny. The main assault was ordered for October 19.

English-language accounts of First Ypres have focused on the BEF, by now seven divisions that did indeed stand and die in their tracks during those waning weeks of October. They had gallant buttressing by the two-division Indian Corps, and from a French contingent drawn from across the Empire: Senegalese from Africa fighting alongside Breton *fusiliers marins*, both barely able to speak French. And the often overlooked Belgian Army retreating from Antwerp held the line of the Yser around Nieuport and Dixmude until the only option was to deny a thousand years of history and open the sluice gates. That shifted the German offensive's decisive point south to Ypres—and put the new divisions at stage center.

On October 20 at 9 am three German corps crossed their start lines: Objective Ypres. They struggled forward to within two miles of the city, and confidence levels were high, though the next day promised to be worse. The objective was the Yser River. In the way was the village of Langemarck, itself strongly defended and with surrounding terrain that offered excellent killing zones—a fact apparent even to the almost-virgin soldiers facing it. "There were odd feelings inside," recorded one private, "really sharp anxiety that bit and gnawed away at us."[3] Routes to the assembly areas were choked as traffic control disintegrated. One regiment took five hours to cover two and a half miles. Men designated to attack at dawn got to sleep around 3 am. Others had

had no hot food for three days and were living on abandoned Belgian rations. Everyone went in with full packs and no orders to drop them. Untrained gunners provided uncertain support for the attack. And yet one volunteer declared, "I felt myself immune … nothing could happen to me." Another affirmed that "When someone went down he was certainly wounded. Or he was dead …."A Belgian cemetery worker dryly commented, "they were drunk."[4] Company officers lacked maps. When they stood up, whether to survey the terrain or—more often—to set an example, they were shot within minutes. The NCOs on whom command more or less devolved knew no more than the privates. The combination of adrenaline in the ranks, disorganization in command, and above all the terrible British fire led to a response arguably hard-wired in the millennia when humans were prey, before they became predators: bunching up, herding together like bison or wildebeests under threat from predators, moving in inchoate mass lunges, then milling around once more.

The Short Magazine Lee-Enfield remains the best quick-firing bolt-action rifle ever designed. In contrast to Mons and Le Cateau, the Germans in front of Langemarck did provide mass targets for the "fifteen rounds rapid" that was the BEF trope. In contrast as well to those earlier battles, German accounts and reports are replete with vivid images of impenetrable machine-gun fire where British records note no more than a gun or two present.

In sector after sector the German advance was literally blocked by the mounds of its own dead and wounded. Regiment and division commanders responded by pushing up reserves. As had been the case in Lorraine, the Argonne, and on the Marne, this "building up the firing line" did not prefigure the drill regulations' final victorious charge, but only enhanced confusion. Attacks broke down into small groups scattered across meadows and behind hedges. Attempts to get forward devolved into a few men crawling or rushing until they too were shot down or reduced to stationary targets.

Perhaps those that died quickly were the lucky ones. The medical services of the new corps were no more developed than anything else about them. Hospital corpsmen were figures of fun in the peacetime army, something less than real soldiers. On the fields around Ypres, "*Sani*" (medic) was as familiar a cry as "*Mutter*" (mother). The way the men with Red Cross brassards responded began a new myth of "*Sanitätsgefreiter* Neumann," who in between treating casualties invented a miracle cure for gonorrhea and developed a hundred ways of facilitating uniformed sexual encounters. The grim reality was evacuation that ranged from difficult to impossible in daylight with litter teams able to make little headway over fire-swept terrain. Field hospitals became charnel houses as overworked, over-age doctors were submerged by wave after wave of the kinds of traumas a normal civilian practice might experience once or twice a year.

These conditions were replicated day after day for three weeks around Ypres, from Dixmude in the north to Messines in the south. As the new corps bled out, Falkenhayn brought up reinforcements: Bavarians and Württembergers, a composite division of the Prussian Guard, some of the peacetime army's best troops. They too attacked, faltered, and died in the face of the last stand of the original BEF, the "Old Contemptibles." Many legends arose around First Ypres. If one seeks a defining aphorism it might be that the Germans advanced over the British—but never through them. Battalions were routinely reduced to eighty or ninety men. But the line held. If there was a decisive moment, it came on October 31 around the village of Gheluvelt, where a lieutenant-general and his staff rode towards the crumbling front because there was nobody else left, and when a desperate counterattack by what remained of a battalion, fortified by a rum ration, took by surprise Germans worn out and disorganized by success and threw back Germans who believed they had done enough for the day.

For the Germans, sorting out the confusion and evacuating the wounded was followed by a week of an activity increasingly characteristic of the developing battle line in all sectors: digging in to get as much cover as possible from shell bursts and rifle fire. The generals on the ground around Ypres were convinced that one more good try would secede the issue. One corps commander declared it clear that the British surrendered when under determined attack. Therefore future offensives would be made with bugles blowing and regimental bands playing. Sector-level attacks continued into November. Again, Gheluvelt was the focal point when on November 11 the Prussian Guard attacked across broken ground, in mixed rain and sleet, over acres of decomposing bodies, and with poorly coordinated artillery support. The Guards were picked men selected for height and recruited from across the Reich. They had suffered fewer casualties than many other first-line formations. They broke in but could not break out, as another last-stand counterattack by another hard-hammered British battalion closed another temporary gap and forced the attackers back from yet another initial gain.

Falkenhayn was—finally—growing less sanguine. The infantry was exhausted; there was only enough ammunition for six days of combat; and the weather was worsening to a point of making large-scale combat virtually impossible. Ypres remained untaken. On November 10, Falkenhayn informed William he intended to close down an operation no longer promising decisive results.[5] That made him the second German commander in a matter of weeks to run out of ideas relevant to the Western Front.

It was from Ypres that one of the war's signature myths emerged. Its taproot was an army report for November 10 that described "young regiments" singing "*Deutschland über alles*" as they stormed the enemy line. A more elaborate version in a regimental history describes a similar incident inspired by an abandoned piano. The story became an intrinsic part of the "matter of Langemarck," the body of literature, lore, and legend that developed into a master narrative during and after the war. Searches were undertaken for the hero who had first raised the song. The Nazis incorporated the story into their own master narrative as a meme for heroic youth betrayed by an undeserving fatherland.[6]

After 1945 the event was downgraded to myth, then to fiction. The task was not difficult. Apart from the Nazi connections, two world wars had made the notion of going singing into battle into a bad joke. Wading through mud and stumbling over bodies, loaded down like a pack mule, left little breath to waste on harmony. Yet the ironic reality fact was that the *Deutschlandlied* and similar songs echoed and reechoed across the fields of Ypres from the beginning. Given the general confusion of the initial attacks, signs and countersigns often were never given, or quickly forgotten. Singing was about the best way for a group to make its presence and identity known. Nor was it the worst way, particularly at night, to keep up spirits shaken by the day's experience. Not enthusiasm but necessity was the matrix of legend.[7]

II

Christmas in the trenches was recognized by a special issue of chocolate and tobacco, celebrated by opening and sharing the packages that managed to make it through the army's postal system, and commemorated by another subject of myth: the Christmas truce. In the French sector of the front, direct fraternization was exceptional; the truce was essentially an affair between the Germans and the British. The informal and episodic suspension of hostilities, with its exchange of carols, its meetings between the trench lines, its posing for group photographs, and its collecting of bodies for decent burial, was a one-time event, reflecting nostalgia for home and desire for normalcy.[8]

Nor was that surprising. The German Army was a citizen army. An overwhelming number of its rank and file had solid elementary educations that incorporated cogitation as well as indoctrination. A high number of them had civilian experiences that encouraged situational awareness; neither shops nor factories, not even family farms, rewarded dullness. In other words German soldiers were reasonably accustomed to working things out for themselves. Most German soldiers were also literate above the functional level. Most of them had anxious families and friends. As an initial flood of letters written in boxcars and billets dwindled when the fighting started, people turned to rumors and newspapers—in practice much the same thing. Especially in the smaller cities and towns, letters from men at the front were frequently published. Most, as such letters are likely to be in any war, were written, indeed composed, to spare their readers. But as the front stagnated and men had a bit of time for reflection, words like "murder," "annihilation," and "slaughter," with phrases such as "we just had no idea of what to do," and "the feeling was that we had been senselessly sacrificed and were being treated like cannon fodder in the most contemptuous meaning of the word," began filtering back home through a military censorship still anything but comprehensive or systematic.[9]

As yet, disillusion with the war and rejection of its waste and stupidity were minority perspectives. Two specific loci of heterodoxy nevertheless existed. One was the war volunteers, not only the students but the others not fully socialized into the worlds of work and deference. The other, less visible but no less vigorous, was social democracy, whose prewar compromise with conscription was expedient at best. Youth and ideology provided matrices for observing the shortcomings of a system that seemed increasingly unable to bury the dead, succor the wounded, and feed the living.

One could hardly speak of a decline in morale, but by the turn of the year endurance had replaced enthusiasm as the lodestone. "We didn't want the war; we didn't start it; but we have to see it through," comes as close to the new defining meme as can be done with a catchphrase.[10]

The home front underwent its own version of traumatic stress. Casualty reports were erratic and slow in emerging, partly for the sake of domestic morale, partly because the war machine had more immediate concerns, and partly because even the vaunted German military administration had simply lost track of the tens of thousands listed as "missing." Lists of names were seldom posted, notifications were individual, from concern for enemy intelligence keeping score—and perhaps as well to discourage Germans from expressing awkward emotions and asking awkward questions.

On September 30 a German mother wrote, "it seems so stupid that the boys must go to war ... yet they must, must!"[11] The defense of Germany required it. Käthe Kollwitz spoke from the heart. Her youngest son was a *Kriegsfreiwilliger* who had enlisted in August, and was killed in action around Dixmude on October 23, aged nineteen. Kollwitz's sculpture *Die Eltern*, a mother and father hewn out of stone by the force of pain, stands in the German cemetery at Vladso, Belgium. At least the Kollwitzes had a gravesite. When the final exhumations and consolidations were complete in the Ypres salient, 25,000 unidentified bodies were interred in a "Comrades' Grave." It is a paradox that in a period when it became increasingly important to recognize individual soldiers' graves, anonymity became an increasingly common signifier of death in battle.

II

Numbers taken at random tell their own story. France counted almost 400,000 casualties by the end of September. German dead alone in 1914 totaled around 150,000. Turning to specifics, the BEF lost over 54,000 men in six weeks at Ypres. The German figure for the same space and time was 80,000. Neither such losses nor the mentalities behind them could be sustained. From a mixture of pragmatism and expedience, the combatants began moving underground.

Like those of its opponents, the German Army's trench system was an improvisation. German doctrine, mythology, and conditioning had since the Seventeenth Century focused on open warfare and offensive operations. The General Staff was, however, well aware of the increasing role field entrenchments had played in the Russo-Japanese War a decade earlier. Professional literature was saturated with articles on the technical and moral aspects of the subject. Institutionally, however, the army remained impervious. In part the political and strategic imperatives impelling open warfare resisted systematic challenge. In part Germany indulged the same kind of superiority complex that explained away aspects of the American Civil War challenging conventional continental thinking: what was to be learned by the grappling of Orientals and semi-barbarians? In part, like any institution, the German Army of 1914 believed in itself—in its capacity to fix mistakes, replace weak links, and overcome obstacles. And in part the pace of the autumn campaign allowed no time for reflection; tomorrow's fight was the one that mattered.

The first trenches correspondingly amounted to shell holes connected *ad hoc*, one- or two-man foxholes, and improvised strong points based on rubble.[12] They acquired an economy-of-force dimension during the "race to the sea," as formations were transferred or leapfrogged north and the resulting gaps needed to be plugged. Trenches, however, were first taken seriously during the blood-soaked stalemate in front of Ypres. A useful case study is offered by the 43rd Reserve Division. A wartime creation, it was recruited from Berlin and Brandenburg. It had a high proportion of *Kriegsfreiwilligen*, including many students. It had been shot to pieces in late October around Dixmude, to the point where one sober historian refers to a postponed attack as "a stay of execution." With its regiments reduced to half strength and morale badly shaken, the 43rd was given a makeover from the top down, starting with a new division commander and two new brigadiers. All were from the active list, experienced in combat command, hands-on, physically vigorous, and not least professionally ambitious. They reconfigured the front line, connecting isolated positions and using the division's pioneers to show the infantry how to construct secure trench networks as opposed to holes scratched out more or less at random. Bridges restored supply routes disrupted by flooding, enabling hot meals to be brought forward once or even twice a day. Systematic patrolling provided up-to-date information on enemy activity and restored confidence shaken by earlier fiascoes. Rear zones were systematically searched for the hundreds reported "missing." Not merely corpses and identity disks, but a fair number of wounded were recovered—another significant morale-booster. On November 10 the division attacked Dixmude, this time with solid artillery preparation and a pervasive sense of having a fighting chance. It was a significant local success—featuring no quarter for the garrison's Senegalese. It also had no context. The capture of Dixmude had originally been intended as the first step in a war-deciding sweep along the channel coast. Now victory amounted to five hundred prisoners, a few machine guns, and control of a heap of rubble. Was this anomaly or portent?[13]

Situational awareness of a similar kind was emerging among staff officers as well. In October and again in January 1915, for example, III Corps' chief of staff combined brief but systematic preparation, massive artillery support, and tactical surprise in successful attacks for limited objectives.[14] Hans von Seeckt would be heard from again. But could his methods be applied on scales larger than a division or two? Or did they amount to sector-level housekeeping? Senior commanders were unobtrusively weeded. The three royal princes predictably remained, all sporting new decorations. However, Hausen was relieved in September. Bülow, since autumn acknowledged as a figurehead, departed in March 1915. Kluck was wounded and evacuated the same month. Their replacements were and remain anonymous—usually appropriately so. The same holds for the increasing number of new corps commanders, most of whom defy identification even in this age of electronic records. What they had in common, apart from being in better health and more emotionally vigorous than their predecessors, was that they were "company men," not likely to be a source of fresh ideas even at operational levels.

Rudolf Binding was a reserve officer recalled in 1914. "The war," he declared, "has got stuck into a gigantic siege. Neither side has the force to make a decisive push."[15] This over-age cavalry lieutenant was nevertheless thinking along lines similar to Erich von Falkenhayn. The new chief of staff had begun reaching a conclusion by November that a decisive victory in the west was not possible in the immediate future, given the existing balance of forces and resources, and given the ability of even rudimentary defense systems to frustrate the most determined attacks by the most committed troops. In the tactical context, Germany had achieved Schlieffen's mantra in reverse. The flank man of the right wing was indeed brushing the Channel with his sleeve, securing the German right, as neutral Switzerland, with its mountains and its militia, secured the left. In between, the great offensive had secured large stretches of eminently defensible terrain from Vosges to the Chemin des Dames to the Somme valley in Picardy, terrain that could be controlled at limited cost by making local adjustments.

Local adjustments were a long way from a Grand Design. But if *Weltpolitik* was an imprecise concept, it was not merely an abstract one. From the Great War's beginning, Germany mounted what Hew Strachan describes as a global strategy of broadening the conflict war by striking at its opponents' perceived weak points in Asia and Africa. India, Persia, and Afghanistan, the Suez Canal region, French North Africa—all were targets of German and German-sponsored initiatives, political, military, even religious, beginning in the war's early months. None, however, generated the kind of prompt, large-scale payoffs that might have lifted them from shadow/sideshow status.[16]

Of more significance was the diplomatic victory that secured the Ottoman Empire's participation on the side of the Central Powers. Its frontier with Russia had been a mutual running sore for years. The seesaw fighting that began in the Caucasus in November 1914 diverted enough Russian resources and generated enough Russian concern about an internal Muslim uprising that it encouraged pursuing a second form of indirect approach. For two decades prior to 1914, Russia had played an increasingly limited role in German strategic thought and planning. Reduced to a basic theorem, Russia was understood as an unlikely theater for the quick, decisive victory that was the lodestone of German military policy. Plans for Russia as a primary objective existed and were regularly updated until 1913, however, when Moltke declared their updating a waste of effort on an unlikely contingency and entrusted the defense of eastern Germany to the Reich's military leftovers. Their mission was to hold Russia in check until the victorious armies could redeploy from France and settle the matter of mastery in the east.

Russia's strategy *vis à vis* Germany was shaped by diplomatic considerations. Since Russia could under no circumstances stand alone against a German–Austrian coalition, its most prudent behaviors were to see that France was not hopelessly crippled, and that Britain would support an alliance concluded only in 1907. That called for an offensive as proof of good will. And the sweeping military reforms implemented after the Manchurian debacle suggested Russia was capable of attacking Germany and Austria simultaneously with favorable odds.[17]

Russia's war plan against Germany involved sending two armies into the East Prussian salient, the first advancing west across the Niemen River and the second northwest from Russian Poland. The intention was to destroy the German field force of the province, and establish conditions for a further advance into Germany. Initially both halves of the offensive were successful against indecisive opposition. The Russian commanders, however, failed both to coordinate their movements and to press their numerical and geographic advantage. A new command team was dispatched: Erich Ludendorff, freshly decorated for his "hussar's trick" at Liège, as chief of staff; and Paul von Hindenburg, a retired general who owed his appointment in part to having retired on the main railroad route from Koblenz to East Prussia, and in part to a reputation for the kind of imperturbability that seemed necessary in the situation. Building on—or it might be said appropriating—the plans developed by the Great War's most brilliant General Staff officer, Colonel Max Hoffmann, they concentrated their forces against the Second Army. In five days of hard fighting between August 26 and 30, 40,000 Russians were casualties, 90,000 more were prisoners, and Germany had its first heroes of the war.

Hindenburg and Ludendorff then turned against the First Army, routing it between September 5 and 13 in the battle of the Masurian Lakes and driving it back across the frontier with over a hundred thousand casualties. The two corps conveniently dispatched by Moltke contributed significantly to this achievement. Like Tannenberg,* however, the Masurian Lakes was a local victory. Neither one opened the way to a significant operational or strategic objective—only to a further advance into the swamps and forests of Russia.

---

* The first great German victory of the war, won against a Russian Army as unprepared as it was overconfident.

Generalleutnant Wilhelm Gröner, in about 1917. He succeeded Ludendorff as Quartermaster General in October of that year. (Getty)

Portrait of the German emperor, William II, from the field. (ullstein bild via Getty)

Kaiser William II (left, with knitted cap) during the award of decorations for the fighters at Cambrai. (ullstein bild via Getty)

Prussian War Minister and later German Chief of the General Staff Erich von Falkenhayn. Published in *Zeitbilder*, 1915. (Photo by Albert Meyer/ullstein bild via Getty Images)

The Germans, moreover, had their attention distracted by an ally that had marched blindly into catastrophe.

Austria-Hungary's offensive north from Galicia into Russia was at best a high-risk enterprise. The risk was compounded by Chief of Staff Conrad von Hötzendorff's belief that he could use his strategic reserve in two places sequentially, shifting it from Serbia to Russia as one might move counters on a map. But apart from having been urged to the operation by the Germans as recently as May, the initial balance of forces in the Russian sector made a Habsburg offensive imperative by the standards of August 1914. Austria enjoyed a temporary advantage in men, and only a slight inferiority in guns. To sacrifice the initiative was to risk giving Russia time to mobilize an overwhelming force, overrunning the Austrian forces in the field and forcing the remnants into the fortresses of Lemberg and Pryzemysl or back against the Carpathian Mountains. The result was a mutually badly managed series of brutal encounter battles that crippled the Austrian Army by mid-September. There were just too many Russians in too many places. His soldiers exhausted, his officers bewildered, Conrad accepted retreat as the only alternative to annihilation, and appealed reluctantly but desperately for German support.[18]

Hindenburg and Ludendorff brought four corps south into Poznan, utilizing the excellent German railway network, and struck the Russian rear on November 11. This time the Russians traded space for position, retreating, concentrating, and counterattacking as rain and then bitter cold and snow slowed both sides to a near-crawl. A reinforced German corps was cut off, and the Russians had ordered up boxcars to transport the prisoners they expected to harvest. Instead, the Germans fought their way out at a cost of nearly 50 percent casualties, bringing out most of their wounded and 16,000 prisoners. As a footnote, the formation that accomplished this long-forgotten feat of arms was one of Falkenhayn's creations, sent east almost by accident to highlight the potential squandered in the mud of Ypres.

As winter set in, the Austrians, driven into the Carpathians, fought a series of back and forth battles that cost them another quarter-million men shot, frozen, or eaten by wolves, while Conrad sought to cobble together a new field army out of the remnants. The German sector stabilized until February 7, when High Command East, Hindenburg and Ludendorff's official title, mounted an attack on the Russians still in Masuria. It was a rousing success tactically, a model of bad-weather campaigning that inflicted 100,000 casualties, took 110,000 prisoners, and drove seventy miles into Russia before bogging down in the face of winter storms and desperate resistance. Strategically, however, the offensive was irrelevant. It had no direct objective. It was uncoordinated with anything the Austrians planned or might intend. The second Masurian offensive, however, did have a significant political dimension.

The closing of the Western Front had thrown the German Army off balance. The emerging continuous front prefigured not merely an attritional war, but mounting a series of head-down breakthrough battles against an entrenched, alert, and capable enemy. The German Army's perceived strengths were mobility, flexibility, and imagination. A school of "Easterners" developing around Hindenburg and Ludendorff asserted that, beginning with Tannenberg, conditions in the East, where the balance between space and numbers had not yet created stagnation and where "flank" and "rear" remained meaningful operational concepts, meant the German Army would have a chance to do best what it did well—*if* it were appropriately reinforced.

Falkenhayn was anything but indifferent to that prospect—albeit from a fundamentally different perspective. He considered that the limited forces at Germany's disposal in the context of the overall strategic situation rendered a decisive battlefield victory anywhere, west or east, unlikely to the point of impossibility. Instead, his thinking echoed that of the elder Moltke in linking force and diplomacy, focusing on a battlefield victory sufficient to prepare the ground for a negotiated, and therefore a moderate, peace. Theobald Bethmann-Hollweg was no Bismarck, nor was Falkenhayn Helmuth von Moltke. However, though aware that the Entente powers had pledged not to consider a separate peace, Falkenhayn was also aware of the historic weakness of such grand coalitions, especially those formed on a negative basis. On November 18 Falkenhayn met with Bethmann and recommended he negotiate peace with either Russia or France. That would enable a decisive concentration against the remaining continental power and Britain—which Falkenhayn regarded as Germany's true implacable foe.

Falkenhayn was confident that given a few more thrashings, Russia could be brought to heel with the diplomatic equivalent of beads, blankets, pots and pans. Bethmann was less sanguine and more suspicious—specifically wary that Falkenhayn sought to evade the army's responsibility for lack of success by shifting the burden to the politicians. In December he visited High Command East and found articulate and ambitious generals who believed the army could achieve a peace on its own. Bethmann, a military amateur, was willing to be convinced—particularly since he saw an opportunity to drive an exploitable, perhaps a Bismarckian, wedge into what since August had appeared a uniformed monolith.[19]

For the next six weeks, the Great War was forgotten as the German high command embarked on a bitter internal conflict. The failure at Ypres, and the casualty rates accompanying it, encouraged suggestions that Falkenhayn possessed neither the ability nor the gravitas to succeed Moltke and Schlieffen in this ultimate emergency. Holger Herwig appropriately speaks of the implosion of a command structure that, like so much of Germany's prewar military system, proved over-tempered metal: inflexible and brittle under stress.[20] Falkenhayn retained his post, less by the merit of his ideas or his skill at intrigue than because William, for the first time in the war and the last time in his reign, decisively exercised the royal command authority on which he insisted and refused to appoint someone like Erich Ludendorff, whom he described as a dubious character driven by personal ambition, to the Reich's top military post. Events would prove William's evaluation all too close to the mark. But the affair's resolution did not generate a strategic decision. France or Russia? The question remained open.

III

The issue involved more than an internal struggle for power at high levels. The temporary Russian occupation of East Prussia was both traumatic and galvanizing. In contrast to German behavior in the west, which was fundamentally generated by combat and its aftermath, the Russians combined unsystematic looting with a policy of deportations that removed around 13,000 inhabitants of the province to a miserable fate in the Russian interior. The number would have been larger but for a well-organized evacuation program that temporarily relocated almost a million East Prussians as far west as Schleswig and Westphalia. The refugees were tangible evidence of the consequences of defeat. Their experiences lost nothing in the individual telling and reinforced the position that Germany was fighting a just war against alien barbarians. A massive fund-raising campaign to alleviate the exiles' hardships and compensate their losses indicated the stiffening—and the systematizing—of a national resolve whose initial manifestations had been more or less spontaneous.[21]

This public spirit was as comprehensive as it was unexpected by the authorities. Both the nature and the depth of public commitment to a future war had been sufficiently questioned by the government and the army to make the concept of a short decisive conflict a socio-political necessity as well as a military one. These prewar anxieties about domestic unrest had proved exaggerated. Social Democrat parliamentarians had voted for war; Social Democratic reservists had reported to the depots in the same percentages as the general population. Plans for incarcerating potential revolutionaries were correspondingly pigeonholed—but not forgotten.

Michael Neiberg describes a general pattern in Europe of hardening attitudes: frustration and bitterness, revenge, hatred and fear sufficient to ensure (the war's) progress to its bitter end.[22] But an underlying question remained: what would that end be? The answer depended in good part on where the emotions generated by war would eventually focus. And that depended on relations between homeland and fighting front. Letters of grievance and complaint in either direction could be interpreted as threatening an extending war effort no less than anything the Entente armies could do. Soldiers' mail was censored at unit level until April 1916, and afterwards centrally, but always sporadically, by samples. Noteworthy as well was that censors were supposed to concentrate on serious criticism of the war effort and serious breaches of secrecy and discipline. They were not to pursue general complaints about conditions, or to interfere with private exchanges of opinion—between spouses, for example, or parents and children.[23]

In part that made a virtue of necessity. By best calculation almost thirty billion letters were exchanged during the war. The number seems initially absurd until one remembers that as trench war became routine soldiers and their families wrote almost daily. The sheer amount of mail made comprehensive censorship impossible, given contemporary technological and administrative resources. But the Second Reich was built around consensus rather than compulsion. Monitoring correspondence was a major way of keeping track of personal opinions, as opposed to the public statements of politicians, preachers, and journalists. Holes perceived could be plugged. Stress points noted could be alleviated. And in the war's first eighteen months, four interrelated stress points emerged.

The first was disruption: the physical removal from civil society of four million men in an economically and socially critical cohort. Families with primary wage earners in uniform found themselves constrained to move in with relatives or relocate to humbler quarters. Factories and offices, schools and hospitals, were forced to improvise as key personnel disappeared overnight. Farms adjusted in the middle of harvest season to the absence of the muscle power, animal as well as human, central to bringing in the year's crop.

Emotionally as well, war brought disorganization. While the patriarchal nature of Imperial German family life can be exaggerated, the absence of fathers, uncles, and older brothers forced women into dual parenting roles always unfamiliar and often uncongenial. The educational structure changed as well. With school days shortening, curricula becoming increasingly war-related, and class sizes doubling, elementary and secondary students alike were cast increasingly on their own resources, or drawn into participation in patriotic celebrations and war work ranging from repairing old clothes to assisting with the harvest. As the war became what amounted to a permanent fixture, and as an increasing number of paternal absences became permanent, questions of upbringing began surfacing. How was the rising generation to be socialized into family lives that were being fundamentally eroded from all sides? A Bavarian farm wife wrote for legions of her sisters, urban and rural, in October 1914: "Regarding our children, they do as they are told all right with the help of the cane ... I could tell you a thing or two, but I'll hold my tongue. I have my cross to bear and no doubt I've earned it."[24] Might victory come too late for the old order of things at home as well as in the field?

It would certainly come too late for the burgeoning community of war widows. They were one of wartime Germany's forgotten cohorts—not least because their existence was a frightening reminder of a very real possibility for the women who still had husbands to write to and prepare packages for. But one of the corps districts that became responsible for much of the wartime-generated administration collected statistics on its new-made widows. The IV Corps district was Prussian Saxony. Almost two-thirds of the heavily Protestant population lived in small towns of fewer than 10,000 people. With a prosperous mixed economy based on agriculture and light industry, it was about as representative of the Second Reich as any of the empiricists' administrative divisions. Ninety percent of the women widowed in the war's first year had been married fewer than ten years. Almost sixty percent of them had been married less than four years. Almost all had children, usually one or two. Three fourths of these orphans were under six; half were under three. The individual stories speak of optimism: finding a better apartment, getting a better job. The women mentioned their husbands with affection and their marriages with satisfaction. "And then came the war," was a common caesura. It would become near-universal by 1918.

The second stress point involved food. With the outbreak of war, Germany's food supply, domestic and imported, became insufficient to sustain the rate and nature of peacetime consumption. Open-ended demand for scarce goods means rationing, whether by market pricing, government fiat, or something in between. The Second Reich began by regulating the pricing of foodstuffs. But there were too many vectors of production, distribution, and consumption to enable effective central control, given all the state's new responsibilities. Differences in production, management, and distribution meant surpluses in some places, shortages in others; this was accompanied by universal discontent at government-fixed prices seen as confiscatory at one end of the food chain, extortionate at the other. In Posen, by the end of 1914 the cost of bacon had increased by a fifth, potatoes by an eighth—and Posen had the closest thing to an agriculturally based economy in Germany. On the other side of the scale, Berlin experienced shortages of bread at the end of 1914, potatoes in the new year. The fear of a potato shortage led in turn to a massive slaughtering of pigs in early 1915. Once the sausage was eaten, meat shortages became chronic in towns and cities.[25]

Bread rationing was introduced for Berlin in January 1915 and for the entire Reich in June. Avner Offer describes two types of rationing: survival rationing for everyone, subsistence rationing for those who work and fight.[26] There is a third type as well. Sustainability rationing is the level required to keep a population on track with minimum government compulsion. That last point was crucial in 1914. The *dirigiste* state of the Twenty-First Century, with its extensive involvement in every aspect of society, was still very much in the developmental stage. Even Germany—or perhaps better said Germany in particular—was not in a position to wage foreign and domestic war simultaneously. And the German people were increasingly accustomed to doing themselves well, whether calculated in terms of calories, nutrition, or enjoyment. Consistent shortages and consistent inconvenience increasingly made food a focal point of discontent during 1915. Bertold Brecht in *Die Dreigroschenoper* eventually coined the aphorism,*"erst kommt das Fressen, dann kommt die Moral"* (first comes food, then comes morale). What might be the social consequences if relative deprivation became absolute?

Contributions were a third source of stress. More than any major combatant, Germany from the beginning emphasized direct, personal civilian sacrifice. From the start of the war municipalities collected garbage. Germany was a high-wastage society, and kitchen scraps could feed animals. Textile shortages were endemic, given the seemingly inexhaustible demands for uniforms, bandages, and footwear combined with blockade-induced shortages. Household metal from kitchen utensils to gutters and roofs was mobilized for the war effort. Gold was sought: coins and jewelry down to wedding rings, with a sideline in gems that could be sold on neutral markets.

Above all cash was solicited for every purpose conceivable, in every way from lotteries to cash boxes, and in every milieu from churches to—so rumor often had it—brothels.[27]

The collections increasingly morphed into a nuisance. They were inefficient. Above all they were insufficient to underwrite the war Germany was waging as opposed to the war Germany had hoped to fight, even before rising inflation ate into the actual returns from the pledges and donations.

Germany was a federal system, with many financial matters under control of state and local authorities. Germany relied heavily on indirect taxes for public income. The standard prewar option for addressing tension between tangible income and desired expenditure was borrowing, at a level that even before the war made German bonds a higher risk than their European counterparts. But with the outbreak of war Germany was largely cut off from international money markets. More systematic and more profitable were war bonds. The first issue was in late September 1914. During the war there were seven more, at six-month intervals: presumably to give the shorn sheep time to regrow at least some wool. Each bond drive was accompanied by a spectrum of exhortations, sermons, leaflets, and public assemblies that made them central public rites, at least in the cities. Moral imperatives like patriotism and duty had a practical counterpoint, with interest rates higher than those paid by banks, and by extensive tax exemption for dividends. Doing well while doing good is an irresistible combination. In 1914–15 the war loans were consistently oversubscribed, reflecting enthusiasm and determination—and underwritten by the conviction that victory would bring repayment with interest.

One overriding caveat persisted. Cashing in required winning the war. The Reich was borrowing from itself—or in gambler's parlance "betting on the outcome." That behavior is as risky in war-making as at the gaming table. Metastasizing immediate costs made sufficient nonsense of budgeting, so that even in 1915 printing presses were beginning to fill the gap with inflationary paper. Inflation was not exactly unknown in the Second Reich, but its impacts were selective and temporary. Wartime inflation was collective and enduring, not to say permanent. The corresponding questions were whether, and for how long, a sense of duty, an ethic of sacrifice, and a determination to stand behind the men in the trenches would counterbalance salaries, pay envelopes, and sustain household budgets already feeling the pinch of growing shortages.[28]

The fourth leg of the stool of stress was health. Before the war the central vectors were increasingly positive. German medicine and German public health set world standards. Urban slums, bad enough, were less toxic than those of Vienna, London, or Manchester. Workplace safety was unrivaled from Chicago to St Petersburg. Infant mortality was shrinking, life spans extending. Quality of life, still an ephemeral concept, had enough positive indices that it was undermining the revolutionary elements of Social Democracy: fat cattle do not usually stampede.

This synergy of wellbeing was challenged, then denied, by the war. Casualties had not been part of the public reckoning when mobilization was decreed. This omission was based on memory as well as denial. The losses in the Franco-German War had been limited in number and impact. Improvements in surgery, anesthesiology, asepsis, and sanitation had saved lives and limbs, reduced deaths from disease, and generally marginalized war's human costs.

This war was different. The opening two or three weeks featured casualty rates that swamped the medical system in terms of both numbers and traumas. A good proportion of those listed as both missing and killed in action actually died of wounds before being treated, or expired in overburdened field hospitals. By the end of August, as the fronts began to stabilize and the systems to adjust, another characteristic of the Great War was beginning to emerge. Military medicine had made enough progress in both treatment and care that men who in earlier wars would have died quickly even with treatment were now surviving—surviving not merely in larger numbers, but even though grossly mutilated. Multiple amputations, destroyed faces, fragment-shredded torsos, joined the "normal" wounded on hospital trains to Germany. And rumors of worse things circulated widely—of men confined to special secret hospitals because of their hideous deformities.

Evacuation to the homeland was a simple process, using existing rail connections, taking little time, and offering better facilities than those available even in the large stationary hospitals in occupied France and Belgium. Cities, towns, even villages accommodated increasing numbers of wounded. By April 1915 a single corps district included almost 200 hospitals and convalescent facilities. In the early weeks hospital trains stopping for any reason in a station were surrounded by crowds ranging from the sympathetic curious to those seeking news of someone, and the wounded were feted as heroes. Even for those able to appreciate the sentiment, the sense of being zoo animals was strong, and grew stronger as with time morbid curiosity seemed to motivate more and more of the onlookers.[29]

To prove things could always become worse, an increasing number of cities sought to limit the numbers of wounded allowed to appear on streets and in parks, theaters, even bars—their presence was described as affecting civilian morale. This was merely one manifestation of a growing question: How to deal with human wastage that did not conveniently remove itself by dying.

The long-standing case that the Great War was "good" for medicine in general has been comprehensively and convincingly challenged by a body of recent scholarship demonstrating the distortion of both research and priorities: focusing on treating abnormal traumas and moving medical care away from patient treatment towards management of warfare and the welfare of the "national body." In concrete terms and German contexts, that meant growing emphasis on rehabilitative treatment and the socialization of the severely disabled through medical processes. "Recycling the disabled," still in its developing stages during 1914–15, meant both returning them to the war effort, whether behind desks, on farms, or in factories, but it also suggested the reintegration into society of a category of people who in prewar years had been relegated to the dustbin of misfits.[30]

One branch of medicine was particularly affected as the war progressed: psychiatry. Otto Binswanger was one of Germany's leading neurologists and psychologists. Shortly after the war's outbreak he wrote that he had had a large number of weak-nerved youths as patients: obsessed by their emotions and focused on their egos. Then came the war and their debilities vanished. They volunteered—and what impressed Binswanger most, all but one "proved themselves" at the front.[31]

Exactly how that proof was demonstrated remained unrecorded. Better documented is the impact of unexpectedly long-term front-line conditions that challenged sense and meaning both in physical and moral contexts. Two-thirds of the men killed in 1914 were between twenty and twenty-nine. Another 20,000 were under eighteen: the war volunteers. Their replacements included more and more men over thirty, with established lives whose norms were as far away from those developing in the trenches as is possible to imagine. Nor was it possible to speak of phobic reactions, the kinds of symptoms associated with what are colloquially described as the "worried well." Add to this constant physical exhaustion and the sheer randomness of death in the trenches, and during the war's first days the result was a steadily increasing number of emotional breakdowns.

Military medicine is focused by its nature on returning as many men as possible to duty, whatever the nature of their disability. The medical and military systems initially synergized efforts to address symptoms before they became habits: seeking "field cures" by keeping cases close to the front line. Prefiguring the American experience in World War II, it became increasingly apparent that the deeper a psychiatric case became involved with the system, the less grew the chances that he would return to the front. But the overloading of the medical system meant that those without visible traumas were frequently sidetracked, slipping between the cracks of the front-line medical system. It was easier just to ship them home.

Once back in the fatherland their experiences varied. To a greater extent than in France or Britain, German doctors applied early versions of talk therapies and drug therapies borrowed from peacetime practice: hypnosis and persuasion, complemented by doses of sedatives like valerian and bromide. Results were sufficiently episodic and unpredictable to generate an alternative perspective during 1915. Before the war, academicians and soldiers alike had voiced concern that modern civilization was producing a race of "girly-men:" labile, sensitive, self-reflective, ill-adapted to appropriate masculine roles in peace or war. This image was reinforced by blunt pragmatism. "They shell you, and of course you're shocked!," to borrow a British aphorism from the war's early months. In the sense of Joseph Heller's *Catch-22*, traumatic symptomology that removed one from the front could well be interpreted as *prima facie* evidence of sanity—or, depending on the observer's perspective, subconscious malingering, an escape into illness. Doctors influenced by Social Darwinism and heroic vitalism insisted that "character" and "will power" ultimately defined a man, and were best restored by direct methods. Sensory deprivation, induced suffocation, massive electric shocks: the list of "treatments" regularly applied to German psychiatric casualties reads like a torturers' handbook.

Yet there was another aspect to the issue. A common pattern of "war neurosis," the all-purpose diagnostic/descriptive term that was the German counterpart of "shell shock," was withdrawal. It could be physical. One patient described pain and paralysis in his legs and in his right arm that made it very difficult to move. It could be emotional. Another man wrote, "I am completely shattered ... I am so tired and weak, I would like to go to sleep and not wake up until there is peace in the world, or not wake up at all." And these were the ones able to communicate. A third "case" did not answer when asked nor react on eye contact, staring into emptiness. Violently invasive therapies developed in a socially constructed effort to restore a sense of duty to army and fatherland were continued as an attempt to break through loss of affect, to reach men otherwise condemned to spend their lives trapped behind their eyes. In this psychiatric climate, short-term cruelty might be perceived as a long-term kindness. It was a trope epitomizing a war effort that within a year was straining Germany to the limits of its human resources. It also became an anodyne camouflage for medical procedures whose inspirations seem a cross between the contemporary Richard von Krafft-Ebbing and the medieval Inquisition. One physician describes a treatment for "hysterical deafness:" "Berthold ... injected saline solution into the ears then ... applied galvanic current surges of up to five amperes ... the patient had, metaphorically speaking, only one decision left: either to regain his hearing or to suffer from further and increasing pain." Comment is superfluous.[32]

One of the stronger arguments against a deliberate German intention to go to war in 1914 is the absence of anything resembling systematic preparation for even a short victorious conflict. The military mobilization proceeded with precision and efficiency. Specifics directly connected with that mobilization went well enough. At the start of the war, for example, the artillery had a thousand shells per gun—enough, according to Moltke, for thirty to forty days of sustained combat. By then the German guns had used more ammunition than during the entire Franco-German War. By the end of October Falkenhayn declared that the army was on the verge of running out of shells altogether. With 60 percent of the state's ammunition delivered by private contractors—Krupp was fulfilling foreign contracts after the outbreak of war—Falkenhayn described an unlimited supply of ammunition as a matter of life and death, and the output increased 400 percent by December 1914. By October 1915 the figure was 1,300 percent.

There were, of course, a significantly larger number of guns to supply, but a reasonable balance between barrels and rounds had nevertheless been achieved. Shortages and bottlenecks plagued supplies of other crucial materials as well, ranging from copper through saltpeter to cotton. The War Ministry responded by contacting industrial magnate Walther Rathenau. He had previously minuted the ministry on this issue and proposed establishing a Raw Materials Office (RMO) to register supplies available in conquered territory.

He now became head of an office under the War Ministry responsible for surveying and allocating raw material necessary for the war effort. Beginning with a staff of three, the RMO metastasized into a complex bureaucracy responsible for monitoring available supplies, supervising their allocation, requisitioning, and seizure as necessary, setting price ceilings to control profiteering, organizing importation, creating a growing number of War Raw Material Corporations, private joint-stock companies producing war-related material under government supervision—and that is only a short list of its most significant administrative functions.[33]

The RMO had a developmental aspect as well. Nitrate, an essential component of shell production, could no longer be imported because of the British blockade. Building on prewar research, German chemists were able to produce a synthetic equivalent first in laboratories, then on an industrial scale. A similar process occurred in the militarization of chemistry, giving Germany a significant lead in the development of the Great War's first new weapons system: poison gas.

This synergy of citizen enterprise, management influence, and state regulation provided an initial working matrix for bridging the gap between the unprecedented material demands of industrialized war and the government's initial belief, hope, and expectation that the civil society and the civil economy would be able to respond to a short war by taking up the slack: becoming more efficient with limited government involvement. The actual course of events is indicated by a comparison of the prewar percentage of state expenditure in the Net National Product, 18 percent, with the 1917 figure of around 75 percent. The adjustment was less traumatic than might be expected. From their inceptions, German liberalism and German capitalism had shown themselves accommodating to state influence. By 1914 the same point could be made about the unions in particular and Social Democracy in general. Richard Bessel makes a strong case that the improvised mobilization of 1914–15 was more successful, relatively and absolutely, than its comprehensive successor.[34] From the soldiers' side of the desk, the War Ministry and its new subsidiaries proved, initially at least, more about management than militarism, more committed to problem-solving than to following procedure. The "temporary commands" established in the corps districts were under senior officers excluded from field commands on the grounds of age, health, or ability. Their staffs were small, the positions often occupied by anyone able to fit into his old uniform, the issues addressed alien. Proposals to create a single controlling agency, a kind of civilian counterpart of the General Staff, were rejected for constitutional and practical reasons. The deputy war minister enunciated the key point: such an institution could not be improvised. We must, he declared, work with what is at hand and solve problems as they arise. That meant turning to bureaucrats and executives for counsel and personnel. Flexibility, even the involuntary kind, could be as useful as a system in a total war.

IV

To say Germany's resources were stretched does not imply their exhaustion. About 180,000 men, convalescents and recruits, were reporting every month. By 1916 the army would count nearly 6,800,000 men. The first reinforcement began in December 1914, when a third wave of reserve formations were organized: nine divisions, one of them Bavarian. Reflecting the ill-camouflaged disaster around Langemarck, each of the new regiments was assigned ten NCOs and 300 men from active regiments as mentors and stiffening. Their training period was extended by several weeks. Their weapons and equipment allocations were complete. Nor was it necessarily a disadvantage that few of the new recruits had any illusions about the kind of war they would be fighting.

The most optimistic back-of-the-envelope calculation could not deny the numbers. This was the last sizable tranche of new formations Germany would be able to raise and sustain. But internal reconfiguration was still possible. Before the war, reducing the size of German infantry divisions to create handier, more flexible entities had been hotly debated. Tactically the initial stages of trench warfare indicated that German divisions were too large for optimal deployment under the developing conditions of the Western Front. Operationally and strategically Germany needed more moveable pieces.

Colonel Ernst von Wrisberg of the War Ministry began by withdrawing from each division on the Western Front one infantry regiment and a proportion of its guns. When the shuffling was completed, by fits and starts across the theaters of war, a standard German infantry division had three regiments, one field artillery regiment of thirty-six guns and a battalion of a dozen mediums, and supporting units supplemented as necessary from higher headquarters.[35] With their similarly reorganized French counterparts, they set the pattern of division organization for most of the century: around 12,000 to 15,000 men, a reasonable balance among flexibility, striking power, and endurance. As for commanders, the brigade had long been criticized as an unnecessary link and the smaller divisions made fewer demands on their staffs.

The permanent army corps, the traditional measuring stick, was ill-adapted to trench warfare, especially in the context of the massive Allied offensives of 1915. On one hand, to gain the advantages of familiarity with specific conditions it was well advised to fix corps headquarters in a particular sector. On the other, when a sector came under attack modern-style it required prompt, heavy reinforcement. Even then, with divisions being worn down over increasingly shorter times it was necessary to relieve and rotate them more frequently. The result in practice during 1915 was that the restructured division increasingly became the German Army's unit of movement and calculation, with the corps evolving towards an operational headquarters.

The new divisions were put together more or less *ad hoc*, and could include both active and reserve regiments. Whenever possible these drew replacements more or less from their original district, decentralizing but preserving the local identity the army historically regarded as important for both efficiency and effectiveness. Otherwise the titles of "active" and "reserve" lost most of their meaning. All the divisions and regiments were armed identically as fast as weapons could be made available; each drew from a common regimental pool that included men with every kind of military preparation and experience. In the final analysis the reorganization took place with a limited amount of heartburning, especially when compared to the British experience in early 1918.

Falkenhayn's initial intention was to use his new reserves in the west. The French had mounted a major offensive in Champagne at the turn of the year—part of Joffre's stated intention to "nibble at them."[36] The initial nibble cost a quarter-million casualties, changed nothing of significance, and returned the initiative to Germany. Falkenhayn requested plans from the commanders on the ground. Krafft and Kuhl, by now established as the best of the field army *chefs*, responded with tactically focused proposals that initially seemed to invite the same fate as Joffre's recent operation. Falkenhayn turned to Seeckt. As part of the general reorganization a new army headquarters, the Eleventh, had been organized with the expressed intention of executing a genuine breakthrough in the west. Johannes Friedrich "Hans" von Seeckt was chief of staff; Max von Fabeck was commanding general. Both had earned notice as cool, clear heads in the final months of 1914. The plan Seeckt submitted reflected his belief that the crucial problem of the fall campaign had been excessive dispersal of limited forces, creating a front that in retrospect might indeed, in Napoleon's phrase, have been designed to stop smuggling. Its final version proposed a breakthrough to be implemented and exploited by no fewer than fifteen corps, supported by every gun that could be made available.

Kuhl, Krafft, and Seeckt had more points in common than fundamental differences. All of them emphasized the importance of attacking into open terrain with no major natural features on which a defeated enemy could rally. They stressed the importance of a strong secondary attack to draw off reinforcements, the necessity of the main offensive securing absolute surprise, the use of short, intensive bombardments of key targets like command posts and artillery positions, and the close cooperation of infantry and artillery.[37]

It is not impossible to perceive here the outlines of the German offensive of March 1918, under significantly more favorable circumstances. The BEF of 1915 was very much a work in progress, with virtually everything to learn about high-tech war on a continental scale. Had a full-scale attack, supported by every heavy gun that could be dredged up, been launched in March between Lens and Armentières, it might have achieved a breakthrough. It might have compelled fundamental revision of French strategy for the year. It might even have opened the way for the negotiations Falkenhayn considered essential.

Falkenhayn did not dismiss those prospects casually. The math, however, seemed against him. Only fourteen new divisions could be formed initially by the regimental transfers—a small number by Western Front standards. Nor did a *de facto* test of the offensive's prospects prove promising. The Second Battle of Ypres was arguably an exercise in gestures. It was a test run for some of the new tactical ideas percolating at army and corps headquarters. It was an effort to eliminate the salient created and held by the Allies in 1914. It was a search for payback, requiting the dead of Langemarck, Messines, the Menin Road. It had a technological aspect as well. Gas had been employed on small and amateurish scales by the French since 1914. OHL decided to pursue its possibilities after the Battle of the Marne, to no practical effect until Fritz Haber of Berlin's Kaiser Wilhelm Institute for Physical Chemistry built on his prewar research and recommended deploying chlorine gas against enemy forward positions. Rather than divert scarce shell casings to the project, Haber suggested moving the highly toxic substance in compressed form to the front in cylinders and releasing it when the wind was blowing westward—the normal meteorological condition in northern France and Flanders. The Allies, he believed, would be unable to develop a comparable instrument and delivery method in time to keep from losing the war.[38]

Legally and morally, Haber's innovation crossed carefully drawn prewar lines that OHL found little difficulty obfuscating—perhaps because the soldiers saw little promise in this variant of "professors' war," perhaps because they saw too much. Rudolf Binding reflected, "I am not pleased with the idea of poisoning men. Of course the entire world will rage about it first and then imitate us."[39] The initial use of cloud gas at Ypres was to support a local offensive, using none of Falkenhayn's prized new divisions. Any broader contexts involved working out the inevitable bugs and glitches before employing gas on a wider, more decisive scale in Russia.

Chlorine gas is an asphyxiant, affecting the respiratory system by destroying lung tissue through hydrochloric acid formed as the gas dissolves in the water present in lungs. In effect the victim suffocates by degrees. Beginning in March 1915, German pioneers laid 5,500 cylinders of this along the front of a single corps. On April 22 the valves were opened and a yellow-green cloud four miles wide drifted slowly towards trenches held by French troops, metropolitan and North African. War has seldom been filthier—and for less reason. The troops directly affected by the gas fled in panic. But the line held. Gas was used three more times in the course of the battle, primarily against a green Canadian division, with essentially the same result. Improvised protection, including urinating on a handkerchief, diminished the chlorine's effect. Nor is it melodramatic to say that the Canadians in particular refused to be daunted by this new horror.

On the evening of May 24, OHL suspended further large-scale operations in the Ypres sector. In an anomaly for the Western Front, the attacker's casualties were lower than the defender's: somewhere around 50,000 compared to 70,000. The Ypres salient had been reduced. The Germans now held most of the high ground surrounding the salient. What remained of Ypres was within easy reach of German artillery. That was all. The salient, whose strategic and operational value had always been questionable, was now more of a death trap than ever. But for the British, the lives lost in sustaining it made withdrawal unthinkable. For the Germans, the lives lost in attacking it made neutralization impossible. In other words, by mid-1915 Ypres was the Western Front in microcosm.

As for the projected war winner, Britain and France set to work and almost within weeks had produced their own, arguably nastier, versions of the Germans' secret weapon. Over 400 cloud-gas attacks were conducted on the Western Front between 1915 and 1918, despite the relative ineffectiveness of the method. Shells became the normal means of delivery and gas became a normal feature of offensive operations: around a third of all artillery ammunition. Eventually poisons were complemented by vesicants: "mustard gas" that clung and burned. Scholars of gas warfare legitimately describe it as evolving—or rather devolving—into a deterrent and a disabler, useful for rendering designated target zones passable only with difficulty, hospitalizing far more often than killing, responsible for no more than 5 percent of the Western Front's total casualties.[40] That is well enough. But it takes no account of waiting in a hospital's darkness with bandaged eyes to discover whether the gas blindness was permanent. Nor does it erase a child's memories of hearing an uncle gassed in 1918 hawking, spitting, and strangling on a damp Minnesota day. Fritz Haber received the Iron Cross and a captain's commission from the hands of William II. He merited both of them.

V

The immediate prospects for extending the use of gas on the Western Front were rendered moot by the virtual collapse of the Austro-Hungarians in the east. A series of futile offensives in January and February finished off the peacetime professional cadres, reducing the army to an agglomeration of home guards and militia, barely trained, poorly equipped, and obviously unmotivated. Falkenhayn's liaison officer at Conrad's headquarters asserted the Habsburg army could withstand a Russian offensive only if supported by German troops or commanded by German generals. On the diplomatic stage, both Romania and the Central Powers' erstwhile ally Italy were being assiduously courted by an Entente able to make more alluring promises than the Central Powers.

Conrad's pleas for help culminated in a threat to seek terms from Russia should Germany not come up to scratch in Austria-Hungary's need. Falkenhayn, studying his options in late March, concluded that Austria-Hungary was simultaneously becoming an increasingly heavy burden and an increasingly indispensable ally. Weaker partners in a coalition always have the option of withdrawing—or collapsing. Conrad might be bluffing but calling his hand was a high-level risk. Falkenhayn decided Germany's least worst option involved mounting an offensive in the east. But it would be an offensive on his terms. Austria's situation left no time for grand strategic combinations. Were German support too generous, moreover, Austria-Hungary might continue her policy of alliance brinkmanship.

Falkenhayn was making his decision as well in the context of the persistent toxic crisis in high command. Hindenburg and Ludendorff had continued their demand that the new corps and as many of the reorganized divisions as possible be assigned to the east, even if that meant the drastic shortening of the Western Front through local withdrawals. With those reinforcements Ludendorff guaranteed to end the war with Russia in early 1915. Falkenhayn for his part remained convinced that "the East gives nothing back." His decision was to relieve the pressure on a desperate Austria by the direct insertion of German formations. The Russians seemed sufficiently overextended and disorganized by their recent successes that a relatively small shift in the balance of force might achieve disproportionate results quickly and put some fight back into the Habsburg soldiers.

As much to the point, direct intervention would frustrate Hindenburg and Ludendorff's scheming ambition. The new sector would be under Austrian command—but Falkenhayn took care to see that the Germans would do the heavy lifting. He sent eight divisions east, most of them organized in the new-model triangular form, most of them as well qualified to execute and exploit a breakthrough as any in the German Army. The 11th Bavarian Division, for example, was organized in 1915 from three war-tested regiments, two active and one reserve. A memorandum of April 4 summarized nine months of blood-bought experience as follows. Bring the assault positions as close to the enemy front as possible. Carry out extensive reconnaissance, making maximum use of aircraft. Build the attack plan around the closest possible coordination of infantry and artillery. Ensure ample phone and visual communications among front line units and headquarters. And not least: define and limit objectives *precisely.*[41]

The mantras might be easier to recommend than execute. Nevertheless, this was an ideal handbook for a well-brought-up division in this phase of the war, or indeed in any other. Nor did Falkenhayn depend entirely on doctrine. He also dispatched the newly created heavy artillery reserve originally intended for the west: 150 guns, no mean force by the standards of 1915. And he gave the 11th Bavarian Division and the rest of the rescuers Germany's best field command team. The Eleventh Army headquarters was assigned to execute the eastern offensive with the redoubtable Seeckt continuing as chief of staff. The new commander complemented his *chef.* In most of his pictures August von Mackensen looks like a caricature, with his hawk eyes glaring and his elaborate mustaches bristling under a cavalryman's fur busby featuring a death's head insignia. In fact Mackensen had shown solid ability to learn from experience, never making the same mistake a third time. He believed breakthrough battles could be won, and he was willing to accept casualties to prove a point. No less significant, Mackensen was sufficiently Nineteenth Century in manners and character that he was likely to prove more congenial to his Austrian counterparts than someone from the emerging generation of technocratic Prussians.[42]

On May 2, 1915, Mackensen turned his artillery loose in one of the heaviest bombardments the Eastern Front experienced. By May 4, the Russian defense system had been penetrated on a twenty-five-mile front and their Third Army virtually destroyed. The Russians staggered backwards. With no time even to improvise rear positions, they held exposed sectors until blown out of them by the increasingly sophisticated German artillery. As the Gorlice–

Tarnow sector developed, the Seeckt–Mackensen team proved masters *avant la lettre* of what their British counterparts would later call "bite and hold." Their tactics were slow but devastatingly sure.[43] By the third week in June, three-quarters of a million prisoners crowded Mackensen's cages. Hundreds of thousands more Russians were dead, in hospitals, or unaccounted for. The army's cadres of regular officers and NCOs had been virtually annihilated. Its supplies of artillery ammunition were so low that even before the German attack a battery was allocated only ten rounds daily for its eight guns. Small-arms ammunition was usually replenished from the dead and wounded; the familiar story of Russian soldiers being regularly sent to the front without rifles originated with the Great Retreat, when it was no latrine rumor.[44] Rear echelons, never particularly stable, had virtually disintegrated, with civilians of all ethnicities sent onto the roads by a policy of deportation as cruel as it was foolish, intended to deny their labor to the Central Powers and punish "Jews and suspicious peoples."[45] All men of eighteen to fifty, for example, were ordered evacuated from the Southwestern Front on June 6. Two weeks later the entire population was ordered to be sent to the rear by any means necessary.

With Russia seemingly on the verge of collapse, Hindenburg and Ludendorff urged a finishing stroke in the direction of Petrograd (renamed from St Petersburg at the outbreak of war), backed by every division that could be transferred from the Western Front or created on the home front. Conrad advocated stronger concentrations south of the Gorlice–Tarnow sector.

Falkenhayn's final decision was heavily influenced by the launching of an Allied offensive in Artois on May 9, long expected but mounted in a force unexpected in the aftermath of Second Ypres, and by a failure of negotiations with Italy that prefigured that state's entering the war on the Entente side in a matter of weeks—May 23 to be exact—and the near-simultaneous British attack on Gallipoli. He was if anything even more convinced that the East would give nothing back—at least in purely military terms. At OHL, Gröner had spoken of a "second act" to elevate Mackensen's tactical victories to an operational level. Now Falkenhayn coordinated a plan with Hindenburg and Ludendorff to concentrate available Central Powers resources against the Polish salient and the five Russian armies deployed there. His contributions were minimal: the experienced staff officers of the First Army, temporarily considered surplus to requirements in the west, and 400,000 rounds of artillery ammunition—the latter given to someone who knew how to use them.

The Twelfth Army was a new organization commanded by a new man. Its commander Max von Gallwitz was a vigorous sixty-three-year-old, an artillery specialist ennobled shortly before the war. At the head of a corps he had demonstrated the ability to handle heavy guns in a static situation during the siege of Namur. He had exhibited steadiness in the Masurian fighting. On July 13, 1915 Gallwitz showed what he could do in open warfare, breaking through the hinge of two Russian armies and inflicting 70 percent casualties in four days.[46] Gas played only a limited role; what counted was weight of shell. Warsaw was lost on August 4. The Russians withdrew to the network of fortresses constructed before the war as a barrier to a repetition of Napoleon's thrust to Moscow in 1812. These fell to the Central Powers like beads pulled from a string: Ivangorod on August 3, Kovno on the 18th, Novogeorgievsk on the 19th, Brest-Litovsk on the 26th. For High Command East, this synergistic tsarist disaster was a potential first stage of its long-projected Grand Offensive into Russia's heartland. Falkenhayn, for his part, ironically and probably unconsciously, was asking himself the same question Moltke had posed the previous September: was Russia showing signs of disintegration as opposed to symptoms of stress?

Russia's army was still in the field. Its commitment to the Entente seemed fixed. Falkenhayn believed the way to use the summer's victories was as the "Moltkean" half of a military/diplomatic operation that would result in a separate peace. But could Bethmann-Hollweg play Bismarck's part? "Russia remains the puzzle," wrote the chancellor. Reports on its prospective behavior were "uncertain, changing, and contradictory." Like Falkenhayn, Bethmann accepted the postulate of Russia's immense military potential. He found no difficulty in assuming a strength and coherence in Russia's strategic policy formation that did not exist in the context of the threats and promises Germany was offering.[47]

Michael Geyer puts the Bethmann–Falkenhayn approach in the context of nuclear-age deterrence strategy: balancing the realities of limited interests against the risks of general catastrophe.[48] Experience suggests, however, that deterrence succeeds less from actual strength than from perceptions of it. By mid-1915 what remained of Russia's government resembled nothing so much as a gambler seeking to recoup an initial loss by increasing the stakes. In such a context the game assumes a life of its own, independent of any initial wagers. As long as Russia's allies would back Russia's bets, even only with promises, the Russian Empire was likely to remain at the diplomatic–military table.[49]

That situation highlights the fundamental weakness of German grand strategy. Germany had made no provisions for winning the war as opposed to waging it. The war aims stated in the 1914 September Program were designed to bring onside as many factions and interest groups as possible: generals and admirals, intellectuals, imperialists, and industrialists. Specifics amounted to little more than the Christmas wish list of a five-year-old.[50] The program's stated goal was ensuring the security of Germany for the foreseeable future through a grab bag of projects ranging from the comprehensive economic and geographic reconstruction of central Europe to the establishing of a colonial empire in central Africa. Russia's reaction to all this would be evaluated later.

"Later" was the summer of 1915. Bethmann's initial overtures were pawn moves, involving frontier rectifications as opposed to drastic changes of sovereignty. Neither Tsar Nicholas II nor his foreign office was indifferent to the German overtures. But since August 1914 Russia, more than any of the major belligerents, had been internally drained by the war's unprecedented demands and sacrifices. Its effort was increasingly sustained by hopes and promises. More and more of the empire's political, ethnic, and ideological interest groups were advancing specific, frequently contradictory, aims and outcomes even before military defeat and social dislocation amounting to an eastward migration of the front transformed Russia's political and administrative scene from discordant to chaotic.

A government confident of its military and domestic positions might have risked cutting its losses by cutting a deal. Russia, which had entered the war largely from a sense of its own weakness, was in no position to take such a risk. Instead, deck chairs were shuffled on the *Titanicheskiy*. Russia's minister of war was cashiered, convicted of treason, and imprisoned. Tsar Nicholas assumed personal command of Russia's armies—arguably the most fraught decision of its kind since the emperor Caligula named his horse a consul of Rome. But hope of succor emerged on the horizon. In the spring of 1915 Britain had offered to fulfill a centuries-old Russian dream: Constantinople, with its guaranteed access to the Mediterranean and its implication of a Balkan sphere of influence. To sweeten the pot, the Allies guaranteed Russia an undefined but significant share of the reparations to be extracted from the Central Powers after the war.

Bethmann's efforts to balance the Allies' offer prove that one cannot always beat nothing with something. His proposals seemed so dreadfully mundane compared to the Allies' soaring counterparts. The German chancellor was further handicapped in the second half of 1915 by an increasingly acrimonious dispute with Austria-Hungary over how, specifically, the postwar restructuring of central Europe was best to be accomplished. As for persuading Russia by military means, a newly belligerent Italy was mounting an offensive against an Austro-Hungarian frontier initially defended in some sectors almost literally by teenagers and grandfathers. The Ottoman Empire's entry into the war had put Serbia astride the Turks' major supply route to Europe, a situation that could not be ignored. Even when Bulgaria's September entry on the side of the Central Powers opened alternate logistical possibilities, Bulgarian support was not a free gift.

The immediate result was renewed juggling of the eastern theater's limited resources. Austria-Hungary moved troops from its Russian front to shore up—successfully—its position against Italy. Falkenhayn despatched a half-dozen German divisions and the proven team of Seeckt, Mackensen, and Gallwitz as the core of a combined Central Powers campaign against Serbia. In an overlooked proto-blitzkrieg through extraordinarily unpromising terrain, a command and staff system at peak effectiveness employed state-of-the-art materiel—aircraft, heavy artillery, and bridging technology—to drive a semi-modern Serbian Army into the Adriatic Sea and harry its hastily deployed Anglo-French reinforcements into the "internment camp" of Salonika.[51]

In the eastern theater, 1915 had been a very good year for the German Army. Over two million Russians were out of the war. The front was 200 miles further east. Serbia was occupied; Bulgaria was an ally. Romania was still neutral. The Ottoman Empire had driven the Allies off the Gallipoli Peninsula thanks in no small part to the German officers who had been a vital part of the command and planning teams. Austria might be weaving but was still fighting, and the opening of the Italian front had to a degree restored its military and public morale.

Ever since, Falkenhayn has been criticized, and not merely by German scholars and soldiers, for failing to seek a final decision in a theater that seemed to offer so many opportunities. At the same time, paradoxically, his confrontation with Hindenburg/Ludendorff has given him—and by extension Bethmann—something of an image as the polar opposite: an advocate of at least relative moderation and perspicacity compared to the heedless advocates of an apocalyptic military solution.

In fact, the major protagonists in that faceoff were operating in a common matrix. Their differences involved means and methods rather than ends. Those differences were, however, real enough. Bethmann regarded the political reconfiguration of Central Europe as an end in itself, securing, at least in Europe and perhaps in wider spheres, German hegemony for the reasonably foreseeable future. Falkenhayn saw the projected new order in tactical terms: a means of winning the war by creating a militarily and economically self-sustaining entity that would neutralize the maritime and economic weapons of Germany's fundamental enemy, Great Britain. Hindenburg and Ludendorff had risen to the top by a combination of competent generalship, obliging enemies, skillful intrigue, good fortune, and watching each others' backs. In the process they had narrowed their focus to a German victory by military means, whatever the cost and whatever the consequences. The September Program indicated that powerful economic, political, and ideological forces in the Second Reich were viscerally hostile to even temporary compromises. Should they coalesce, Germany's war effort would become not absolute but total.

And the Hindenburg–Ludendorff team might become a potential rallying point if Falkenhayn could not win the war his way, and quickly. The central problem of Great War offensives was the ability of an entrenched enemy to bring up enough reserves to limit any attack if given enough time. Falkenhayn had presided over and facilitated a lethal combination of planning, surprise and firepower that successfully addressed that situation in a Russian context. Strategically, the Russians had retreated as far as 200–250 miles. Operationally, Russia's offensive capacity seemed crippled. In terms of policy, however, Russia was still in the war. And the additional divisions that might have either finished off its army in a series of set-piece battles or dazzled it into paralysis with grand campaigns of maneuver were fixed on the Western Front by an Allied strategy that had progressed from fumbling nibbles to savage bites.

— VI —

Whether the French offensives of 1915 reflected strategic necessity or irresponsible doctrine remains an open question. They began in mid-February when 155,000 men of the French Fourth Army struck a three-mile front in Champagne. The intention was to make a limited breach, then expand right and left. A stubborn defense and two dozen local counterattacks left the French commander trying to make a case that holding ground once gained cost fewer casualties than retreating from it: Château generalship at its apogee. The result was three square kilometers bought at the cost of over 40,000 casualties. A similar, near-simultaneous attack against the salient of St Mihiel produced similar results, this time at the price of 65,000 casualties. Joffre nevertheless believed French methods had improved and French morale was "marvelous." In May he tested both at Notre Dame de Lorette.

Notre Dame de Lorette, Lorettoberg, is the name of a low ridge north of Arras. Combined with its neighbor Vimy Ridge it is the dominant terrain feature of Artois, dominating the plains around it. The Germans had occupied the ridge during the "race to the sea," held it in December/January 1914–15 against a slapdash French offensive, and developed the Lorettoberg–Vimy position into a salient threatening communications with northern France. On the other hand, a successful "bite attack" could cut the lateral railways behind the German line that were the capillaries of the invaders' logistic system.

On May 9 the initial attack went in. On June 25 Joffre halted the offensive. The French had gained high ground on the ridge of Notre Dame de Lorette—a microscopic tactical inconvenience to the Germans. Total gains in the principal sector amounted to less than two miles on a five-mile front. Over two million artillery rounds had been fired. When secondary and spoiling attacks are included, French casualties totaled over 140,000.[52]

Joffre kept the faith in the face of a torrent of criticism from professional and political sources. On September 25 he mounted an even larger operation, with the main effort in Champagne and with a supporting attack in Artois. The French demonstrated a steep learning curve, coordinating bottom-up and top-down initiatives. Tactics were improved, infantry and artillery coordination was systematized. The German first lines were regularly broken. But the supporting lines just as regularly held.[53] On October 3, Joffre ordered the cessation of attempts at a breakthrough. On November 6 he closed down another failure. This time over three and a half million artillery rounds had been fired, exhausting French reserves and overstraining French production capacity. This time French casualties in Artois and Champagne totaled almost 200,000. Including the 90,000 British casualties endured at Neuve Chapelle, Aubers Ridge, Festeubert, and Loos while the BEF was learning how to fight a technologically and administratively sophisticated war makes the result a summer of attrition—attrition on the wrong side of the balance sheet from Allied perspectives, despite the mutual congratulations exchanged regarding all the valuable lessons that had been learned.

From an Allied perspective, the usual approach to the Western Front in 1915, the French and British took the initiative, sought to break the stalemate, and failed more or less catastrophically. In that context the Germans usually emerge as schoolmasters, charging a high price in blood for tactical tutorials, mastering the field to the point where during one particularly disastrous attack at Loos the Germans ceased firing out of pity for their feckless targets and sent medical personnel into no man's land, treating the wounded and allowing those able to move to make their way to the British line. As many as fifteen days later, other wounded were still crawling into the trenches of one German battalion, whose commander noted, "we were not in the habit of slaughtering the defenceless."[54]

The Germans also emerged on top in the Great War's developing third dimension. Aircraft had made their first appearance in Germany's order of battle when maneuvers showed the previously favored zeppelins unable to meet operational standards and were highly vulnerable even to improvised ground fire. The general staff turned by default to the airplane, and from Moltke downwards became rapid and enthusiastic converts. Between 1909 and 1911 budgets increased exponentially; civilian aircraft companies received subsidies; a flight command was created; and pilot training began. There was no shortage of volunteers—including several dozen general staff officers—for a service that offered something other than routine duty. By 1914, staff planners had developed no fewer than nine roles for aircraft in wartime, including ground attack and troop transport.[55] Over 250 planes were available for the observation, liaison, and reconnaissance duties that lay within their actual technical limits. But the doctrinal framework for expansion only required the engineers to catch up.[56]

In the East, air reconnaissance provided vital intelligence during the Tannenberg campaign. In the West air assets, evenly distributed with six to an active corps and none for the reserves, were spread thin, especially on the right, where the airmen were unable to track the concentration and movement of the BEF with any consistency. As the front stabilized, the High Command sought wider opportunities. An improvised bomber unit, with the innocuous cover name of Carrier Pigeon Detachment Ostend, began short-distance night raids into France and laid plans for expanding operations to Britain once aircraft with a suitable range and payload should come on line. In the interval, zeppelins began bombing London in January 1915, averaging around two raids a month against little opposition, with limited material effect but enough psychological impact to remind the city there was a war on.[57]

Initial hopes that the raids might force Britain out of the war proved ephemeral—not the last time a projected technological quick fix collapsed in the Great War. A series of attacks on Paris proved no more productive, but did confirm Germany's post-Schlieffen Plan commitment to developing an alternative strategic option. More familiar, and certainly more immediately significant, was a breakthrough on the tactical level: the development of the single-seat fighter as an effective instrument of war. The specialized fighter plane emerged as a result of a growing recognition that effective aerial observation, increasingly important in the context of a stable front where a minor advantage could seem significant, depended on aircraft being able to get there and back—or not. On April 1, 1915, a French pilot, Roland Garros, achieved the first kill with a machine gun from a single seater.

His innovation, attaching deflector wedges to his propeller blades, was a high-risk option even for those daredevil days. As early as 1912, Moltke had enquired how best guns could be mounted in aircraft. An early version of a synchronization gear was patented a year later, and a Dutch designer working in Germany, Anthony Fokker, developed a more reliable version. Demonstrated in May and June, it was mounted on another innovation: a single-seat monoplane that was strong enough to dive on a target and recover without tearing its wings off, and fast enough to repeat the maneuver if the first strike missed. These Fokker *Eindeckers* were initially deployed by ones and twos to observation squadrons in mid-1915. In the next six months they became the "Fokker scourge" to Allied observation planes, the optimization of which for stability rather than maneuverability drastically limited their survivability.

The *Eindecker* was what later generations would call a "hot" plane, a "widow-maker." It was a young man's weapon, whose virtuosos, like Max Immelman and Oswald Bölcke, were in their mid-twenties when they became national heroes and public figures, recipients of every award a grateful empire could bestow. That included the *Pour le Mérite,* the Reich's highest military honor, previously in practice reserved for senior generals and royal princes, which was now open to commoners for shooting down, initially, eight enemy planes—and received a new nickname from the youthful pilots who wore it or aspired to it, the insouciantly irreverent "Blue Max."

The Fokkers' actual successes were limited—around sixty kills all told. But they secured near-absolute air superiority until early 1916, with corresponding alarm and despondency among Allied air crews and their senior officers. As much to the point, they created the war's first generation of youth heroes in a Germany that prior to 1914 had been a *de facto* gerontocracy, where young men in particular were expected to wait their turns. The youth movement that emerged around the turn of the century was about escape and withdrawal, not participation. The initial inchoate dreams and hopes of the "war volunteers" had been trodden into the mud of Langemarck. But one need not be a futurist to be engaged by the notion of literally transcending the limitations of high-tech ground war. One might be an infantry lieutenant recovering from trench-induced rheumatism. Or a seventeen-year-old who spent the war's first months as a volunteer driver for the army. Or a cavalryman facing transfer to the quartermaster service who indignantly declared that he "had not gone to war to collect cheese and eggs." Hermann Göring, Werner Voss, and Manfred von Richthofen would be heard from again.

From the German side of the front, however, the experiences of 1915 brought more reflection than celebration. For a full year the Allies had maintained consistent pressure all along the front, from the Hartmanswilerkopf peak in Alsace to the war-created marshes of Flanders. The unheard-of price they paid demonstrated the political and ideological necessity of recovering the lost provinces of France (Belgium had become a very secondary consideration), and structuring the conflict for control of a Franco-British alliance that was still as much a relationship of convenience as commitment.[58] And the Prussian/German Army had been forced into a reactive mode for the first time since the darkest days of the Seven Years' War.

In tactical and operational contexts, again the advantage seemed to lie with Germany. The Maxim 08 machine gun was far from an ideal weapon for position warfare. Its sled mount was too clumsy for the typical trench. The gun was too heavy to be brought into position quickly from a dugout. There were never enough of them: a quarter of the 8,000 guns in service were captured Allied weapons—mostly Russian. But the Maxim was reliable as long as it had ammunition and water—most of the latter being supplied in emergencies from canteens rather than the often-mentioned field improvisation of urination. If only by default, the M08 in the hands of an experienced crew was master of the battlefield in 1915. The railway system behind the front, its capacities restored and enhanced, was a major force multiplier, enabling the timely lateral redeployment of severely limited reserves and barely adequate heavy artillery from sector to threatened sector. Time and again German combat reports and regimental histories credit the last-minute arrival of fresh troops, even in small numbers, with restoring a line or a situation. Battlefield logistics had also significantly improved since the days of the Schlieffen Plan. The evacuation of wounded and the arrival of hot food hardly occurred by timetable. Both, however, were regular enough to be understood as systematic, making significant contributions both to morale and to the image of the army's culture of competence, shaken by the events of 1914. One enterprising paymaster even brought payday cash to a front-line battery in the midst of the fighting at Neuve Chapelle! There may have been nowhere to spend it, but the gesture was nevertheless appreciated.[59]

Ferdinand Foch, in a painful position to know, described the consequences in analyzing the May fighting for Vimy Ridge. The Germans, he declared, brought nine fresh divisions into the sector in only ten days. They established new lines of defense to replace those captured. Above all, "on May 9 (the beginning of the French attack) we dominated the enemy heavy artillery. After May 20 it dominated us and we never overcame that."[60] Essentially similar evaluations characterized Allied reports the entire year.

Enemy praise did not affect the acute embarrassment felt by regiment, division, and corps commanders unwillingly constrained to emphasize the defensive. With the end of the war of movement in November 1914, as soldiers' worlds shrank to a few yards' worth of holes and ditches, myth and ego filled the vacuum at higher levels. Competition is the breath of life in any army worth maintaining, and the peacetime Second Reich was a Petri dish of rivalries both for professional advancement and for placement in a no less significant informal pecking order. On the developing Western Front that translated into holding and recovering ground. *"Halten, was zu halten ist"* (hold what is there to hold) became a mantra similar to, albeit far more costly than, body counts in Vietnam. Loss of ground was seen as damaging the propaganda war, unit morale, and above all the career opportunities of the officers held directly responsible.

As trench systems became more complex and comprehensive, this reflex behavior came under increasing criticism from the front lines and from students of tactics who understood that economy of force was central to addressing the dominance of firepower. Holding ground with the smallest number of men enabled the formation of reserves for local counterattacks and, eventually, major offensives. As early as January 1915, Falkenhayn declared that French assault tactics required not lines of fixed defenses but a fortified zone permitting some liberty of action, utilizing terrain and taking account of its potential and disadvantages.[61] This concept may have foreshadowed the later development of defense in depth, but was overshadowed by Falkenhayn's insistence that forward positions however defined must be held at all cost and any ground lost be retaken promptly. Casualties were not to be a factor.

The chief of staff's reasoning was that citizen soldiers whose morale was increasingly dubious and whose training was increasingly sketchy could not be trusted to employ more flexible tactics effectively. Nor could a junior officer corps whose professional elements were being steadily reduced through casualties and promotion be expected to make up for the shortcomings of their rank and file. The practical result was a tendency to deploy as many as two-thirds of a regiment, plus the machine-gun company, in the front lines, on the common-sense grounds that holding on in the first place was easier and less costly than recovering ground lost.

The tactic worked well enough in the winter of 1914–15, when Joffre sent his divisions back into the offensive without either the equipment or the training for it. Over a quarter-million *poilus* died between December and March, and on the whole the increasingly developed German defenses held well enough. That began to change in the spring, as the French deployed a steadily increasing number of guns from fortresses, arsenals, and museums. Most were obsolescent at best. But given a target no more complex than an obvious trench line, and a week or ten days of time, they could demolish even a sophisticated position.

On May 9, 1915 two battalions of the 10th Bavarian Reserve Regiment were holding the village of Neuville St Vaast. Between 7:30 am and 10 am over 2,000 shells landed in the sector of a single company; the 10th was forced into a corner of the village and the French pressed their attack. Days of hand-to-hand, see-saw, grenade and bayonet fighting followed, regiment relieving regiment as the High Command insisted Neuville, "perhaps the most important point on the Western Front," must be held at all costs. On June 8, Neuville finally went under, despite desperate German counterattacks. One of the companies involved in the final fight began with 120 men. Forty-five came out. The authorized strength was over 250.[62]

The course of events in Neuville St Vaast can stand as a case study for tactical-level war in the West during 1915. Allied battalions and divisions could break in, if willing to pay the price. They could not break out; their successes remained marginal. As casualties mounted, confusion grew, and water and ammunition ran out, *ad hoc* German combat teams, sometimes a spontaneous group, sometimes the remnants of a platoon or company, supported by a machine gun or two and sometimes a few artillery pieces as well, plugged the gap and restored the situation.

That scenario was predictable enough to make it plain that this war was not 1870 written large. But if the concept of elastic defense was still embryonic, increasing numbers of regimental officers, and even some staff types, no longer felt impelled to retain every anonymous terrain feature in northeastern France. Killing Frenchmen and Tommies seemed more important—particularly when they seemed so willing to cooperate in the process. The commander of the 107th Infantry, deployed in the remnants of Neuville just before its fall, made an eloquent case that the position was untenable, its trenches collapsed and dugouts blown in, its retention achieving nothing but increased casualty lists and debilitated morale as men realized their sacrifices were achieving nothing. He recommended withdrawing to the final defensive position established outside the village. But Colonel Löffler made that case only when the order for his regiment's relief had arrived![63] Official doctrine and official policy remained the same: hold ground, retake it, or fertilize it. It would take most of a year, and much more blood, to begin changing the army's institutional mind.

CHAPTER IV

VERDUN AND
THE SOMME:
END OF AN ARMY

At the turn of the New Year 1916, Germany's overall military position could have been far worse. Its armies stood deep in Russia and the Balkans. Allied initiatives in the Middle East had to date achieved only marginal success. The Italian theater seemed permanently stabilized. Austria-Hungary was wobbling but no longer staggering. The Ottoman Empire was doing well enough with German infusions at command and staff levels supplemented by minor direct military assistance. Domestically, Germany's morale and economy alike, though unexpectedly highly stressed, showed no serious signs of erosion, much less exhaustion. The navy was still a fleet in being, if it had not yet achieved successes commensurate with its cost. Above all the Second Reich's trump card, the army, had shown itself the Great War's most comprehensively effective fighting force—even if in part by default. Strategic planning was not its forte. Its high command's record was at best questionable. But the same could be said for its opponents. And in the crucial categories of administration, operational art and tactics, above all fighting spirit, the German Army stood at the head of the list. At Neuville when the final order to evacuate the town resulted in a near panic, it was a *Sanitätsgefreiter*, a Landsturm medic officially well over-age for the front line, armed with nothing deadlier than bandages and iodine, who restored calm in his hard-hammered company.[1] Every engagement, large or small, seemed to produce similar examples among junior officers, NCOs, and rear-rank privates.

I

All these positives nevertheless added up to a negative. Germany was, after eighteen months, without any reasonable doubt fighting a war of attrition, the kind of war history, theory, and statistics alike indicated the Reich ultimately could not win. In early January 1916, Falkenhayn summarized his position to Bethmann: Germany's political and economic circumstances made it "extremely desirable" to end the war before the end of the year.[2]

In a more immediate, practical context, from Falkenhayn's perspective the military and political capital of Hindenburg and Ludendorff had never been higher. In particular Hindenburg, the duo's front man, was a household name. His short-cropped hair and prominent stomach suggested a man "in the best years," undiminished by the inroads of time, epitomizing the older generation's virtues and virility. There was talk in high circles of having Kaiser William deposed and hospitalized, with the Crown Prince becoming regent and Hindenburg as imperial administrator (*Reichsverweser*). No one doubted who would exercise the real power in that structure.[3]

Falkenhayn was an easy man to dislike. His manners and his grooming were alike impeccable, inviting characterization as a soft-shoed carpet-knight. His manner in public and private was courteous, ironic, casual—and inscrutable. By comparison with Hindenburg and Ludendorff, Falkenhayn could readily appear a self-centered, desk-and-papers general ill-placed in charge of a real war. Instead he emerged in 1916 as Schlieffen's spiritual successor, with a plan that was no less a gambler's gambit: a plan he saw as a chance to decide the war and dish his opponents at the same time. It involved a shift of emphasis to the West, albeit not in quest of a decisive victory in the traditional model. Germany lacked the resources to overthrow both Britain and France. Instead Falkenhayn proposed to win the war by inverting its attritional character, increasing the military pressure on the Allies to unbearable, or at least unacceptable, limits and thereby impelling negotiations in the style of Bismarck.

The consistent failure of the French offensives in 1915 had convinced not only Falkenhayn, but many of his close General Staff associates, that the Third Republic was near the end of its resources. In particular, French soldiers were morally and militarily inferior to their German opponents. On the other hand, German experience indicated that even significantly weaker forces occupying typical Western Front positions could hold off and see off the mass attacks that were the norm in 1914/15. The risk of seeking to invert attrition was to reverse the past year's circumstances: bleeding Germany while storming French defenses.

It was a Hegelian conundrum: offense-defense, thesis-antithesis. Falkenhayn saw the synthesis as involving a shift from tactics to psychology: breaking the French will by overloading and short-circuiting the French psyche. Demonstrate that France's military situation was hopeless, and its labile national character would collapse. Britannia's best sword would be struck from her hand, and—with a little help from the U-boats—Germany's real archenemy would be ready to conclude peace as well.

The next question, the critical one from Falkenhayn's perspective, was how best to force France's breakdown? His answer was to weaken the French army by compelling, or impelling, it to repeat the behavior of 1915 and take high casualties attacking German positions. A large-scale breakthrough attempt was likely—indeed almost certain given Germany's continued overall inferiority in men and guns—to suffer the same fate as the Allied efforts of 1915: an initial break-in that turned, in Falkenhayn's words, to a mass grave. The chief of staff initially considered mounting a series of small operations sufficiently threatening or embarrassing to generate immediate French responses. No combination seemed likely to be appropriately provocative, and Falkenhayn increasingly turned to a single initiative centered on Verdun. Since Roman times it had been a fortress covering the Meuse Valley. Logistically, the area was well served from the German side by rail lines. Operationally, Verdun was the focus of a French salient so narrow that it could readily be turned to a killing ground by German heavy artillery. Strategically it was difficult to reinforce, being connected to the rest of France by one road and a single railroad line. In a policy context, Verdun was sufficiently important militarily and psychologically—at least from a German perspective—that the French would have to make every effort to retain it. Verdun, moreover, lay in the sector of the army commanded by Crown Prince William. Placing him in command of the attack would reinforce Falkenhayn's position with the heir and his father, who though by now a figurehead still occupied the Imperial throne.

A traditional recipe for rabbit stew begins with the instruction "catch one large, plump rabbit." Falkenhayn's intention was to commit initially only ten divisions to the attack—a modest force by Western Front standards. The real work was to be done by a mass of heavy artillery, assembled with the greatest possible secrecy and unleashed with the largest possible surprise. The infantry would advance to the high ground on the east bank of the Meuse, within easy artillery range of Verdun, but short of the city itself. Falkenhayn proposed to force the French into an inescapable dilemma. They might abandon Verdun when casualties inflicted by the German guns became unsupportable and hand the Germans a major prestige victory. They might seek to relieve pressure on Verdun by attacking on other sectors, inviting a repetition of the blindfolded butcheries of 1915. Or they might seek to retake the high ground around Verdun under the heaviest barrages of the entire war, with their own artillery unable to deploy effectively in the salient. The élan of the French soldiers would become the means of their destruction—this time not by desperate close-quarters fighting with rifles, grenades, and machine guns, but under German artillery at long range.[4]

Falkenhayn expected the third alternative with anticipation that at times seemed more than professional. His constant references during the operation to "bleeding them white," "bleeding them to death" and "blood spurting" disturbed even Crown Prince William, never exactly remarkable for sensitivity on any subject.[5] Perhaps the chief of staff sought to convince himself. No one at general headquarters remembered much of this kind of talk during the planning stages. Did it matter to Falkenhayn exactly what happened at Verdun, as long as the Allies were weakened? Support for that hypothesis can be drawn from his reaction to Fifth Army Headquarters' proposal for the attack. This expanded Falkenhayn's initial plan, first by following up the attack on the east bank with one on the west and then by setting the objective as taking either Verdun itself or the heights directly dominating it. Knobelsdorf, the Crown Prince, and their senior subordinates understood well enough Falkenhayn's intention of wearing down the French without concurring in the details.[6] The Fifth Army, however, regarded reducing the salient and neutralizing the fortress as primary objectives whose achievement would best secure an eventual decision.

Falkenhayn expressed reservations, but in the end not only accepted the revision but agreed to provide two more corps for the attack—at a time of his choosing. Perhaps he was more concerned with possibilities and eventualities than specifics. Thus Verdun's capture would be acceptable, perhaps even welcome, if it contributed to weakening the Allies, whether in futile direct counterattacks or equally futile offensives elsewhere, to be followed by Germany's resumption of a war of movement: a series of initiatives to break what remained of the Allied armies—assuming France did not, as expected, sue for peace earlier.

Strategically, Falkenhayn's conception was a departure from both the massive frontal breakthroughs that had proved so expensively futile for the Allies in 1915, and the battles of envelopment on the Schlieffen model that had been no more decisive for Moltke in the west and Ludendorff in the east. Nor did he overlook that if the Crown Prince were hailed as the victor of Verdun, it meant a transfusion for a monarchy also suffering from "bleeding," and corresponding reinforcement of Falkenhayn's position.

The chief of staff was confident that he had created a no-lose situation that would impel the Allies, whatever they did, to assume the role of an obliging enemy: behaving as though their orders were being written by the German High Command. His code name for the operation was *Gericht*. Like a good few German words, *Gericht* has variant connotations. It means "law court." It means "judgment", as in Last Judgment. And it is the root for "execution ground."[7]

II

Making offensive preparations in absolute secrecy, difficult to achieve in any war, was nearly impossible on the Western Front. German security measures nevertheless succeeded admirably.[8] Allied intelligence believed the main German effort would be in the east. In particular the French high command had shown little interest in Verdun, systematically removing troops and guns throughout 1915 for the offensives in Champagne and Artois, expressing confidence in the position's continued ability to see off even a major German attack. Taking full advantage of the French railroads, the Germans deployed 1,200 guns for the offensive's first day. No fewer than two-thirds were classed as heavy, from 15-cm howitzers and naval guns to the 42-cm casemate-busters that had done so much damage in Belgium. Most were modern, manufactured in the previous decade. The High Command and the Fifth Army emphasized that fire was to be continuous and comprehensive, engaging permanent fortifications and field positions, supply routes and assembly areas, and above all the French artillery, on a twenty-four-hour basis. A network of observation balloons and observation aircraft would provide target acquisition while the Fokkers controlled the sky. Ammunition expenditure was calculated as two million rounds a day, mostly gas and high explosive, for the first six days, then the same number for the next twelve. To guarantee sustainability, thirty-four trains a day would deliver shells and specially equipped front-line shops would take care of the expected wear on tubes and carriages. The expected result was permanent fire superiority, with enough surplus firepower to keep trenches under bombardment, defeat counterattacks, and give direct support to the infantry—more or less simultaneously.

Not volume of fire, but accuracy, was the ultimate objective. French strong points were the primary targets. It was vitally important to avoid friendly fire, the "blue on blue" that had so often disrupted attacks in 1914. Forward observers would accompany the riflemen, with telephones, flares, or colored balloons signaling positions occupied.

Falkenhayn's emphasis on carefully controlled artillery supported on a tactical level his operational concept of a managed battle in which he would control the levers and determine the calibrations. Concepts like "attack" and "storm" did acquire different meanings when 42-cm mortars would be used against front-line strong points. Verdun was not projected as an example of "artillery conquering and infantry occupying." The infantry was the principal arm, the defining mission of which remained capturing or retaking ground. The number of machine guns per unit had been steadily increased in 1915 on an improvised basis: a quarter of the available weapons were captured ones. As they were replaced, in 1916, the regimental machine-gun companies were disbanded and each battalion received an organic company, initially of six guns, later increased to nine, and eventually to twelve.

In 1916 the infantrymen received two powerful direct-support assets. The *leichter Minenwerfer* (light mine-thrower) had begun as a pioneers' weapon. Bulkier than its Allied counterpart, the British-designed Stokes "stovepipe," the *leichter Minenwerfer* also threw a heavier shell, and on a wheeled mounting could more or less keep pace with the infantry. It was correspondingly welcome in the close-support role as a substitute for artillery and increasingly decentralized to the infantry. In the winter of 1916/17 it became official: every battalion was assigned four of them. The flamethrower had been spectacularly and successfully tested on a small scale in 1915. At the start of Operation *Gericht* two hundred of them, manned by volunteers in a special regiment of the Prussian Guard, were deployed to help the infantry forward. They proved terrifying in aspect and horrible in effect. But they were short-ranged and their crews were obvious targets.

Personal equipment also improved. By 1916 every front-line soldier had a gas mask, the best of its type developed on either side. And during the year the cloth *Pickelhaube* gave way to the steel helmet Model 1916. In quality and design the "coal scuttle" surpassed all its competitors, particularly in offering protection to the back of the neck. Despite symbiotic identification with the Third Reich, the helmet has influenced successors from the US Army's 1980s Kevlar design to the headgear of the imperial storm troopers in the *Star Wars* film series.

Despite these improvements, from the infantry's perspective Verdun and the Somme would remain low-tech: riflemen's battles, with the rifle increasingly making space for the hand grenade as a second principal weapon. The standard German grenade, one of the Twentieth Century's signature weapons, was dubbed the potato-masher from its similarity to the kitchen utensil. It consisted of a thin steel can filled with high explosive attached to a hollow wooden handle containing a pull cord and a five-second fuse. Introduced in 1915 as a specialized pioneers' weapon, the *Stielhandgranate*'s light weight and wooden handle made it easy to throw and gave it a range of thirty or forty yards. At first used principally by squads of six or eight picked men, the potato masher, eventually complemented by the smaller, lighter, easier to carry and throw, oval-shaped "egg grenade," became standard throughout the infantry platoon at Verdun and on the Somme. Depending on blast effect rather than fragmentation like its British counterpart the Mills bomb, the potato-masher was as effective as any similar weapon of the Great War against a machine-gun nest or for clearing a trench. At closer quarters, knives and pistols, clubs and sharpened trench spades supplemented rifle butts and bayonets for what increasingly amounted to random grapplings in near-liquid muck.

The evolving nature of infantry attack put heavy burdens on quality— spirit, strength, and skill—in an army that initially had been primarily concerned with numbers. The volunteers and reservists of August 1914 had been evaluated casually, and for enthusiasm as much as fitness. The unexpected need for replacements and the simultaneous raising of new units at the end of 1914 had led to the call-up of a disproportionate number of the physically unfit and the emotionally questionable. In the course of the next year physical criteria, at least, were overhauled. Recruits and convalescents were systematically categorized as fit for the front, for garrison duty, or for labor service: or as "unsuitable for war." Increasingly rigorous, increasingly frequent reexaminations had a corresponding effect on what their disgruntled victims called *Heldenklauerei* (hero-theft).

The experiences of Verdun and the Somme also induced significant personnel reshuffling in the combat units. The original system of categorization by age had been obscured as the war progressed with replacements being assigned as needed, which usually meant on a basis of immediate need, which in turn usually meant more or less randomly. The result in the companies and batteries, especially in the drawn-out fighting of 1916, was increasing numbers of men simply and obviously unable to stand the strain, burdens and dangers to the rest through no discernible faults or flaws, often willing enough but nevertheless such liabilities in the trenches that discipline and punishment were wasted effort. Beginning in August 1916, younger replacements were sent to divisions the records of which indicated they were most likely to be engaged in offensive combat. Their older men in turn were exchanged for younger counterparts in the Landwehr and other second-line formations. Systematic evaluation of 1916's combat led the High Command to order in April of the next year that no one over thirty-five should be assigned to infantry or pioneer units on the Western Front.

Peacetime standards of training had been trampled first by the need to take the field as soon as possible, and then by the need to replace the drastically unexpected casualties. Instead of two years it was initially cut to two months, with consequences demonstrated most drastically at Langemarck, but everywhere the improvised Ersatz divisions were committed as well. Yet for the first half of 1915 the replacement system continued to operate in the context of a short-war illusion. Since the Prussian constitutional crisis of the 1860s, German liberals had argued for reducing peacetime service on the grounds that extended stretches in uniform were unnecessary to produce effective soldiers. The fundamental problem in the Great War's first year, however, was ineffective cadres. The professionals as a class wanted to get to the front for varying mixtures of idealism and careerism. The officers and NCOs left in the depots tended to be the regiment's expendables. In March 1916, the army responded by making home depots responsible only for eight weeks of training in the basics of drill, discipline, and fieldcraft. The next step was a month at a field recruit depot, responsible for what today would be called "advanced branch training," most of it focusing on infantry skills. These depots were initially improvised. Verdun and the Somme encouraged their proliferation, and in early 1917 every division was ordered to establish one. They were staffed by officers and men temporarily rotated from the front. They had a corresponding incentive to do their best for men who would soon be assigned to their regiments and companies. The recruits for their part, after two months of being too often chivvied around for no apparent purpose in Germany, could appreciate the difference in attitude even when the lessons were imparted with the assistance of boots, fists, and vocabularies.[9]

But the question remained: what were the replacements supposed to learn? The German Army's approach to doctrine heavily emphasized giving scope for original thought and initiative by subordinates. Superiors were, indeed, directly forbidden to issue orders restricting that latitude. Evaluation processes emphasized discussion as opposed to instruction, explaining the reasoning behind decisions made. Seeking a right-or-wrong dichotomy was discouraged.[10] These approaches were reinforced by the constant surprises imposed by the rapidly evolving conditions of the Western Front. What the depots taught reflected what their parent formations considered important and their instructors considered effective. Cadres learned from each other and took the new insights back to their parent units. Divisions produced memoranda used internally as training guides and shared with neighbors. There were enough differences in these documents that Falkenhayn tried to restrict their circulation until they had been vetted by higher authority. But the stabilization of tactical conditions during 1915 fostered sufficient homogeneity in experiences to make these reports much sought after, not only by formations new to the war, but in those rotating back to the line that were interested in knowing what new tricks each side had introduced since their previous tour.[11]

Most of the reports and recommendations from the front were pragmatically defensive in orientation. How best to improve trench systems? What were the optimal uses of obstacles like barbed wire? Where did machine guns belong in fighting positions? How could mining operations be coordinated with above-ground attacks? The High Command's long-term concern, however, was overcoming the tactical stagnation that was the Western Front's defining characteristic. In March 1915 the War Ministry ordered the formation of an experimental Assault Detachment (*Sturmabteilung*) to focus on technologies, tactics, and techniques applicable at the small-unit level. But it began developing into a combination school and laboratory only when Captain Willy Rohr took command in August.

In addition to testing every weapons system and item of personal gear from flamethrowers to body armor, Rohr introduced new tactics and new structures. He replaced the linear advance based on companies and battalions by "assault squads" of ten or a dozen men. These *Sturmtrupps* were to advance independently, taking advantage of local terrain features and tactical opportunities without concern for keeping contact and securing flanks. Fire support would be direct and immediate, coordinated at low levels as opposed to controlled from the top down. To keep the attack from dissolving into a jumble of squad actions, participants were oriented on large-scale maps and rehearsed on full-scale models of the objective.

The storm troop model confirmed the noncommissioned officer's status as a junior leader. It affirmed the prewar injunction "to educate the soldier to think and act for himself." Two crucial questions, however, accompanied the innovation. Were the preparations so elaborate that they could be employed only on small-scale levels? And to what extent could the methods be introduced to a mass army, as opposed to an elite, chosen or self-selected? The first external training course was held for a Landwehr division in December 1915. It lasted six days, and was more of a demonstration than an exercise. With *Gericht* only weeks away, Rohr's vision would remain in abeyance—temporarily.[12]

Helmuth von Moltke the Elder said no plan survives first contact with the enemy. *Gericht* was sidetracked by first contact with the weather. The offensive was scheduled for February 12, but a winter storm neutralized the comprehensive observation on which the fire plan depended. For ten days the gunners waited, the infantry suffered in place—and the French reinforced their positions. While intelligence had no full idea of its scope, they were sufficiently aware of the concentration of men and guns to realize that a major attack was brewing in the Verdun sector and increased the defenses accordingly: eight divisions in the salient, three in reserve, and more available as needed with artillery in proportion.

Meeting an alert, prepared enemy influenced the tempo of the attack that went in on February 21. For most of the day German guns hammered French positions. Not until late afternoon did the infantry advance—to take unexpectedly heavy casualties against positions unobserved, unengaged, or undamaged by the barrage. But as artillery observers moved forward, targeting improved. Assault teams exploited and created gaps. By February 24, despite a number of iconic French last stands, the front was around five miles from Verdun. Over half the defenders were casualties. Front morale was eroding. Fort Douaumont, a key point of the defensive system, fell without a fight on February 25, a consequence of fog and friction on the French side, aggressiveness and initiative on the German.[13] By the 27th, German infantry had reached the heights east of the Meuse, on the river's right bank. German guns were beginning to advance to their next firing positions. Tactically and operationally, the French might have been well advised to withdraw to more defensible higher ground instead of holding on to defending a salient under fire from three sides. Retreating across the river, even abandoning Verdun, were options seriously considered. But modern war is also a matter of policy and politics. Premier Aristide Briand threatened to dismiss the whole high command if Verdun fell.[14] Public morale and parliamentary stability had been deeply shaken by the failures of 1915. Another disaster might fatally erode support for the war. In more immediate terms, Briand's government was even less likely to survive.

As the initial shocks wore off, Verdun's defenses began to reshape, mythologically and operationally. The city became a symbol of stoic heroism, inviting comparisons to Thermopylae and overwhelming any consideration of such mundane matters as strategies and casualties. Joffre and his brain trust came up with such presumably inspiring slogans as "We'll get them!" and "They shall not pass." Verdun received a new commander. General Philippe Pétain had made his reputation and learned from his experience in the offensives of 1915. He understood two things. There could be no more withdrawals around Verdun, and France needed to husband its reserves. His solution was the systematic rotation of divisions through the sector, relieving them before they were worn down to groups of survivors. Between February 27 and March 6 almost 200,000 men and over 20,000 tons of ammunition would be brought up by trucks running day and night along a modest prewar secondary road—the "Sacred Way."

The French Army in 1916 included 330 infantry regiments; 259 would see action at Verdun. Rotation did not solve the problem of attrition, merely extended it in terms of time and force structure. The bill would come due the next year. But French resistance stiffened, underwritten by supporting artillery heavily reinforced and aggressively employed. The German infantry was increasingly left to its own devices as its supporting guns fell behind in the cratered slime their shelling had created. With over 25,000 casualties in two weeks, almost all in the forward regiments, the offensive's fighting power was eroding significantly. On February 27 the German High Command admitted that the operation had been brought to a halt: temporarily, to be sure.

In fact Falkenhayn faced the beginning of a paradigm shift. The French decision to hold the right bank of the Meuse was theoretically an optimal condition for *Gericht* as a killing ground. But the Germans were stalled in front of the Meuse heights and suffering heavy losses from French artillery positioned across the river. Fifth Army headquarters demanded more men and more guns—do any generals think they have enough?—with the intention of expanding the offensive to the river's west bank. Knobelsdorf had supported this option from the beginning, for tactical reasons.

Falkenhayn had his doubts. His goal was the French Army's destruction in an economy of force context. He could not see marginally expanding the scope of *Gericht* as contributing to either end. Instead he considered shutting down the operation, shifting his focus to another sector with the same goal in mind.[15] But German doctrine and German experience supported deferring to the commanders closest to the action, and on February 29 Falkenhayn agreed to release two more divisions to the Fifth Army.

The attack on the west bank was planned as a two-phase operation. It began on March 6, executed by two corps with massive artillery support. It was the first downward step on a long, steep, and slippery slope. The artillery's general preparation and its direct support of the infantry were first rate by previous standards, thanks in good part to improved methods of long-range fire control. Though the German Army was still a long way from what the British called "slide-rule gunnery," consulting systematic weather records combined with improved gun calibration incorporated variables like wind, temperature, and humidity, and significantly improved accuracy.[16] But this time the Germans were unable to get much beyond the forward positions. Later attacks shifted from the broad fronts of February to smaller scale "bite and hold" operations the objectives of which were captured incrementally. The costs, however, remained heavy.

Since the first days of the offensive, the Germans faced a problem that had tormented the Allies for a year: the lapsed time between the artillery's halting of a bombardment and the infantry's arrival on the objective. The solution, first tested in the Balkan Wars but then ignored by Western armies, was the rolling or creeping barrage, moving forward in a sequence of "lifts," usually around a hundred yards or so, as the infantry advanced.[17] This was an improvement, but not a panacea. The lifts were in theory coordinated by observers working with the forward infantry, their own command posts, and the supporting artillery's battery positions. But communications were at best random. Electronic links, telephone and telegraph, were erratic. Visual signals, flags, flares, and rockets, were obscured by the literal fog of battle. Carrier pigeons were spectacular but unreliable. Casualties inevitably interfered with the program. Infantry could lose touch with the barrage if held up, or face "friendly fire" if the barrage failed to lift.

The defenders, moreover, had been constrained almost inadvertently to adopt a defensive system well suited to frustrate the rolling barrage. It began with an improvisation by French Colonel Émile Driant during *Gericht's* initial stage. With his fixed defenses crumbling under German guns, he dispersed his surviving infantry among shell holes and rubble. It took the Germans over a day to clean them out. More and more battalion and company commanders followed the same pattern: organizing their forward positions as a network of small, mutually supporting strong points, sometimes based on a machine gun or two, with reserves dispersed almost randomly in the deepest cellars and dugouts that could be contrived.

The result was to deprive the German artillery of clear targets and the German infantry of tangible objectives. The initial reaction was to employ longer, heavier area bombardments that cost ammunition, wore out guns, and sacrificed surprise. Meanwhile French counterfire shredded assembly areas and forward positions. French counterattacks impelled the Germans to keep as much as two-thirds of their strength in reserve, further diminishing an assault's initial impetus. To compound the problem, bad weather again shut down German artillery observation, whether by plane or balloon.

Not until March 14 did the Germans take and hold part of the sector's key terrain feature. The ridge line known as Le Mort Homme, "Dead Man's Hill," had been named before the war. Its cognomen was prophetic: almost 200,000 men would be killed and wounded on or around it from first to last. As the attacks continued, moreover, it became clear that Le Mort Homme was covered by massive artillery fire from the neighboring Hill 304. To the Fifth

Army headquarters, at least, the logical solution was to shift the focus of the attack to Hill 304 and keep up the pressure.

By the end of March, however, a month of doing the same thing the same way and expecting different results had increased *Gericht's* casualties to more than 80,000 and Verdun seemed as distant as the far side of the moon—at least to Falkenhayn. The Fifth Army was more optimistic. It now argued that the French Army was on the edge of exhaustion, capable of no more than local offensives. Falkenhayn gave his subordinates the rope they requested. The new series of attacks failed to get much beyond the forward French positions, and lost much of the initial gains to increasingly determined, increasingly powerful, increasingly well-supported counterstrokes.

By April Pétain had concentrated enough troops to match German strength. The "*noria*" system of systematically moving divisions into and out of the combat zone like buckets rotating down a well maintained effectiveness and sustained morale at acceptable levels of desertion and madness. In the face of these developments, Rupprecht and Kuhl, even Crown Prince William, were openly expressing doubts. In early April Falkenhayn, comparing casualty lists with operational and strategic gains, took counsel with his subordinates on the wisdom of breaking off *Gericht* altogether. Knobelsdorf and the Fifth Army's corps commanders responded that the moral and physical effect of French artillery fire made it impossible to remain in the positions currently occupied. Knobelsdorf remained convinced a series of large-scale attacks with wider objectives would make the kind of progress that would fulfill the kaiser's boast that the war would end at Verdun. He was not, however, reflexively arguing for a bigger hammer. He agreed that further attacks must be carefully prepared. He showed visible concern observing—through a telescope—the failure of one of the many attacks on Mort Homme. But, Knobelsdorf asked, what would be the effect on army and home front alike, of withdrawal after such heavy casualties— and the propaganda campaign that accompanied the offensive?[18]

It is a familiar, arguably a universal, military aphorism that the first duty of a commander is to command. For the first time in his career Erich von Falkenhayn faced a simple choice: up or down. He listened to Knobelsdorf. By the end of April, 21 divisions and the High Command's entire artillery reserve were committed to Verdun. The Western Front's reserve was reduced to a bagatelle: eight divisions.

For a while the French continued at least to some extent to play the role assigned by Falkenhayn. Douaumont had become almost as much a symbol as the citadel of Verdun itself, and in mid-May the French planned its recapture on the pattern established by the Germans: a massive local bombardment to obliterate the defenders—who had recently almost managed that themselves by a carelessly ignited internal explosion—with the infantry mopping up what remained. All this was to be done, moreover, by a single division. On May 22 the French broke into Douaumont, but an assault force decimated by German artillery were isolated by counterattacks and forced to surrender. The attacking division lost over half its strength, mostly as usual from its infantry. The Germans finally overran the last defenses of Le Mort Homme on May 29. On June 7 Fort Vaux fell. Under attack since March, targeted by as many as 2,000 shells per hour,[19] its small garrison held almost to the last man and literally to the last rounds of ammunition and the last drops of water, fighting hand to hand inside the fort when the Germans breached the outer defenses.[20]

Fort Vaux was Douaumont in reverse, and as such epitomized a crucial fact. Initially almost without anyone in higher German headquarters becoming aware of it, Verdun was becoming just another exercise in trench warfare. Falkenhayn's original intention of the French exhausting themselves against German defenses and German firepower was being turned inside out. Now the Germans were attacking against equal numbers, with the French expected to oblige with improvised counterattacks. Now Knobelsdorf, with the bit in his teeth, insisted on pushing every attack to its limits. This was not mere bullheadedness. The further the Germans advanced into what was both an operational and a tactical salient, the more vulnerable they became to French artillery increasingly able to keep the rear areas as well as the forward positions under what seemed twenty-four-hour bombardment. Driving forward seemed the best way to address the problem—somewhat like accepting shredded flesh and bone as the price of halting a buzz saw by hand.[21]

This approach also served to make Verdun to the Germans what Falkenhayn had intended it be for the French: an objective in itself, with failure to capture it a physical and moral defeat for the German Reich and the German Army.

With his reputation and his legacy on the line, Falkenhayn grew ever more committed to what Napoleon called "making pictures," repeating beliefs until in his mind they became realities. In particular, he remained convinced that French casualties were over twice as heavy as the German ones: 525,000 to 250,000 by May. This facilitated an insouciance increasingly disturbing in a GHQ where everything did not seem as normal around Verdun as it did to a chief increasingly focused on preparing for the major Allied relief offensive he expected, and on increasing pressure for an unlimited U-boat war against Britain. Bethmann successfully held out against the latter.[22] But while preparations for a major joint offensive had been observed in the British sector since early April, German intelligence accurately reported that Verdun had reduced significantly the French forces available for the operation.

From Falkenhayn's perspective at mid-year, things might be worse. Since the French had begun limiting their commitment to Verdun rather than risk locking up their entire army in a single sector, the city's capture seemed increasingly feasible. Falkenhayn continued to insist that French collapse was only a question of time. He considered an expanded program of annexations on the Franco-German border. He juggled, if not invented, figures to keep Bethmann on side, insisting that the French had suffered 800,000 casualties by June 1 and that the government's collapse was imminent. Falkenhayn went so far as to declare the war might end by the close of the year—more or less the time frame pessimists had discussed in secret before 1914. He ignored the increasing number of critics in GHQ who asserted more and more forcefully that he was seriously overestimating the army's capacities. He could not, however, dismiss the weight of intelligence that by mid-June indicated that not only was a major British attack developing in the region of the Somme, but that the French would be contributing heavily to an operation involving around forty divisions plus an unprecedented amount of artillery.

Though Falkenhayn had anticipated an Allied offensive to relieve pressure on Verdun, the newly threatened sector was held by only thirteen German divisions. Falkenhayn began transferring reserves from across his front. On June 24, the chief of staff also informed Knobelsdorf and the Crown Prince they must seriously limit their use of men, material, and munitions—but not immediately. The capture of Vaux had opened the way to the last barrier before

Verdun. Falkenhayn supported the Fifth Army's recommendation to continue its attack until that barrier, the ridgeline from Thiaumont through Fleury to Fort Souville, was reached, impelling the French to bleed themselves white with counterattacks. William and Knobelsdorf had accepted, if only by osmosis, Falkenhayn's original concept of victory through attrition.[23]

On June 21, the German artillery began a full-scale barrage along the right bank of the Meuse. It included a high proportion of gas shells filled with phosgene, more toxic than chlorine, which wrought particular havoc among the horses bringing ammunition to the French batteries. Beginning in April Rohr's assault detachment, expanded to a battalion, had been operating what amounted to a tactical school in the front lines. Time and again the storm troopers demonstrated the efficacy of Rohr's approach: reconnaissance, initiative, coordination of fire and movement.[24] Their example institutionalized what had more or less become a general response to the French dispersion and decentralization imposed, ironically, by the effectiveness of German artillery mentioned earlier. The skirmish lines prescribed in peacetime regulations and used in combat since August 1914 were now consistently disrupted by improvised strong points. They correspondingly gave way to *ad hoc* combat groups, operating independently, bypassing defended obstacles and taking them in flank or rear. These tactics were in turn taught to replacements in the divisional recruit depots and imparted to units new to Verdun in a specialized training center supervised by the Rohr Battalion.

Both processes were still in the beginning stages on July 23, when the Fifth Army's infantry went forward on a four-mile front in the Thiaumont–Fleury sector. Fleury—or most of it—was captured by a Bavarian regiment, the first to wear steel helmets and using storm troop tactics practiced for a solid month previously.[25] Not only were the spires of Verdun cathedral visible, but by the end of the day German machine guns were firing, albeit briefly and randomly, into the city's streets. Pétain the Imperturbable warned GHQ that general withdrawal to the right bank of the Meuse might be necessary. But the French reacted promptly, defying the phosgene, stopping the Bavarians with counterbarrages, throwing them back with counterattacks—and in the process demonstrating an enduring shortcoming of storm troop tactics. Even mounted in regimental strength, the further an assault on the infiltration model progressed, the more disorganized it became and the more vulnerable grew its own flanks.

Again there was no breakthrough. Not until July 11 did Fleury fall entirely into German hands. And the French continued to counterattack what became as much a symbolic objective as Douaumont itself. What was once Fleury changed hands by some account as many as eighteen times before it finally fell on August 18 to become one of the "lost villages" of Verdun: officially existing but never rebuilt.

Falkenhayn's original intention of the French exhausting themselves against German defenses and German firepower was being turned inside out. Now the Germans were attacking against equal, sometimes stronger, numbers. Their heavy artillery was being transferred to the new front on the Somme that had opened on July 1. The air superiority they had enjoyed in February eroded as the French improved their organization and introduced a second-generation fighter aircraft. The Nieuport 11 rendered the Fokker not merely obsolescent but a deathtrap, giving French observation planes a degree of security that significantly improved their effectiveness, and more or less blinded the German guns that had been so crucial to *Gericht*'s initial successes.

Falkenhayn and Knobelsdorf acrimoniously debated responsibility for the contretemps. On August 21 Knobelsdorf was decorated and reassigned. Falkenhayn was dismissed a week later. In November the Crown Prince was percussively sublimated: kicked upstairs to an army group. His successor in the Fifth Army command, Max von Gallwitz, had long and publicly favored assuming the defensive at Verdun. On September 2 the High Command ordered the termination of offensive operations at Verdun. But a familiar German proverb warns against adding up the bill without consulting the waiter.

While Verdun might be marketed as a moral victory in France, the government was not content with half a loaf. Pétain had been promoted to command of an army group in May. His successor, General Robert Nivelle, was as fervent an apostle of the offensive as though 1915 had been merely another year on the calendar. And it seemed he could make it work. The by-now superior French artillery spent a month silencing German batteries and demolishing German positions from Douaumont to Vaux. On October 24 the attack went in. The French took every objective, including Douaumont, which since the Germans captured it had been hit by around 120,000 shells, including 3,700 of 155 mm and larger.[26] Most of the garrison had evacuated the battered, blazing fort a day earlier. That only confirmed the French recovery in a day of what the Germans had spent four months capturing. To cap the triumph and confirm Nivelle's reputation, Vaux was retaken on November 2. Another attack on December 15 retook still more ground before winter weather and plans for spring offensives finally ended the Battle of Verdun. The front line was almost exactly where it had been at the start of *Gericht*.

III

Three-quarters of the French Army passed through the trenches of Verdun: seventy-three divisions, twenty-three twice and seven of them three times. Forty-eight German divisions fought there, enough of them twice to produce a total of seventy-five divisional commitments. The blood price on each side was almost even. Official French figures were around 61,000 dead, 216,000 wounded, and 101,000 missing—many of them dead and never accounted for. German losses totaled 142,000 killed and missing, 187,000 wounded. Verdun was the grave of illusions on both sides. But the Germans had more to lose. Like their American counterparts at Hamburger Hill, Dak To, and a hundred other nameless places in Vietnam, German soldiers were dying on alien soil for what at best they understood as abstractions. They gave their tactical objectives names like "Golgotha" and "Coffin Lid." Pistols were eagerly sought, not for use against the French but for a mercy shot at the last extremity.[27] At least since the Wars of Liberation the Prussian Army had never regarded its men as expendable ciphers. At Verdun they were treated "much as a businessman looks at his balance sheets."[28] Falkenhayn had projected regular reliefs, and initially four to six days in the forward positions were the usual stretch. As Verdun developed, that time could extend to three or four weeks as a matter of course. Exact calculation was difficult, since ostensible "reserve" trenches were often no more than four hundred yards to the rear: easy range for French guns. Woods and villages vanished virtually without trace in what became a constantly shifting landscape of craters and torn-up earth. In 1914 Hill 304 stood precisely

304 meters above sea level. In the course of Verdun its height was reduced by nine meters; the French and German artillery between them blew all the topsoil away.[29] Shell holes could be almost fifty feet across, deep enough to shelter over thirty men—if one accepted the increasingly inaccurate mantra that shells never landed twice in the same place! The heavy clay soil that predominated in the sector made constructing trenches and shelters difficult even when by chance the guns were silent. High explosives and wet weather transformed that soil into a heavy mire that could suck down men as readily as the more familiar liquid muck of the Ypres salient, and was judged worse than its counterpart on the Somme by men who experienced both.

Suffocation and drowning were anything but exceptional. Mud to the knees was a trench norm, with hip-depth common. Army-issue boots were a correspondingly familiar casualty. The dead were in theory brought to collection points where they piled up "like logs" until evacuation to cemeteries in the rear might be possible. In practice many remained unburied or were hastily covered over near where they fell, to be thrown around in later bombardments until only pieces remained. The closer to the front, the more bodies and parts of bodies there were—German or French, who could tell. "You noticed it first when you stepped on something soft, something pulpy." Sometimes a corpse cried out—but it was just the air forced from the trodden-on lungs of someone decaying for two or three days.[30]

These conditions were not specific to Verdun. Arguably, indeed, Verdun was no worse, objectively considered, than a dozen other major battlefields of the Western Front. Yet account after German account depicts "a solidified gray sea," where death was omnipresent and a living man felt "like a beetle on a corpse." Day and night were inverted. By day no one who could help it showed himself. To move in groups amounted to "three times the deaths, a hundred times the fear, a thousand times the exertion."[31] It was at night when defenses were repaired, when working parties transported ammunition and construction material to the front. It was in darkness when now and then the field kitchens cautiously found their way forward to deliver hot food and bring back sick and wounded on the wagons. Early morning was usually the quietest time of day—unless the French mounted an attack. But by day and by night the stink remained and prevailed. It was strong enough and distinctive enough to let a messenger know whether he was going in the right direction: an unforgettable compound of decaying humans, dead animals, blood, gas fumes, high explosives, and shit.

Ralph Peters, retired US Army officer turned defense analyst and novelist, has perceptively commented that those who write about war at the sharp end neglect bodily functions.[32] With some notable exceptions, that was certainly true of the Germans. In the front lines a man could go weeks without washing or changing underclothes. Any clean water that appeared was used for drinking. Bowels were moved in small trenches dug for the purpose or into empty cans. In supporting positions the rule was *Massenlatrinen*: long ditches with poles on which users half stood and half sat. These facilities, serving a dozen or fifteen men at a time, offered enough sociability to be a major source of gossip: literal "latrine rumors." They were also open to rain and snow. They had an overpowering stench in warm weather. The poles were usually fouled in all seasons.[33]

Circumstances were made worse by the omnipresent diarrhea. Most food that reached the front was cold and greasy: badly smoked bacon, poorly preserved meat, bread just fresh enough to disturb digestions. Those fortunate enough to be evacuated might occasionally be treated with warm red wine. The rest tried not to foul themselves—with limited success. In particular an attack of diarrhea during a barrage could be fatal; even during brief pauses men took their chances in the open, running back and forth in a crouch, trousers half down, "an image of human misery."[34]

"One aspect of human misery" might be a more accurate construction. An army's culture of competence is judged heavily by how it treats "wastage." Each German soldier carried field dressings—simple bandages sufficient at best to staunch bleeding from light wounds one could quickly reach. As was the case in all armies, it was forbidden to drop out of an attack to assist casualties. "I still hear it today when someone called 'comrade, help!' And we had to say 'comrade, the medics will come.'"[35] When contact was line-of-sight, both sides seem to have more or less respected the Red Cross brassards and the men who wore them. But that meant little under the constant heavy bombardments that defined Verdun. In the words of an American Civil War song, "a cannon ball/ don't pay no mind." Neither does a high-explosive shell. In the words of one veteran, "whom God wished to punish especially was wounded at Verdun."

Another reflected, "If only it was quick. Not to lie helpless and slowly bleed to death."[36] A casualty unable to move under his own power was likely to be blown apart by shells, or die from shock and loss of blood before he could be evacuated. Those who survived never forgot the fear that tortured them in the hours before they were found and brought to an aid station.

The medics went from case to case, giving injections and applying dressings in the open or in shell holes and trusting for survival to luck and providence. But stretcher-bearers were always overworked and always at high risk. Nor was it a routine task, moving a helpless man across Verdun's moonscaped terrain even when the guns were relatively quiet. Almost always it was only in the brief time before dawn broke that wounded could be brought in without, in Kipling's words, "gettin 'em killed as we raised 'em." Even then it could take days before they were moved down the line.

Hours could be too late. The very soil of France was contaminated, laden with bacteria from centuries of fertilization by animal waste. Infection, particularly tetanus and gas gangrene, raised amputation rates to mid-Nineteenth Century levels and death rates to as high as 40 percent. Wounds, moreover, seemed at times to be the least of the medical system's problems: three-quarters of the nineteen million casualties treated during the war involved illness or injury. "Trench fever" and "Verdun fever," generic names for debilitating sicknesses transmitted by lice and flies respectively, added to soldiers' misery—without, as a rule, the compensation of hospitalization.

The German system was as good as the best—in principle. Aid stations, established even in the forward positions, were staffed and equipped well enough to perform emergency operations. After basic treatment casualties were evacuated through a network of clearing stations, dressing stations, and hospitals, depending on the nature and severity of their wounds. Always there was the necessity of triage, sorting casualties into three categories: those who could be helped by immediate treatment, those who could afford to wait, and the hopeless cases set aside to die. Lightly wounded men might be returned to their units after brief periods of convalescence immediately behind the front. Serious casualties were sent to stationary hospitals in the rear echelon, or when necessary returned to Germany and its network of permanent hospitals as quickly as possible for treatment, convalescence, and eventual recycling.

The medical service coped more quickly and successfully with Verdun's conditions than did the combat arms. They were able to draw on more developed, more relevant doctrinal and institutional matrices. Prewar German medicine had focused strongly on public health: hygiene and sanitation, vaccination and disinfection. Comprehensive bathing and delousing facilities brought trench fever and typhus under control. New vaccines eventually reduced typhus and tetanus to single-digit percentages. Hospital and laboratory facilities multiplied, and so did personnel. Around 24,000 doctors wore German uniforms in the course of the war. They were supplemented by late-term medical students, and by over 200,000 attendants, mostly women and most of those nurses. As surgical techniques and post-operative treatments improved, amputation rates and shock-related deaths declined.[37]

These developments, however, were in early stages during the heaviest fighting at Verdun and on the Somme. Too often there seemed only three possible exits: a POW camp, a "home shot" (*Heimatschuss*), or death. The first was too random and too high-risk to be seriously considered. Even "passively deserting" by allowing oneself to be overrun in an attack depended heavily on an incalculable variable: enemy willingness to take prisoners. The third alternative was too grim to be a serious subject of discussion, though between February and September 1916, twenty-nine members of the Fifth Army committed suicide. All, in passing, were enlisted men; according to the official records at least, officers died on the field of honor. A home shot, a "million-dollar wound," was on the other hand a frequently uttered wish, and perfectly acceptable as long as one did not go looking for it. A "gentleman's wound" in the arm or leg merited particular congratulations, accompanied by hopes, expressed or concealed, that the luck might rub off on one's comrades.

Self-infected illnesses, from dysentery to typhus, and self-inflicted wounds, usually involving hands or feet, were less drastic but could cost as much as a year at hard labor in a military prison. Shirking was far more familiar. A man on his way up the line could claim he had lost his way, or a messenger could take a few hours longer than absolutely necessary to report. These kinds of dodges seem to have usually been good for at most a day or so. The rear was stiff with *Kettenhünde* ("chain dogs," MPs so cognomened for the distinctive gorgets they wore) who checked passes and papers even for walking wounded.

Reporting back to the company with a plausible alibi was usually a better alternative. German military culture could be surprisingly flexible the closer one got to the front, despite the army's alleged (often exaggerated) peacetime emphasis on *Kadavergehorsamkeit* ("corpse-like obedience"), and for all the elaborate lists of punishments, including firing squads, which were authorized in regulations. Officers were as a rule not particularly eager to report subordinates for absence without leave, disobedience, or any other military offenses that might reflect on their own ability to command.

The German Army was, moreover, a citizen army of an authoritarian society. On one hand it could not rely for motivation on the "liberty, equality, fraternity" public ethos of the Third Republic and the accompanying draconian penalties for failing that Republic. On the other, in contrast to Great Britain, German regulations were not designed to control a volunteer force disproportionally drawn from purportedly lower and less disciplined classes that was believed ultimately to best understand force.

The Second Reich, moreover, was a state of law. It was specifically relevant that the penalties in German military codes for limited unauthorized absences involved terms not of imprisonment but arrest. Since removal from the front was the goal sought in the first place, commanders were likely to return the slacker immediately to the front "to redeem himself," with an added diet of pack drill and extra duty.

A reasonable conclusion is that at this stage of the Great War the German Army's system of discipline and control functioned effectively. No instances of "collective indiscipline" went into the official histories. They existed, nurtured as much by frustration as from self-preservation. By May and June, men were refusing to leave their trenches in obviously futile assaults. Officers were telling their French captors of having to compel movement at pistol point. But the scale remained small and the occurrences never became systematic. After over a year of a kind of war unimagined in nightmares, there had developed an increasing level of recognition, however unacknowledged publicly or officially, that men had limits, whether from exhaustion, sleeplessness, stress, or fear. The period from Bismarck to Hitler has been described as an "Age of Nervousness" in Germany: a combination of cultural construction of anxiety and genuine experience of suffering.[38] Since Goethe published *The Sorrows of*

Young Werther in 1774, a degree of sensitivity had been considered part of the emotional equipment of young men, at least those of the cultivated classes. By now German psychiatrists emphasized the emotional impact of permanent positional war. The traditional war of movement was "muscle war," but the spatial and emotional restriction of the trenches made greater demands on the nerves: on courage, endurance, flexibility, and above all will. Werner Beumelberg, whose right-wing orientation and Nazi sympathies did not entirely distort his insights into the World War I experience, said it as well as any: "Verdun devoured the nerves from a living body."[39]

Considered in terms of the ratio of shells fired to human targets, the actual chances of being hit during a barrage were surprisingly limited. It was the sense that one *would* be hit that created an "inhuman emotional strain." The relatively restricted size of Verdun's battle zones further enhanced the effect of the dying, the dead, and the fragments that inescapably reminded men of their own vulnerability. Official medical records described overt symptoms: disturbed sleep and awareness, headaches, trembling, convulsions. Apathy, loss of affect, were no less familiar: "faces were dead in living men."[40] Only the eyes twitched—"barrage eyes" was the trench phrase—or were fixed in the "thousand yard stare" that meant never again having to experience anything worse.

Soldiers of the armies that fought in World War I developed distinctive styles of expressing the experience. The tropes in each case were set by those men conditioned by their civilian experiences to observe and discuss their situations. Most of these were educated; most belonged to the middle classes, but beyond that their visions had little in common. For Americans the Great War was a Grand Tour of their cultural homeland. For the British it was a test of the ethos of "service, sacrifice, and sticking it" inculcated by the public schools, their imitators, and the boys' literature they inspired. For Germans the war fitted the concept of *Bildungserlebnis*. More than most German words, this one defies precise definition. "Developmental experience" comes reasonably close in English. The sense is of processing events so as to foster maturation and insight. All has meaning if one seeks it. All can define and liberate a person by shaping character.[41]

For the boys of 1914—and many men as well—the war offered unrivalled opportunities to apply those concepts, and not only in the initial stages.

Verdun, however, tested them to the limits and beyond. Verdun was the matrix for an alternate perspective in prose, poetry, and correspondence. One novelist depicted a ranting mob with empty eyes and open mouths, waving arms and legs torn off by shells. He described a soldier standing in the sanctuary of a shattered church waving a crown of thorns and proclaiming he had slit the barbed wire from Christ's forehead.[42]

Literary inventions? Almost certainly. But in them Hieronymus Bosch challenged Wilhelm von Humboldt and Hell was a universal metaphor. In the short story "Ils ne passeront pas," science fiction author Harry Turtledove introduces an outpost preparing for another day at the front when a new sound is heard. It is the seven trumpets of the Book of Revelations. The events foretold in the Apocalypse are played out at Verdun. And no one notices! The supernatural manifestations of flaming mountains and falling stars seem merely new weapons. The monsters and the angels are effortlessly destroyed by machine guns and artillery. At the end a great voice says "It is done!" And the Battle of Verdun goes on.[43] The tale's perspective is French. The Germans could have told it just as well, and in their fashion did.

IV

Both Falkenhayn and his subordinate commanders awaited the Allied offensive on the Somme with a confidence that with hindsight it is tempting to call insouciance. Compared, however, to Artois, the Champagne, and Loos in 1915, the German situation was far superior. The "race to the sea" had resulted in a stable front around fifty miles long developing in the Somme valley between the villages of Gommecourt in the north and Mauricourt in the south. While not exactly a "live and let live" sector, combat had been sufficiently localized that in particular XIV Reserve Corps, responsible for what would become the crucial Gommecourt–Fricourt sector, managed nicely with its original organic formations: the 27th and 28th Reserve Divisions from Baden and Württemberg. For over a year their regiments and battalions had rotated in and out of trenches and dugouts, constructed by men still becoming accustomed to war, which were initially risky places to be, prone to collapse under rainfall or shell fire. But the fighting on Vimy Ridge in the spring of 1915 generated a plethora of instructions and memos, circulated down to company level, on the design of trench systems. The men from southwest Germany included high proportions of farmers accustomed to working with earth and factory workers used to working hard. Self-interest was sufficient to make them so proficient in constructing the positions in which they would have to take regular turns that specialist pioneers were needed only as foremen.

Over several months in 1915 and 1916, XIV Reserve Corps constructed three separate, mutually supporting systems of front-line trenches, mostly on reverse slopes, well linked by communications trenches. The soil of that part of Picardy is largely clay, and the water table deep. That enabled construction of large, complex dugouts, *Stollen*, the standard depth of which was twenty-five feet and more, many concrete-built or concrete-reinforced. Used not as fighting positions but as headquarters and for sheltering reserves, *Stollen* often featured electric power, and their own individual water supplies. Over time their occupants fitted them as well with small comforts that amounted to unheard-of luxuries to the French and British.

So comfortable indeed were these dugouts that training emphasized the risks of what in later wars would be called "bunker psychosis." Training emphasized the necessity of leaving relative safety instantly, to man the parapet in the interval between the ceasing of the artillery and the arrival of the infantry. Routine casualties were just high enough to ward off slackness; doctrine and orders stressed holding the front line and retaking any ground lost immediately, and at all costs. Commanders responded by concentrating their men—and their machine guns—forward, despite an increasing number of suggestions based on the experiences of 1915 to man those positions thinly in the interest of limiting casualties.

The defense was kept up to date on enemy movements by a network of radio and telephone interception systems that enabled the Germans to boast of knowing opposing company commanders by name. Staffs, commanders, and men understood the terrain intimately: roads, landmarks, danger zones.

Anchored by fortified villages like Serre and Ovilliers, and by strong points with names like Schwaben Redoubt and Mouquet Farm that would become all too familiar to British, Australians, and Canadians, by any standards the Germans on the Somme were prepared to stay a while.[44]

The barrage that prepared the way for the Somme offensive has inspired what might be called a drumfire of criticism from the Allied perspective. For over a week, more than 1,500 guns fired over a million and a half shells into the German positions. The figures were impressive but arguably *faute de mieux*. The BEF would carry the main weight of the attack, and its high command did not consider the artillery a primary assault arm. Guns were intended to destroy trenches and wire and neutralize strong points, clearing the way for the infantry to do the real work. Initial ideas of achieving this with a hurricane bombardment were abandoned when it became clear that the BEF lacked enough guns for that alternative. In any case, the shift to a longer artillery preparation was widely expected to deprive the German infantry of rest and food to a degree that would make the attack, in the unfortunate phrase of many a British officer before July 1, a walkover.[45]

From British perspectives the bombardment's effects are generally presented as limited. There were too few heavy guns and too few shells. Inadequate quality control in British factories meant as many as a quarter of the rounds fired were duds. Others were the wrong type for the fire missions. One British survivor of July 1 noted dryly that lead shrapnel balls were singularly ineffective against steel barbed wire.[46] Target acquisition, fire control, and command were still all at the low end of their respective learning curves. Heavy rain and reduced visibility limited effective air observation. Preparing the Somme was, in short, a learning experience for the BEF's gunners at all levels. The same was not true of the French, who profited greatly from their recent and ongoing experience at Verdun. Their fire plan was based on a phased attack, with the artillery preparation determining what the infantry could be expected to achieve. The combination of trench mortars concentrating on forward trenches and heavy guns seeking out supporting positions was devastating from the beginning. Admittedly, however, in the target zones it could be difficult to discern the difference between Allied methods.

The German pattern of keeping the same formations in the Somme sector more or less permanently meant few of the defenders had experienced anything remotely resembling the bombardment heralding the offensive. The Somme sector had been so stable and so quiet for so long that the elaborate defensive works could seem more to keep the troops busy than preparation for a real contingency. From their perspective the barrage seemed the road to the end of the world—especially because it was in good part a surprise. A new and formidable British fighter had made its first appearance in April. The pusher designs of the Dh 2 and the Fe 2b look comically antique today, but proved dangerous adversaries. A "Fee" accounted for Max Immelmann on June 18; another dropped a memorial wreath a few days later. In a sector already drained of first-line planes to support Verdun, the new British fighters quickly gave the observation crews a clear field, providing the artillery a critical advantage in target acquisition and ranging while German reports described British aircraft circling trenches at low level, observing movements in detail, and calling in barrages on all of them.[47] A single British bomber scored a lucky hit on an ammunition train in the St Quentin railway station, destroying sixty carloads of shells and blocking the movement of an entire regiment. Other small-scale bombing raids disrupted headquarters, troop columns and supply dumps, none of them prepared for war in a third dimension—or arguably any other.[48]

As early as June 28, the Second Army reported that the British guns were in a position "to flatten our positions and smash our dugouts … our infantry is suffering heavy losses day after day."[49] A divisional history said, "What we experienced surpassed all previous conception. The enemy's fire never ceased for an hour. It fell night and day on the front line … It … made all approaches to the front hell … It … smashed men and material in a way never seen before or since." A Bavarian captain reported relieving a company near Montauban that had been reduced to thirty men and forced to abandon two lines of trenches under French drumfire. Heavy shells penetrated dugout roofs over twenty feet thick. A twenty-year-old *Kriegsfreiwilliger* in the Thiepval sector wrote on June 29: "The tongue sticks to the mouth in terror. Continuous bombardment and nothing to eat or drink. No sleep. How long is this going to last and little sleep for five days. How much longer can this go on?"[50] The youngster got his personal answer on July 1. British soldiers scavenged the diary from his body.

The first day of the Somme has gone down as the greatest, bloodiest disaster in Great Britain's military history: 60,000 casualties, almost 20,000 dead, most suffered in the first couple of hours. A long-standard explanation has been that British infantry, inadequately trained, incompetently commanded, and incontinently laden with superfluous equipment, were mowed down in line and *en masse* by German machine-gun fire. Recent research indicates that in fact only about a dozen of the eighty battalions in the attack's first wave did not either approach the German trenches to close range during the night or drop their burdens and form *ad hoc* combat groups under fire.[51] Reality at the sharp end was nevertheless a race for parapets and redoubts between the British crossing no man's land and Germans emerging from dugouts. The Germans won—not by much, but enough. Both sides agreed that the machine gunners and their well-sited weapons were the backbone of the defense in sector after sector. Reality was also shaped by German artillery that had been silenced but not suppressed by a British barrage that proved more diffuse than intense. Counterbattery, taking out British guns, was less important than exacerbating confusion and disrupting movement by keeping trenches and lines of communication under fire, and shelling those sectors where the British established footholds. Some batteries fired as many as 3,000 rounds to hold the line—or most of it. Neither reinforcements, ammunition, nor water—vital in July's heat—could get through (the main reason, in passing, why the British assault waves were so disastrously loaded down was to make them self-sufficient when they gained their objectives).

In the offensive's southern sector, around Montaubon, the British were more successful, but with losses too heavy to enable any follow up or follow through. The French on the Allied right did even better. Thanks to infantry tactics and artillery techniques learned at Verdun and pitted against a German defensive system less well-developed south of the Albert–Bapaume road, the French Sixth Army advanced five kilometres, about three miles, in four days, halfway to Berlin by previous standards.[52]

From the perspective of a century later, had the British Army not been so taken by surprise the German defenses might have broken, generating a regional Allied victory, if not necessarily a decisive one. Certainly Second Army headquarters, evaluating the first day's sketchy and random reports, concluded that its positions had been severely ruptured, and that only the desperate resistance of the front line's survivors had averted catastrophe. An attempted counterattack at Montaubon on July 2 collapsed in confusion. The

Crown Prince William of Germany reviewing some of his troops near Verdun in 1916. (Bettmann)

German soldiers prepare to throw hand grenades from a trench near Chemin Des Dames during the Battle of the Somme in 1916. (Photo by Popperfoto/Getty Images)

Two soldiers in a German observation post on Hill 304 in the Verdun area observe the enemy through their periscopes in November 1916. (Photo by adoc-photos/Corbis via Getty Images)

corps commander confronting the French withdrew his troops from their second-line positions—a crass violation of High Command policy that General Fritz von Below approved.

Retribution was swift. Falkenhayn reminded the Second Army that the first rule of position war must be not to yield a foot of ground, and the second one was to commit the last man to an immediate counterattack. To underscore the point, the Second Army's chief of staff was condignly relieved. His replacement, not entirely by chance or seniority, was one of Falkenhayn's better personnel choices. Colonel Friedrich von Lossberg was deputy chief of operations with the High Command for most of 1915. His section was responsible for evaluating ideas, opinions, and experiences from German operational units as well as captured enemy sources, for the purpose of developing and distributing up-to-date principles. One particular French document described a theoretical defensive system consisting of a thinly held front line, a number of strong points in support, and shelters to the rear for reserves. A number of junior staff officers saw this as a possible alternative to the German practice of massing troops in the front line, which was proving both expensive and inflexible. Some went further and advocated abandoning the front line entirely in the face of an attack, then, reinforced by reserves, counterattacking to expel an enemy disorganized by temporary victory.

Lossberg initially stood more or less in the middle. He argued for maintaining the front at all costs—but in limited strength, with increased flexibility, and while allowing greater independence to commanders on the spot. He got a chance to test his approach during the 1915 French September offensive in Champagne, replacing the Third Army's chief of staff when the latter advocated a major withdrawal. Lossberg was junior for the appointment—in modern parlance a "fast burner." His literal first act at his new headquarters had been to inform a corps commander on his responsibility that the retreat was canceled. An hour later Lossberg was touring the battlefield, talking to senior officers, getting a "fingertip feel" for the situation. A combination of new front-line positions based on the reverse slope of a long ridge with prompt counterattacks supported by accurately observed artillery fire brought the French to a sudden and frustrating halt. Continued attempts to recover momentum only swelled their casualty lists.[53]

Falkenhayn was impressed. When a similar situation threatened on the Somme, he lost no time summoning Lossberg. He arrived at Second Army headquarters at 5 am on July 3, receiving an immediate *Vollmacht* from Below and a warm welcome from the field commanders. Lossberg's record and his reputation had preceded him. As much to the point, July 1 and its aftermath had badly shaken the defenders. The British in particular seemed unexpectedly unaffected by their immense initial losses, saw July 1 as a clear success, and were determined to develop their advantage in the south, first between Fricourt and Montauban, then against the next German positions between Bazentin le Petit and Longueval. A newly committed reserve army would cover the main attack by advancing northeast, towards Thiepval and Pozières. After an acrimonious exchange between Haig and Joffre, the French Sixth Army was committed to maintaining pressure on the Allied far right, in what would increasingly become a parallel operation the steady and overlooked successes of which were restricted by the continued need to maintain a strong presence at Verdun.

Below and Lossberg proved to be the best senior command team the Germans had yet deployed on the Western Front. Working in each other's pockets, they spent most days visiting the front, beginning at 7:30 am, usually with the commanders of the previous day's hardest-hit sector, then preparing the next day's orders, again usually on the ground, and finally returning to headquarters and dispatching final versions by telephone.[54] Facilitated by the relatively limited size of the combat zone, this was as close to "command from the saddle" as was possible under modern conditions. It provided a sense of grip to subordinates that helped them control their own sectors. From the beginning the team had agreed on a three-stage response: holding the front to the last man, retaking lost ground by prompt counterattacks, and eventually mounting a general offensive to make good the losses of July 1 and 2. There was no question regarding stage one. Below's army order of July 3 forbade "the voluntary relinquishment of positions—The enemy must be made to pick his way forward over corpses."[55] Nor was this mere fustian from on high. At 9:30 pm on July 2 the 180th Infantry received orders to defend Ovilliers to the last man, withdrawing not a step without direct orders from division headquarters. It fulfilled its assignment to the letter until relieved four days later, eviscerating a British division in the process. The neighboring position of La Boiselle fell on July 4, at the cost of 3,500 British casualties and the accompanying judgment "the Germans never fought like that again,"[56] made by an officer in an excellent position to know.

The Second Army's major challenge, however, was in the rear: securing and deploying reserves. The High Command was as shocked as the generals on the spot by the force of the Allied attack and still unwilling to shut down Verdun. Even had that decision been made, withdrawing forces from that still close-gripped situation was not an easy task. Nor could the divisions chewed up earlier in "the mill on the Meuse" be rebuilt overnight by superior orders, no matter how urgently phrased. The High Command scraped up reinforcements from across the front, stripping artillery from the Verdun sector and infantry from everywhere. Elements of around twenty divisions were committed to the Somme in the first two weeks, plugged in and thrown in by batteries and battalions to shore up sectors under increasing pressure. From first to last almost a hundred divisions would be cycled through the Somme for almost 150 tours—*noria* in reverse. And as the Germans coped with one emergency after another, they found themselves confronting an entirely new operational situation.

The Allied offensives of 1915 had been time-limited: two or three weeks at the most, with the final stages increasingly episodic, broken-backed. On the Somme "the enemy just kept coming at us, day and night,"[57] with a "grim obstinance" as certain as the turning of the earth, and about as easily stopped. The French had always been formidable in the attack. The British were improving significantly. As battalion and brigade commanders learned their craft the hard way, their infantry was taking more ground and capturing more positions, albeit still at costs high enough and with fiascoes sufficiently frequent that the summer of 1916 is commemorated rather than celebrated in regimental histories. The decreased frontages and the limited objectives increasingly characterizing British planning after July 1 enabled an increased concentration of guns, the crews and commanders of which were also learning from experience.

German casualties increased exponentially. A single battalion lost 700 men in four days "under the violent fire of enemy heavy artillery."[58] Casualties of three and four hundred per battalion in a single tour were common; after two weeks in the line, the 16th Bavarian Infantry was down to fewer than 600 men, a fifth of its authorized strength. When the battle was at its height, two weeks was about the maximum time a German division could remain in the line before being "bled out" (*ausgeblutet*): no longer fit for combat. Even small-scale reliefs were risky, costly, and often random; a regimental sector might be held by three battalions from different units, entirely unknown to each other. Communications were not so much disrupted as suspended. Even deeply buried telephone cables were severed; dispatching messengers amounted to a death sentence for no purpose. The Allies increasingly dominated the entire "battle space." Their artillery and aircraft were reaching well into the German rear consistently and effectively, disrupting resupply and reliefs, punishing local and sector reserves. Regiments pulled out of the line had minimal opportunities to rest, reorganize, and retrain before being recommitted. Fresh divisions—and these grew fewer as the summer progressed—were worn down materially and morally by the weight of Allied firepower even before being committed to combat.

Sustained Allied fire superiority made fixed trench systems increasingly vulnerable. It also made anything like a flexible defense of forward positions through temporary withdrawals an unacceptably high-risk option. Especially as losses were replaced by recycled wounded and inexperienced replacements, flexibility made demands the ordinary infantrymen could not predictably meet. On the other hand, disrupted organizations, ruptured communications, and the consistent Allied artillery superiority randomized counterattacks, reducing them to small scales, battalion levels or less, and making determination a substitute for both shock and sophistication.[59] The British had a platoon-level technical advantage as well: the Lewis gun, a light machine gun that gave even outnumbered men in improvised defenses a useful plus in firepower and morale. Thiepval Ridge and High Wood, Longueval and Pozières, and a dozen other sites of memory and mourning were brutal mutual killing zones. A German officer spoke for them all when he described Delville Wood: "a wasteland of shattered trees, charred and burning stumps, craters thick with mud and blood, and corpses, corpses, corpses piled everywhere … Worst of all was the lowing of the wounded. It sounded like a cattle ring at the spring fair."[60]

On the Somme there was another common denominator: the Germans were increasingly failing to recover lost ground. Max von Gallwitz summarized the reasons: the defending units were exhausted; the counterattacking ones lacked relevant knowledge and training. Results in the French sector, though more or less lost to Anglophone history, were similar. In the process the innovators addressed two general institutional problems not originated on the Somme, but exacerbated there. Both reflected the Somme's fundamental nature as a battle the German Army was visibly and viscerally losing. Verdun might be a meatgrinder, a butcher shop, a mill that ground death. But it was an offensive. The Germans set the agenda; the French responded. The Somme was exactly opposite. The Allies were the attackers. They kept on attacking. And from the beginning of the preliminary barrages, it was increasingly and unpleasantly clear from front-line shell holes to army headquarters that the Germans were on the permanent short end of a "materiel battle" (*Materialschlacht*) unprecedented in the history of war. No matter what resources could be scraped up and thrown in to balance the odds, the Allies seemed able to meet the rise and raise the stakes almost effortlessly. When on July 30 Max von Gallwitz issued an order of the day stating that the next assault "must be smashed before the wall of German men,"[61] he was making an unmistakable point that blood must be matched against steel. The past six months made the probable results impossible to ignore. They also encouraged the questioning of military and national cultures of competence at levels and on scales no less impossible to overlook.

The relationship between soldiers and states has an elementary and significant contractual element. The state is expected to provide those who fight its battles a fighting chance—the best one it can. When that contract is perceived as broken, the "employees" may seek its renegotiation. The French Army would do this in spectacular public fashion in 1917. The Germans on the Somme were arguably a year ahead, using a different method: what the workers in Scotland's factories and shipyards called "ca'canny," or going slow. German intelligence calculated the Allies had thirty-four divisions in the Somme sector. The Germans had at best a round dozen. They faced odds—as long as no one checked official figures too closely—of almost two to one in infantry, one and a half to one in artillery, two to one in aircraft.

And on September 15 the Allies raised the stakes again. "The enemy..." recorded a staff officer, "employed new engines of war, as cruel as effective."[62] Reactions to the tanks varied widely, but of the more than 1,600 casualties taken by the regiment that bore the weight of the attack, almost half were listed as missing—and most of those were prisoners. This was an unheard-of ratio in an army priding itself on its fighting spirit. Was it also a portent? A division of the Prussian Guard, the Second Reich's institutional elite, when ordered back to the Somme for a second tour in August, had its command declare the men were unfit for combat because of the nonstop British artillery. By early September an increasing number of regimental histories speak of having reached the limits of endurance under the never-ending flail of the Allied guns: "Today's fire was the worst ever ... The enemy artillery was firing brilliantly, directed from the air of course. German aircraft were nowhere to be seen."[63] This was death uncontrollable and unavoidable. These were men rendered helpless and out of control by the enemy's technical dominance. In November a British battalion commander described the Germans as "very different Huns to fight than the Delville Wood lot. Boys ... and oldish men. One of his soldiers, escorting prisoners to the rear, discovered that the original seven had become eight: "when he saw us coming along he [just] fell in."[64] Nor is it any disrespect to the battalion involved to describe it as "warriors for the working day," as opposed to shock troops like the 29th or 51st divisions. What had happened in a matter of a few months? And what —if anything—was the remedy?

It is a trope, almost a cliché, that the German Army on the Somme suffered an irreparable loss of its best officers and men. The career professionals, the high-spirited volunteers, the shrewd reservists who had survived the earlier bloodlettings vanished into the mire of the Somme, never to be replaced. To a degree this narrative reflects a dominant aspect of German regimental histories: a tendency to construct their stories on a framework of inspiring leadership.

There were men at the front who saw the war as an opportunity to be reborn and remade in Nietzsche's concept of the "overman" who might be killed but could not be conquered. These were few and far between.[65] The men immortalized in unit histories are better understood as those who met situations while others followed or watched. This is a common, arguably a universal, pattern in mass armies on Western lines: citizen-based, where the ideal is the soldier rather than the warrior, where discipline trumps initiative, and where the average man in the ranks, in Kipling's words, "wants to finish his little bit/and wants to go home to his tea." In that structure leadership tends to be from the front and personal. Casualties tend to be heaviest among junior officers and NCOs. And when the agents, the actors, the visible ones, are lost—a near-inevitable reality, especially in the circumstances of 1916— they tend in any narrative to acquire mythical qualities. German accounts from the Somme for the summer of 1916 in particular tend towards a necrology of the irreplaceable. Thus an undistinguished and indistinguishable regiment of the line commemorates a captain "whose personality and powers of leadership were incomparable, a man apart in the way he rallied his men around him ... He is not dead. He lives on in the ranks of his 2nd Battalion."[66]

The prospect for relying less on individual example-setters than on the cooperative, integrated small group as showcased by the Rohr Battalion was still in experimental stages. It was questionable in any case whether the appropriate training and tactics could be generally applied in an ordinary rifle company, as opposed to an elite of volunteers and picked men. Prussian and German practice since the days of Frederick the Great emphasized a high general average in the ranks and among the units. The previous year had, as previously mentioned, been focused on improving those averages.

Taken together, Verdun and the Somme drove home the same point. German material inferiority was the crucial factor on the Western Front, unlikely to be altered in Germany's favor by continuing the same policies and practices. The most direct and immediate prospects for a balance shift were specific and operational: overhauling structures, doctrines, and tactics so as not merely to take account of the new way of war, but to move ahead of the curve. Robert Foley describes a process of "horizontal innovation." Its transmission system was based on the reports submitted by units from battalions to army groups. These were not narratives, but analytical, lessons-learned documents describing enemy methods and approaches, critiquing what worked and what did not in countering them. In the war's early years they had been *ad hoc*, informally circulated. On the Somme they became a key intellectual force multiplier in a military learning culture that historically emphasized flexibility, independence, and sharing information and ideas.

In particular, German staff officers were not mere subordinate advisors. Nor were they responsible only for a specific function: intelligence, operations, logistics. They shared responsibility for making and implementing decisions. They were a small group, homogeneous in backgrounds and attitudes. Though not precisely a band of brothers, they were accustomed to working with, and getting along with, each other. Prior to 1914, unlike far-flung Russia, distracted Austria-Hungary, and imperial France, they had had a single dominant mission: preparing for and winning a specific kind of war. Within their limits they could and did develop and introduce specifics: how to fight and, in particular, how to fight on the Somme in the summer of 1916.

The Germans reacted incrementally, like a clever boxer being driven towards the ropes. They restructured an overstretched command structure, giving Lossberg and Below the sector south of the Somme with a new First Army headquarters and assigning the quieter zone north of the river to the Second Army under Max von Gallwitz, bringing his own trouble-shooter's reputation from the Eastern Front and Verdun. Gallwitz also donned a second helmet as army group commander, responsible for coordinating operations in the Somme theater. Corps were reconfigured on the now-standard model of being responsible for sectors, with divisions rotated to meet needs and resources. On the tactical level, Lossberg responded to the disruptions of communications caused by Allied artillery and ravaged terrain by decentralization and simplification. Battalion commanders were given complete control over their sectors. Their decisions were final while the immediate fighting lasted. They commanded all reinforcements regardless of seniority. Division commanders played the same role two steps higher, exercising full authority in their sectors, over reinforcements and over almost all their supporting artillery. The latter, a sharp difference from the French and British norm of centralizing artillery command at higher levels, accepted some sacrifice of massed fire support in favor of prompt response to changing situations.

Historically, corps and regiments had been the German Army's most important headquarters. Now they were becoming essentially transmitting agencies, responsible for forwarding reinforcements and supplies. This role reversal was correspondingly revolutionary, regarding significant attitude adjustments and serving as a useful litmus test for the flexibility increasingly demanded of senior officers in 1916. Reducing for practical purposes the chain of command to two links, each in full control of its sphere, also addressed a practical problem of implementing counterattacks. These were increasingly configured on two levels. The counterthrust (*Gegenstoss*) was the battalion commander's province: an immediate, improvised exploitation of the structural confusion and emotional letdown that accompanied even the most successful attack. The counterattack (*Gegenangriff*), methodically prepared and systematically supported, was usually a divisional matter.

The new approach was codified in two manuals. *Conduct of the Defensive Battle,* issued on December 1, 1916, described a zone defense. The outpost zone might be as wide as 3,000 yards in open terrain or as narrow as a few hundred in broken ground. The battle zone was defined by a main line of resistance and a second line 1,500 to 2,500 yards to the rear, both as far as possible concealed from enemy artillery observers and in full view of their own. The normal deployment in a regimental sector of a front-line division was one battalion in each of these zones, with a rear battle zone, as far as three or four miles back, occupied by the third battalion as a reserve. Specifics were outlined in *Generalizations on Position Construction,* issued in January 1917. Overmatched sentries and outposts could fall back on a network of resistance centers, dugouts and shell holes held by a half-dozen men, and regroup for a counterattack. Should enemy strength and shelling make that impossible, the defenders could again fall back and then mount an improvised counterattack (*Gegenstoss*), supported by regimental reserves. Entire *Eingreif* divisions (whose mission was mounting immediate counterattacks against enemy breakthroughs against the *Stellungsdivisionen*—line-holding divisions) could be committed as well and if necessary stage a formal counterattack (*Gegenangriff*) with up to several days of comprehensive preparation.

Initiative, mobility, flexibility, counterattacks on an unpredictable schedule and an increasing scale—these were the keys to achieving the ultimate objective of restoring the original position. The battle was still to be fought *for* the front line, but no longer *in* it. And the ultimate option now involved a command decision. Was the restoration worth the price in casualties? The question could no longer be overlooked, either at the front or at home.

Lossberg's innovations were sufficiently effective even when applied *ad hoc* that one of his junior officers nicknamed him "defense lion"—and even as a captain Erich von Manstein was not easily impressed. But an even more comprehensive example of horizontal innovation was developing at the other end of the German military spectrum, where Lossberg had a counterpart and counterpoint. Hermann von der Lieth-Thomsen was a general staff officer assigned before the war to monitor aviation developments who became an enthusiast. In March 1915 he was named commander of the army's field air forces, and since then had advocated enthusiastically for an independent air arm, on a par with the army and navy. Coming from a lowly major the initiative was quickly sidetracked, but Thomsen made his mark nevertheless on the men and organizations of his embryonic service. The year 1916 brought a spectrum of new challenges as the Allied air forces grew numerically stronger and operationally superior in the areas of observation, reconnaissance, and bombardment. Thomsen's response was to concentrate the fighters. There were not many *Eindekkers* that spring—only ninety or so, distributed by twos and threes among the army cooperation squadrons. Initially they were grouped into *ad hoc* detachments. One of these became Jagdstaffel (Fighter Squadron) 2, under the command of Oswald Bölcke. Bölcke's reputation as a tactician was already high enough that he had been tasked with codifying a set of guidelines for air-to-air combat. He proved no less able to impart these *Dicta Bölcke* to the men of his squadron. Bölcke was a supporter of concentrating fighter power. Most of his pilots were accustomed to lone-wolf tactics. But most of those who survived the summer of 1916 were able to see the advantages of cooperation in the face of superior numbers and superior aircraft.

The *Jagdstaffeln,* in contrast to their Allied opponents, did little escort work. They were conceived as an instrument of air superiority, to counter the observation planes so important to Allied artillery. At Verdun they managed to hold their own. But the demands of the Somme, where the odds were as high as four to one and the Allies dominated the air for two and a half months, stretched the new organization to its limits. As more and more fighters were sent north, by the end of October in the Verdun sector a half-dozen or so German aircraft were facing French formations of up to forty-five planes. The Germans responded institutionally at army levels by giving the aircraft and the ground defenses a common command and a common telephone network. Operationally, the practice of reacting defensively to Allied incursions gave way to an emphasis on carrying the fight across the front—a doctrine easier formulated than implemented, at least initially, given the odds.

Front-line squadrons benefitted as well from an improved training program. Nurtured and galvanized by Lieth-Thomsen, it also gained from 1915's overhauling of the ground forces' training programs. During 1916 it developed to a point where most pilots had sixty-five hours of cockpit time before being sent to the front and to a further one-month course in current combat tactics, taught by men fresh from tours at the front. That kind of instruction gave fledglings something more than an actuarial chance in their first crucial days and weeks on operations. And beginning in autumn 1916 they began gaining a technical advantage as well. For a year German designers, manufacturers, staff officers, and combat flyers had been developing and evaluating not merely a replacement for the *Eindecker*, but a successor. The Albatros D I was the archetype of future Great War fighters. A single-seat biplane with two forward-firing machine guns, fast and maneuverable, it entered squadron service in September and contributed heavily to stabilizing the air battle at Verdun and on the Somme.

What integrated and synergized these improvements and innovations was institutionalization. Thomsen, like Lossow, was a mere lieutenant-colonel. But for over a year his observations, recommendations, and urgings had proved too prescient to ignore. In October 1916 the Air Service—henceforth the words merit capitalization—was assigned control of all aspects of military aviation: production, training, administration, ground defense, communications—even weather research. The Air Service remained under the High Command, but each field army had an Air Service commander and the army's air assets reported to him.

For such a relationship to function effectively, fog and friction must be kept to a minimum. The Air Service benefitted from arguably the best commander/*chef* team Germany fielded during the war. Ernst von Höppner had begun in the cavalry, served on the general staff since 1902, and since 1914 had been both an army chief of staff and a division commander. He knew the system, had the seniority to make it work, and was an enthusiastic advocate of military aviation. His chief of staff, not surprisingly, was Hermann von der Lieth-Thomsen. In a relatively small service where everyone had started the war as a junior officer, it was easier to introduce and implement change and to react promptly to new situations. Air officers with field armies systematically submitted reports and recommendations. The Air Service, like its ground counterpart, also solicited reports from the front, and captains and lieutenants were more likely to be listened to than their counterparts in the infantry and artillery. Beginning in 1917, a series of manuals and instructions provided a clear structure of principles and doctrines.

The institutional result of all this was to enable the German Air Service to maximize its increasingly inferior material resources and hold the aerial ring until the war's final weeks. The first effects would become apparent in the early weeks of 1917 during the Battle of Arras. That, however, left Verdun and the Somme still to be fought out in 1916. Verdun might have slacked off in its final weeks, with fighting becoming as routine as anything ever became at Verdun. The Somme was a different matter. At Verdun, the battle of attrition had been essentially a German initiative. If one emphasized lines on a map and overlooked strategic intentions and casualty lists, in terms of ground gained Verdun might even be claimed a victory. The Somme was an essentially different matter. On the Somme, attrition had been forced on the Germans. The lines on the maps had moved in one direction: backwards.

By the end of September the German Army on the Somme was showing fundamental strain. The artillery fired five million shells during the month. But guns were wearing out and fire control was becoming erratic. Casualties in the same month were close to 135,000—most of them, as usual, in the infantry but with a disturbingly high number of surrenders. In October and November the British were less successful in the center, but on both flanks the Allies pushed forward in the face of worsening weather, despite— and sometimes because of—depending heavily on divisions making their second or third appearance. German divisions rotated back had less time for rest. Their replacements were fewer, too often too old or too young. The mediatizing innovations on the ground and in the air were still in their preliminary stages. As Robert Foley states, horizontal innovations can improve methods—but at best they do so incrementally, as a blood transfusion rather than a cardiac stimulant.

Thiepval, as much a symbol to the Germans as Douaumont had been to the French, finally went under on September 27. Württembergers of the 180th Infantry had held the position on July 1. At the finish they held it still, as close to the last man as made no difference. But six weeks later, on November 13, the British 51st Division overran Beaumont Hamel, Hawthorn Ridge, and Y Ravine, also icons of the first day on the Somme, taking 2,000 prisoners including a whole battalion caught by surprise. In six days of fighting the British accounted for a total of over 7,000 prisoners. The First Army command blamed the defenders' lack of alertness and awareness from divisional headquarters down to the rifle companies; the divisions holding the sector were relieved twice in less than a week.

An unacknowledged subtext of these and similar reports submitted as the year waned was that an improvised army led by amateurs was taking the measure of the world's most professional and self-confident, not to say arrogant, competitor. A trope for German soldiers in the final weeks on the Somme might be the dead man seen with a prayer book in one hand and the other in a bag of grenades. On the other hand, there were lucky ones, like the messenger lance corporal of the 16th Bavarian Reserve Regiment who on October 7, his third day at the front, was hit in the leg and spent the next two months in hospital with a million-mark wound. At the other end of the power spectrum, in December the German government called for peace negotiations. It may have been a trial balloon or a diplomatic feint. It was also a recognition that the balance of war might be shifting in the Allies' favor—one corpse at a time.

CHAPTER V

RECONFIGURATIONS

German casualty figures for World War I remain notoriously difficult to reconstruct. The sheer scale of losses challenged record-keeping at every level. The problem was further exacerbated by, let us say, flexible standards for defining a wound. Those points made, it can reasonably be stated that almost a million German soldiers were killed in action or died of wounds in 1916, at Verdun, on the Somme, and everywhere else from East Africa to Lake Naroch that the tides of war carried them.

———————————————— I ————————————————

Casualties do not of themselves determine who is winning or losing a war. Nor do they determine the competence of commanders or the effectiveness of governments. But neither can they be dismissed as collateral damage, the cost of doing business. As early as midsummer 1916, Falkenhayn was showing signs of stress. The vultures in Berlin and at OHL headquarters were beginning to circle. And the Russian high command tried once more for a conclusion in the field. Russia had made an unexpected recovery from the debacles of 1915. Domestic production of weapons and ammunition reduced dependence on

Allied imports. Grain reserves had more than doubled. Over six million men were under arms. And as the French calls to relieve the pressure at Verdun grew more strident, a new general offered a new plan. Alexei Brusilov, commanding the Southwestern Front, proposed to attack along the entire 350 miles of his four-army sector, each army in a particular zone. This would give the enemy no idea of which was the main effort or where the next blow would be struck. An overextended and demoralized Austro-Hungarian defense collapsed almost immediately. Falkenhayn scraped up ten divisions and enough artillery to stabilize the front, taking *de facto* charge not merely of the immediate fighting but virtually the entire Habsburg war effort.[1]

The military and economic responsibilities accompanying that shift had little time to manifest before they were compounded by Romania's August entry into the war on the Allied side. That kingdom hoped to gnaw the Dual Monarchy's carcass in the wake of Brusilov's successes. Its army proved spectacularly ill-prepared for the kind of war the Central Powers had learned how to wage, but it was Germany that was constrained to provide the bulk of the forces and planning for the Central Powers' offensive against Romania. It furnished the commander as well.

The initial success of Brusilov's offensive had led to increasing pressure from Bethmann-Hollweg and the Foreign Office, and within the High Command, which had relocated to Pless in Silesia, to turn over full command in the East to Hindenburg/Ludendorff. Falkenhayn resisted successfully—as long as he had the support of the kaiser and those of his immediate advisors who as late as mid-July saw Falkenhayn as "a card ... with which one either wins or loses,"[2] whose sacrifice meant the end of William's remaining credibility. Romania's decision for war tipped the balance. At 11 pm on August 28 Falkenhayn received Imperial notice of his relief. The next morning Hindenburg appeared at High Command headquarters. At precisely 1:26 pm Erich von Falkenhayn boarded a train out of Pless.

He did not exactly vanish into obscurity. As a consolation prize and an opportunity for rehabilitation, Falkenhayn was given command of the Ninth Army, the assignment of driving the Romanians back across the border, and the constraint of completing the campaign before winter. Falkenhayn responded by emphasizing "speed and relentless attack." Movement and assault would keep the Romanians so off balance that they could neither plan nor react before the next sequence shifted the paradigm again. This proto-blitzkrieg, implemented in one case by an improvised mechanized force, ranks with the Serbian campaign of 1915 as a tactical and operational cameo: the German Army at its best.[3] On the other hand, like its predecessor, its scale was small. Its enemy was even more obliging in terms of decisions taken and blunders made. Nor did Falkenhayn's cauterizing of a single running sore proffer guidelines to the comprehensive military and political challenges confronting Germany's new command team.

The Hindenburg–Ludendorff appointment reflected and projected Germany's situation. They were worked in as a command and planning team. Hindenburg described their relationship as like a successful marriage: neither party consistently dominant, each bringing something vital to the mix. Ludendorff was a manager and an organizer, talents reflected in his official title of First Quartermaster-General. Intelligent and industrious, a master of detail yet able to maintain a sense of general situations, he was at his best as a problem-solver with no time left over to indulge the irritability and anxiety that were the negative sides of his character. To an army badly shaken by Verdun, the Somme, and their aftermaths, Erich Ludendorff provided a sense of grip as welcome as it was badly needed.

If Ludendorff was a serious version of Gilbert and Sullivan's "model major general," Hindenburg modeled a traditional Prussian general, arguably to the point of caricature. Solid of body, with a near-literally square head and appropriate facial hair and facial expression, he looked the part—a point to be neither overlooked nor mocked in an era of photography and newsreels. He projected an air of imperturbability: nothing seemed able to bring him out of countenance. And Hindenburg was popular, both as a public figure and in the corridors of power.

But were they *hommes connetables*, capable of fulfilling the military responsibilities they were assigned and the economic and political ones they would assume? The overwhelming consensus is that their inheritance was poisonous, nurturing an already potential combination of militarism and expansionism at the expense of wisdom and caution.[4] Too often overlooked is a counterpoint: Germany in 1916 had no one else. When the army is specifically considered, there is an obvious void in the second generation, the mid-levels of staff and command. A first-rate crop of third-generation figures were emerging: Seeckt, Lossow, Rohr, Leith-Thomsen, and those yet unidentified, like the recycled reservist who would revolutionize artillery tactics in the next year, and the infantry captain whose feint-and-strike tactics in the mountains of northern Italy prefigured the methods of a later, greater war. But these were junior ranks: majors and lieutenant colonels. Their counterparts among the movers and shakers in the High Command, officers like Max Bauer and Gerhard Tappen, suffered from over-tempering: an involvement in situations beyond their maturity and judgment that began in the war's early weeks. With the exception of Max von Gallwitz, it is difficult to identify, much less recall, any field commanders who began the war as colonels or *Generalmajoren* and had risen, or would rise, much above the level of what the British called "good plain cooks" and "safe pairs of hands." Germany's war was unlikely to end well in safe pairs of hands.

Though it took time and lives, Britain and France eventually produced significantly deeper pools of senior military leadership that were unspectacular but able to shape the situation they confronted. Some, like Pétain, Foch, and Douglas Haig, grew incrementally into their responsibilities. Others—Fayolle and Mangin, Currie, and Monash—emerged from the ruck of war. Even Italy came out of the Caporetto disaster militarily revitalized, with Armando Diaz succeeding Luigi Cadorna. The parliamentary states, Britain and France, developed as well a body of effective second-generation political leaders. Lloyd George and Clemenceau had no counterparts in the Second Reich. Italy's Vittorio Orlando is less familiar, but he rallied Italy and oversaw the destruction of an enemy army—something neither of the transalpine premiers achieved.

None of these men were especially pleasant—intriguers, manipulators, and schemers all, often with private lives to match. They were, however, competent relative to circumstances. In contrast, compared to Britain's George V, William II cut an abysmal figure as a figurehead. Bethmann-Hollweg's successors as chancellor remain obscure even to doctoral students. And so it goes. Wherever one looks in Germany after 1916, the images are of cut-and-paste, of second- and third-rate people with first-line responsibilities. The structural reasons for that phenomenon are outside the scope of this book, except to note the development of similar phenomena in the other war-making empires, and suggest it was hardly coincidental.[5] For present purposes, a case can be made that the Hindenburg–Ludendorff team filled vacuums as well as arrogated power in what was in good part a response to a comprehensive emergency that bade fair to escalate into a general crisis.

II

The new command team turned first to the Western Front. Hindenburg and Ludendorff had been too focused on events in the east—and on intrigues within the High Command—to be *au courant* with recent details and developments in what, *mirabile dictu*, was proving after all to be the war's vital theater. It was his duty, Ludendorff stated, to adapt himself to the new conditions. He and Hindenburg began with a tour of inspection, visiting as many front-line units as possible, contacting others by phone, and demanding accurate information rather than eyewash and whitewash. Ludendorff came away convinced that the first months of the coming year would bring a battle deciding "the existence or nonexistence of the German people."[6] To meet that challenge, Ludendorff asserted, it was necessary to begin with the basics.[7] German tactics must be revised on two levels: a general shift in emphasis to the defensive, and a specific set of coping mechanisms to check the increasingly effective Allied infantry and artillery team. In early September the High Command began systematically collating and evaluating recent front-line reports. On December 1, as mentioned in Chapter IV, it issued *Principles of Command in the Defensive Battle in Position Warfare.* Ludendorff credited two relatively obscure and even more junior staff officers with constructing the manual that shaped German doctrines of defense in every theater for the rest of the war. But the fundamental ideas were Lossberg's. Max Bauer and Hermann Geyer had previously served under him and absorbed his ideas. This was General Staff procedure at its best. Ludendorff's ego was as large as anyone's who held his kind of post is likely to be, but he applied it to generating and sustaining a corporate effort that had been less evident under Falkenhayn, who preferred keeping his own counsel. Bauer, a difficult man and a difficult subordinate, noted that Ludendorff's style "lifted a great weight" from his working group. That opinion was as general in the High Command as any was likely to be among strong-willed men. It owed something to the Hawthorne effect generated by "an iron will and a firm determination." It owed more to abandoning definitively the increasingly costly, increasingly futile, policy of holding and regaining the forward line at all costs.

The objective of defense was described in the new *Principles* as making the attacker exhaust himself by establishing positions in depth, defended in echelons. As the Allied infantry advanced it would become disorganized. Its communications would be disrupted. It would eventually outrun the range of even its heavy artillery, to find itself caught in a combination maze and net. A complementary accompanying manual on *Principles of Field Construction* gave details: a three-tiered system with a lightly held outpost zone as a tripwire; a battle zone that could be as much as three thousand meters deep with a forward trench position, a network of strong points; and a second trench line protecting the artillery and the reserves in the rear zone which would mount the final counterattacks to destroy or throw back the enemy before he could consolidate his temporary gains and restore the original position, or as much of it as made no difference.

Firepower was the revamped system's framework: machine guns in the battle zone, artillery underwriting the counterattacks that were "the soul of the German defense." Flexibility was the principle: "resist, bend, and snap back." "Elastic defense" is a good capsule definition. So is "offensive defense." But the system's key and its core was human: "stout hearted men with iron nerves"—and individual initiative. Since 1914 falling back from a position had been defined as defeat, and carried an aura of disgrace. But by August 1916 it had become standard German operating procedure on the Somme to establish machine-gun positions outside the trench lines, in shell holes, to provide some protection from Allied barrages. Withdrawal was becoming instrumental, pragmatic: a means to the immediate ends of evading shell fire and wearing down attacking infantry, and to the ultimate one of setting the stage for the counterattacks that would reverse enemy gains.

Promulgating the doctrine did not mean its automatic implementation. Senior officers and their chiefs of staff were expected and accustomed to think for themselves, and the circumstances of the Western Front in 1916 fostered coping more than conformity. Lossberg himself believed the new regulations gave front-line troops and junior officers too much leeway in deciding when and how far to fall back. Ludendorff responded positively to that kind of criticism, asserting that the new system was a work in progress, to be modified when the Allies attacked again. Arguably more important to the reform's credibility was the extent that it codified and systematized much of what was already being done, and proving effective, on the Somme. The point was reinforced in mid-December, when the final French offensive at Verdun owed part of its success to the failure of German sector reserves to respond effectively because they were held too far behind the front.

II

On October 11, 1916, the Prussian War Ministry shook army and society alike when it ordered a census of Jewish soldiers with the intention of determining how many were serving in combat units. Germany's Jewish community had supported the war as an affirmation of a German identity that transcended internal political, social, and religious differences. The number who served remains inexact, though a figure of 100,000, of whom 12,000 were killed in action, is familiar. Less familiar is the extent of Jewish integration in the German Army. Jews, for example, regularly joined Christmas celebrations and were accepted as guests and comrades. "We feel together as one," a Jewish soldier wrote in December 1914.[8] As late as 1917 an army commander attended a Yom Kippur celebration and stood to attention when the shofar sounded. That same year an enlisted man wrote home, "I have never heard a thing of anti-Semitism here." There were certainly instances of overt anti-Semitism, but often balanced by conciliatory or apologetic behavior. Promotion statistics offer a useful indicator. Before the war Jews were accepted in limited numbers as Bavarian officers and barred entirely from holding commissions in the Prussian Army. The Prussian exclusion was dropped on the outbreak of war, and approximately 2,000 Jews were commissioned as line officers by 1918 in the German Army. The process could be frustrating, but military bureaucracy plus the army's policy of commissioning as few officers as possible from any civilian background seems to have delayed individual commissions more than institutional prejudice on religious or cultural grounds. Promotions to noncommissioned grades, while more difficult to track statistically, seem to have followed the same pattern.[9]

In short, it is difficult to show definitively that anti-Semitic attitudes had a substantive effect on the experience of Jews in the wartime German Army.[10] How, then, to account for the *Judenzählung*? It has been described as the consequence of increasing pressure from right-wing groups and individuals attacking Jews as slackers at the front, profiteers and traitors at home. It also reflected a general's desire to impress the new brooms of the High Command. Deputy War Minister General Franz Gustav von Wandel had ignored or downplayed these essentially unsubstantiated accusations. With the appointment of Hindenburg and Ludendorff, War Minister Adolf Wild von Hohenborn, a Falkenhayn man, sought to demonstrate his zeal by ordering a census of Jews in uniform and their specific assignments. That did not avert his being shuffled off to a corps command, but no one in the ministry had any particular incentive to halt the bureaucratic machinery—particularly given Ludendorff's personal anti-Semitism and his near-obsessive drive to collect data of every kind on a war effort he was convinced needed fundamental overhauling.

Objectively evaluated, the census was a fiasco. Some field commands were not interested in another tranche of paperwork. Others rejected it as risking damage to morale, or violating the civic truce proclaimed by the kaiser himself. Still others regarded it as morally offensive: the men under their command were doing their duty as Germans—enough said! The census was so flawed—and so controversial—its results were never released. The Jewish community's concern was that such a census had been authorized at all. Most Jewish soldiers, insofar as it can be determined, were angered or insulted, but on individual bases to individual degrees, depending on particular circumstances. On the home front condemnation was general and vocal. Max Warburg, Jewish banker, advisor, and confidant of the kaiser, demanded—vainly—a public apology from the War Ministry. The major significance, however, of this census was as an indicator of the increasing exacerbation of civic entropies that had been patched but not bridged by the *Burgfrieden* of August 1 1914—William's proclamation that henceforth he recognized no parties or confessions: "today we are all brothers, German brothers." And that in turn foreshadowed a Homeric attempt to revitalize a war effort proving inadequate to its purpose.[11]

Home-front strains had been showing since before the turn of the year. In 1915, when farmers refused to stop feeding animals grain and potatoes— defined as foodstuffs necessary for the war effort—the government had ordered a mass slaughter of pigs that reduced Germany's swine population by over a third and its meat supply in proportion. Prewar Germany had depended heavily on imported food. The combination of the war's effect on Russian agriculture, the Allied naval blockade, and an ineffective system of price controls and distribution combined to produce an *Ersatz* economy of substitute products and an efflorescent black market in edible foodstuffs. With bread consisting increasingly of ground beans and corn meal; with sausage depending on plant fibers; with ration cards required for every conceivable commodity; with lines of wives and mothers standing at shops too often with empty shelves; empty stomachs and aching feet eroded civic morale in synergy with the metastasizing casualty lists.

Things got worse in autumn. Cold weather, early frosts, and heavy rains cut the potato harvest by two-thirds. Turnips became the all-purpose replacement. Its only similarity to the potato was their common status as root vegetables. The turnip was something fed to animals: left to its own devices it was chewy, tasteless, unpalatable—and seasonings of any kind were in short supply or non-existent. The "turnip winter" of 1916–17 became a byword for deprivation even in the latter days of World War II. The winter was among the coldest on record. Coal shortages shut down public facilities; private homes and apartments turned to ice boxes.[12]

The front was little better off. "By far the most important feature of a soldier's life," stated one army morale report, "is food provision."[13] But by the end of the year potato rations were being supplemented, when not replaced, by turnips. Bread rations were reduced in March. Meat became an if-then commodity. Coffee consumption had averaged as high as three kilos per adult before the war. The government took over the supply's management in 1916 with predictable results. Chicory gave way to acorns and beechnuts, then to carrots and turnips. Hot water over oft-recycled grounds was a valued luxury.

Complaints multiplied—complaints focused increasingly on the alleged plenty enjoyed in the rear echelons and by the officers. The even worse fare in homeland camps and depots combined with anger at the privations suffered by their families to sour replacements long before they reached the front.

Complaints proliferated at the top as well as the bottom. The Hindenburg Program arguably had its genesis in the new command team's initial tour of the Western Front. When they asked the generals on the spot to describe their needs, ammunition had a universal high priority. Belts could be tightened but guns must be fed. Hindenburg and Ludendorff found it easy to agree on the importance of shells, not only to stabilize the current *Materialschlacht,* but to reverse it: to enable once more the victorious advance leading to victory and requiting sacrifice. On August 31, 1916, Hindenburg demanded of War Minister Wild von Hohenborn a 100 percent increase in ammunition and a 300 percent increase in artillery and machine guns—by the spring of 1917. Monthly production of powder, until now the crucial factor in determining arms production, was also to double, without considering availability of the necessary raw materials. Almost as an afterthought, the target figures for iron and coal were ratcheted upwards as well. This was less of a shock than might have been expected. The War Ministry had been working on its own plans to increase production since the turn of the year, but was handicapped by increasingly strained relations between a military concerned entirely with winning the war and industrialists committed to maximizing profit, retaining their social position, and not least controlling the skilled workers on whom the first two ultimately depended.[14] Wild outlined the new order on September 16, when he informed a meeting of Germany's major industrialists machines must replace men and Germany, unable to outbreed its enemies, must outproduce them.

The Hindenburg Program called for increased central control of production, material, and labor.[15] It declared that factory construction must be increased to meet the new production requirements. And as a capstone to the entire project, it was proclaimed that financial considerations no longer mattered. The intention was increases in production within a specific time and at any price. Exactly how those increases would be paid for was a matter of indifference. Applied to a complex economy, the Program amounted to doing neurosurgery with a chainsaw. Gerald Feldman simultaneously summarizes and skewers the Program as "having little to do with either sound military planning or rational economics." It was an all-or-nothing gamble that put the German economy on the line for an agenda and a timetable whose practicality had never been calculated, much less evaluated. In specifics it was the direct, comprehensive ignoring of a century-old General Staff legacy of systematic assessment. In addressing the labor question, for example, Hindenburg placated the industrialists by casually promising the army would release skilled workers to the mines and factories at a time when merely replacing casualties was a top priority. To meet that problem he advocated raising the conscription age to fifty, closing the universities, and requiring preliminary military training for boys between sixteen and eighteen. But the Hindenburg Program would require somewhere between two million and three million workers. To save manpower, businesses not considered vital to the war effort, especially smaller ones, would be converted to some form of war production or shut down. The field marshal therefore demanded authorizing the compulsory transfer of civilian workers to war plants, and making women eligible for compulsory labor on the grounds that "(s)he who does not work does not eat."[16]

But there was another potential source of labor, as obvious as it was thus far untapped. As early as August 1914 the government had sought to retain 300,000 or so Russian Poles doing seasonal agricultural labor. In 1915 business and industry increasingly sought to hire workers in Poland and Belgium. Poland produced over 200,000 of them by February 1916, in the context of heavy economic pressure from the occupation administration plus a long-standing subculture of seasonal migration. By November 1916, however, despite an unemployment figure of 600,000, only a few thousand Belgians had been impelled or compelled to accept skilled employment in German and Austro-Hungarian factories. German industrialists importuned the military to facilitate and expedite the process of increasing the number of Westerners, generally literate, numerate, and at least semi-skilled; correspondingly far more desirable employees than Easterners. Ludendorff responded by ordering the deportation of 20,000 Belgians a month. German industries proved completely unable to incorporate them. Complaints were raised in the

Reichstag by liberals denouncing involuntary servitude and socialists protesting at depressive effects on job opportunities and wages. In February the deportations were canceled and voluntary recruitment resumed. Eventually the program brought in around 100,000 workers—hardly justifying its administrative costs, to say nothing of its continued negative effect on occupied Belgium.[17]

Germany's labor question was exacerbated in 1916 by internal problems. As initial hopes for a quick victory had faded, the War Ministry began improvising exemptions, particularly of skilled men. By early 1916 a million and a quarter exempted men were employed in war industries—not a few of them recalled from the front. This gave soldiers opportunities for an honorable way out of a war with no end in sight. It generated resentment among the unskilled and unlucky who remained at the front, and encouraged doing everything in one's power to avoid being put into uniform. And it gave management a Damocles sword to suspend over the heads of dissidents. For the first eighteen months of the war labor troubles had been limited. Going into 1916, however, inflation ate into pay envelopes. Long hours and poorly maintained machinery drove working conditions downward. And as increasing numbers of workers took to the streets in more industrial cities, social and economic grievances took on increasingly political aspects. The 55,000 Berlin workers who went on strike for three days in June that year asserted their aims as "peace and bread." Union leaders complained to the authorities that they were losing influence to unorganized workers and radical leaders. The end result was an Auxiliary Service Law of December 1916 that established mandatory service for all able-bodied German males, in factories or in uniforms.

That piece of legislation was itself a political milestone. Chancellor Theobald von Bethmann-Hollweg, a long-time supporter of Hindenburg and Ludendorff, accepted the concept of compulsory civilian labor only after considerable self-examination and careful consideration of prevailing parliamentary winds. The High Command was insouciantly certain the Reichstag would approve once the delegates understood that otherwise the war could not be won. But the unions and the Social Democrats refused to abandon the right of free movement unilaterally. The direct result was a compromise giving unions the right to organize in war industries and the establishment of joint labor-management committees to settle wage disputes. The negotiations were an entering wedge increasing parliamentary influence on what was becoming, in fact as well as concept, a total war.[18]

In October 1916 a War Office was established with responsibility for controlling the economic mobilization. It was directly controlled by the High Command. Its *chef* was Wilhelm Gröner, by now a *Generalleutnant*. Its staff was a mixed bag of junior officers seasoned with a few civilian PhDs. Gröner had been the military representative on the War Food Office for several months, and had some idea of the complexity of his new assignment.

What he did not expect were the synergized crises in coal production and railway transport in the winter of 1916—choke points that for a while bade fair to derail the Reich's war effort altogether.[19] By February 1917 Germany was producing over 200,000 fewer tons of steel than six months earlier—attrition on the wrong side of the balance sheet. Gröner would perform yeoman repair and recovery work. But the Hindenburg Program's initial damage to Germany's war effort was not to be overcome by further improvisation.

Put together, the Jewish Census and the Hindenburg Program are generally and reasonably denounced as a material and moral paradigm shift, a signpost not only to the collapse of 1918 but to the long-term consequences culminating in 1945. Yet with a century's perspective it is legitimate at least to consider an alternate approach, one not so heavily dependent on the limited perspectives of two very unsympathetic generals and the not much less unsympathetic military establishment they represented. The Jewish Census was a fundamental breach of the Second Reich's social contract, in that sense inviting comparison to America's World War II internment of Japanese. But the census was in progress when Hindenburg and Ludendorff ascended to power. It was neither fully implemented, nor were systematic conclusions drawn from the incomplete results that were never released. Its principal author was permanently exiled to an obscure field command, albeit not for this particular reason. None of that can be described as reevaluation, much less atonement. It does indicate that the census was regarded as a bagatelle rather than a signifier. Nor is it cynical to suggest that war is the province of mistakes and victory enables explanation—again we should consider the Japanese internment. Once the war was won there would be time enough to fix any damage done by an ill-advised, dead-end initiative that was, in context, only one among many taken since August 1914.

Reconsidering the Hindenburg Program involves beginning with its military genesis. President Truman observed when Dwight Eisenhower was elected his successor that "poor Ike" was in for a rude awakening. He would say "do this," and "do that"—but nothing would happen! Government, in other words, is essentially different from the military in that it depends more on cooperation than command. The same trope can readily be applied to 1916. Hindenburg and Ludendorff, that is to say, attempted to improvise and impose a command economy in a literal matter of weeks, arguably as much for public consumption based on the new team's image and prestige as on practical contexts, and as much from a still-ephemeral image of "total war" as from any consideration of social, political, and economic realities.

The question remains, however, whether Hindenburg and Ludendorff really inhabited that "airy empire of dreams" Heinrich Heine described as the Germans' true spiritual home. So much military and academic attention has been devoted to the Prussian/German General Staff that it is easy to overlook its two even more fundamental defining factors: command culture and operational focus. At seventh and last, the former was hierarchic. Generals gave orders; staffs and subordinates implemented them. The Hindenburg Program was obviously a work in progress. It was equally obvious that progress would be supervised and fine-tuned further down the chains of command and planning. That was Gröner's job—he was in place to handle the administrative details that were his forte, and to bring the civilians, whether bureaucrats, businessmen, or politicians, on line. He had demonstrated that talent time and again, before and during the war, as chief of the General Staff's Railway Section.

Gröner's appointment did something even more important. It freed Hindenburg and Ludendorff to concentrate on operations. Arguably since the days of Frederick the Great, certainly since its flourishing in the Nineteenth-Century Wars of Unification, the Prussian/German military system had been focused on war planning and war fighting—downwards rather than upwards, a perspective structured by Prussia/Germany's geostrategic situation as, in

Bismarck's phrase, "a mollusk without a shell." The administrators, the officials in uniform, were summoned afterwards to facilitate the work of the real soldiers. Franz Halder, chief of staff of the Wehrmacht in its glory years from 1938 to 1942, would put it aphoristically: in war, he declared, quartermasters must never hamper operational concepts. The material must serve the spiritual.

In that context, the Hindenburg Program can be interpreted not, as Michael Geyer suggests, as a fusion of the military, industry, and society, a synergy upwards like the one Fritz Lang presents at the climax of his 1927 classic *Metropolis*, but as a mobilization downwards, to provide a bigger hammer for the focal point of the war effort: the army.[20] Nor was that either a shortsighted or a foreshortened perspective. It was certain that the French and British would come again in the spring. The final months at Verdun and on the Somme indicated that the Allies had improved significantly in both material and operational contexts. The Hindenburg Program might indeed best be understood as a desperate effort to restore the former balance, as opposed to shifting it. The best Germany could hope for in the current strategic context was to break even in terms of hardware. And that in turn encouraged the new team to emphasize what had historically been the Prussian/German Army's focal point: quality. Back-of-the-envelope calculation was enough to show that the men potentially available to be put into uniform would suffice to do little more than replace casualties—which themselves must be reduced as far as possible. The solution for both the Prussian soldierly icon and the German technician of war was to fight not harder but smarter: to overhaul comprehensively a system strained to the limits of its prewar matrices. Doctrine, weapons, training, morale, tactics, yes, even strategy, must be fed into the hopper in a situation where there were neither time nor resources to spare.

Ludendorff was convinced, however unwillingly, that during 1917 the war on land must shift temporarily to the defensive, with secondary fronts in Italy and the East essentially shut down and efforts in the West devoted to wearing out the French and British operationally while the U-boats eroded their strategic position.[21] This invites interpretation as an unacknowledged development of Falkenhayn's 1915 concept, with a narrower focus on military options as opposed to diplomatic initiatives. In practical terms it meant shortening the front to a degree as drastic as it was unprecedented. Ludendorff had initially rejected the idea, declaring retreat impossible for political and military reasons: it would devastate morale in the army and on the home front. Rupprecht of Bavaria, since August 1916 commanding the group of armies responsible for the sector from the Somme to Flanders, advocated instead a general offensive from Armentières to Soissons. First Army command was reluctant to abandon the favorable marshy terrain in its Ancre sector. Ludendorff responded that in order to save men and materiel, to make optimal use of the terrain, and to build a reserve for the projected defensive fighting, temporary adjustments were necessary. But the quartermaster-general assured his subordinates, "seeking decision in movement and in great battles remains our future military ideal, on which Germany's future will be built."[22]

Preliminary planning for the Great Reconfiguration began in September 1916. The original concept involved no fewer than five interlocking back lines from the Belgian coast to the Moselle Valley. Work started in October on the one perceived most crucial. The grandiloquently christened Siegfried Line ("Hindenburg Line" to the Allies) extended over eighty miles. Its construction absorbed over a half million tons of rocks and gravel, over 100,000 tons of cement, 12,500 tons of barbed wire—and that was just the beginning. The defenses demanded an infrastructure: supply dumps and depots, hospitals, magazines, housing, a network of access roads. The Siegfried Line was the war's biggest military building product, much of its initial stage completed in four months. That last statistic was especially impressive for what was still, at this stage of construction technology, a labor-intensive project. The original intention was to depend on German firms using contract labor from the Reich and the occupied territories. When this proved impractical the army took over. A normal construction zone required around 10,000 workers, who had to be housed, fed, sustained, and guarded. Entire villages were evacuated; temporary camps were built when necessary. Administration and control was in the hands of officers, mostly older men, rear-echelon types from the Landsturm, whose ideas of order and discipline were solidly military, with a solid middle-class grounding. As a rule they understood that abuse of any kind delayed a project directly essential to the war effort. But at best the work was hard and the conditions spartan. Food, clothing, and medical care were alike in short supply. The guards, also mostly *Landsturmer*, usually ranged from stolidly indifferent to casually brutal in behavior. The workers quarreled and fought among themselves for small advantages. They were a mixed bag. Around 6,000 were contract employees, initially mostly German, later French and Belgian as well. Nine thousand more were conscripted from France and Belgium. Unlike the situation in the Reich, for the pick-and-shovel project that was the Siegfried Line forced labor proved effective—and certainly more "reliable" than the free workers, who quit or walked off the job in overwhelming numbers. In retrospect Ludendorff described forced civilian labor as essential to waging modern war, and by the Armistice over 60,000 Belgians were working under the gun behind the German front, at anything their uniformed masters ordered.[23] The Siegfried Line was an entering wedge.

Even more critical to the project were over 28,000 prisoners of war.

The Hague Convention of 1907, to which Germany was a signatory, allowed POWs to be set to work, but prohibited their employment in anything directly connected with military operations. During 1915 civilian authorities put increasing pressure on the armed forces to allow POWs to be used to replace mobilized Germans. By the end of 1916 over four-fifths of them were working outside the camps. At first the overwhelming majority were assigned to farms. Agriculture in Germany was still largely a matter of muscle; most of the POWs were Russian peasants; and food production if properly defined was not strictly war work. Indeed an increasing complaint was that the POWs fitted a little too well into the family farms, replacing absent German males domestically as well as behind the plow. During 1916, however, increasing numbers of prisoners were assigned to mines and factories, with little or no regard for the war-essential provisions of the Hague treaty. Apart from the fraying, not to say shredding, of international law, the conditions were more demanding and the control more rigid than in the countryside. Less and less consideration was given to prisoners less able to work, and virtually none at all to anyone citing the law of the Hague and refusing to work in a coal mine or a steel mill. The construction of the Siegfried Line, a project fully under military control, contributed significantly to the changing status and image of POWs from subjects of military control to factors of economic mobilization.[24]

Construction was only half of the German plan for strategic withdrawal. Operation *Alberich* was named from the dark side of the *Nibelungenlied*, after the malignant dwarf who renounces love for power. Occupied Belgium and most of the German-conquered regions of eastern Europe had general governments: essentially civilian administrative systems, albeit heavily militarized in personnel and policies. Occupied France, however, was the pure article, an *Etappe* or military region organized behind the front as part of the war zone. The Hague Convention was clear: civil authority and civil law were to be maintained, and civil rights respected, as long as there was no direct military reason for suspending them. That meant civilians were expected to obey occupation regulations and in general remain passive. Occupiers in turn were tenants, expected to maintain their own military internal order and to pay their way. In principle, civilians were like POWs in that they could not be compelled to act against what was still their legitimate government. In reality, determining exactly where that boundary lay was a consistent point of contention. A good number of French were shot on usually vague charges of espionage and sabotage. A good number were jailed for everything from curfew violation to receiving letters from across the front. Kite-flying was forbidden lest it be used for signaling. Requisitions of kitchen utensils generated passive resistance from whole communities. In general, however, everyday relations between the French and Germans in the occupied zone tended to stabilize around poles of habit and convenience: commerce, sex, and "I know a good one."[25]

Alberich was a new paradigm. Its intention was to create "a land completely uprooted," in the words of Ludendorff's original order. This document was interpreted to include complete destruction of anything the Allies might find useful, from electric cables and water pipes to entire villages. It was interpreted to mean the complete evacuation of the entire civilian population. It was a military operation, planned in detail from the top down and executed at unit level with what can only be described with the cliché "Teutonic efficiency." The town of Bapaume was reported as having been destroyed in forty-five minutes. Highways were demolished, railroads dismantled, trees cut down. It took 18,000 boxcars to haul away the "movable items," miscellaneous personal and household goods. A hundred and forty thousand people classified as able to work were deported elsewhere, on foot or by rail in the occupied zone or to Belgium. The 15,000 "unfit," the sick, the old, the children, were evacuated separately.

In the Second Army's sector at least, pains were taken to provide cars and ambulances, with attendants instead of guards, for the latter category of deportees. But however they were implemented, the deportations in particular caused discomfort—even guilt. Rupprecht compared the project to the devastation of the Palatinate by Louis XIV in the Seventeenth Century, and did not want his name associated with it. "Military necessity" was invoked and reinvoked as justification. Russia's scorched-earth policy in the long retreat of 1915 was cited as a precedent. But in that context Michael Geyer makes a telling counterpoint. If the exigencies of war now legitimated destruction and depopulation in a noncombat zone, then civilians were comprehensively subject to military control for the duration of a war.

What developed behind the Somme front at the turn of the year may legitimately be considered a harbinger of the totalitarian repressive systems characteristic of the rest of the Twentieth Century. These depended on three essentials: technology, bureaucracy, and ideology. As yet ideology was absent or marginal, embryonic and subterranean. In Geyer's words, "the language of the concentration camps was present [but] the path to the extermination camps was paved with the good intentions of ordinary people"—or perhaps their self-delusions.[26]

III

If the Hindenburg Program can be interpreted as a "macro" exercise, catching up to the Allies in terms of tons of shells and a number of weapons systems, the quality of the hardware was no less important. In the war's two final years, two new technologies would play increasing roles. Beginning with the Albatros and its sturdily built counterparts in the observation, reconnaissance, and ground-support categories, the Germans, as will be seen, held their own and a bit better up to the armistice. On the ground it was another story.

The British introduction of tanks in mid-September 1916 has generated a cottage industry among students of the Allied learning curve. If the enthusiasm for armor as the focal point of Allied victory has given way to a more modest paradigm stressing the limits of Great War vehicle technology and the importance of combined-arms tactics, the impact of tanks is generally recognized. Ludendorff himself affirmed that perspective when declaring after the war that Germany had been defeated not by Marshal Foch but by General Tank.[27]

In that context it is easy to overlook the German Army's quick and comprehensive success in developing effective antitank techniques. The normative terrain combination of shell holes and muck, plus the vehicles' obvious unreliability, gave defenders a situational advantage. Beginning at Flers, the Germans did what they tended to do best: improvising, taking on tanks like any other target with any weapon to hand. Intelligence officers closely interrogated the crew of a captured tank, and translated a diary lost by another tanker. Within a week Berlin had a general description of the new weapon, plus a reasonably accurate sketch.

For the infantry, the appropriate response to the new weapon was described as keeping calm. This was admittedly easier said than done. Whenever possible, however, the tanks' vulnerabilities were directly demonstrated on knocked-out vehicles. Aim at openings in the armor, use grenades individually and in bundles: the heads of a half-dozen stick grenades tied around a complete "potato masher." Since tanks drew fire like magnets—enough fire to strip away any accompanying infantry—and since their close-in visibility was virtually nil, a quick throw from a short distance was not a suicide mission—not necessarily, in any case. More effective and less directly risky was the K-round. This was simply a rifle-caliber bullet with a tungsten carbide core, designed to punch holes in metal plates protecting snipers and machine guns. Adapted for use by the ubiquitous German machine guns, K-rounds took many a tank out of action by causing confusion and casualties among the crews.

Towards the end of the war German designers came up with a 13mm version, initially fired in a specially designed single-shot rifle, the shoulder-breaking recoil of which made it generally unpopular. More promising was a tripod-mounted machine using the same round. Not ready for service by November 1918, the design and the bullet became the basis for John Browning's 50-caliber machine gun, the "Ma Duce," which had now been in American service for approaching a century. Slightly further back on the horizon were a short-barreled, low-velocity, easily portable 37mm gun, an automatic 20mm cannon the Swiss would develop into the universally deployed World War II Örlikon.

This apparent digression into the details of marginal, specialized hardware is not merely relevant for students of arcane weapons systems. It highlights the continuing German commitment to tank defense—a commitment that rapidly extended to routinely deploying ordinary field guns, whose 3in. high-explosive shells could take out tanks at two miles, in designated antitank roles. A large number of such guns were also mounted on trucks as mobile antiaircraft pieces. They did so well in ground combat at Cambrai in 1917 that the crews had to be officially reminded their primary mission was shooting down airplanes.

When considering German tanks' design, the perspective changes. The committee responsible for the project first met in October 1916. Its members were mostly from the motor transport service. They depended heavily on designers and technicians loaned by the auto companies; seven firms ultimately shared the contracts. The working model demonstrated in May 1917 was a clear winner for the title of "ugliest tank ever built," and a strong contender in the "most dysfunctional" category. It required a crew of eighteen men. Its rectangular, slab-sided box shape was protected by ordinary steel plate instead of hardened armor. Its underslung tracks and low ground clearance gave it almost no capacity to negotiate obstacles and broken terrain, the Western Front's normal tactical environment. First deployed in March 1918, the tank would live down to its appearance.

The apparent fiasco of German tank design is frequently used as a sarcastic counterpoint to Ludendorff's dismissive assertion that High Command had decided not to fight a materiel battle. It is more accurate to assert that the High Command was *unable* to fight a materiel battle after 1916. Given Germany's resources relative to the competition, "materiel war" required a syncretic relationship among Germany's productive forces—a relationship structured and managed from the top down. The High Command did not possess *de facto* that kind of moral authority, even in a deferential society. It is better understood as, initially at least, one among a stable of contestants for position and power. The military was well positioned to improve its position by acting as a fulcrum, a broker, even a croupier, working towards consensual interaction.[28] But the army would have to prove itself by succeeding.

For Hindenburg and Ludendorff, that meant winning the war. Winning the war meant, again initially, standing on the defensive at the critical point, the Western Front. That in turn meant systematically readjusting towards defensive operations. In that context tanks, which at their stage of development were legitimately understood as a one-dimensional offensive weapon, fell at best in the "nice to have" category. Another, far humbler, less spectacular instrument of war would be the focus of the army's reorientation. That weapon was the light machine gun.

The German soldier's primary group during the war's first two years was the company: for much of the war around 200 officers and men, including a dozen noncombatants, as a front-line norm. Lesser units existed primarily for administrative purposes; as a rule, indeed, in the war's early stages squads were formed by height, as was the peacetime practice—the unit looked better on parade! The company was also the primary tactical unit, frequently detached to support another battalion or regiment—a practice contributing not a little to the fog and friction of early trench warfare.

This system was reasonably functional as long as the infantryman carried only a rifle. That made both fire and movement depend essentially on numbers, when not mass. The hand grenade was in practice most useful for keeping heads down, leaving the final assault to be made with close-quarters weapons—an unpredictable process at best. Part of the answer came from across the line, as the British introduced the Lewis gun in late 1915 and the French followed with the Chauchat a few months later. Both were light enough to be moved and served by two or three men. More importantly, both were designed to provide close fire support to attacking infantry, something impossible for the heavier tripod-mounted automatic weapons with which all armies began the war.

The Germans as well had been seeking a solution to the problems of weight and visibility inseparable from the heavy guns. Their result was a direct modification of the Maxim 08. The 08/15 kept the mechanism, the water jacket, and the belt feed. The tripod gave way to a bipod, with a shoulder stock and pistol grip making them easier to control. The High Command and the manufacturers were pleased. The same factories could make both guns. Many essential parts were interchangeable. Men familiar with one could easily master the other. Altogether, the MG 08/15 was a model economy-of-force weapon.

Company officers liked it because it gave them an organic supplement to previously limited firepower. Front soldiers complained—not, of course, an unusual occurrence. The gun weighed over forty pounds, exponentially heavier than its Allied counterparts. Moving it was like dragging an engine block, and only the strongest men could fire it from the hip in an attack. It required water—always a scarce commodity in the line. It was challenging to maintain even compared to the Lewis, which, though notorious for all the ways it could jam, remained a valued prize of war in many regiments. But as it was introduced by ones and twos during 1916, the 08/15 became half the military counterpart of a successful companionate marriage: initial acquiescence developing into respect, then affection, and sometimes even more.[29]

The first guns reached the front in late 1916. Officially at first there were three guns to a company; in April 1917 six became the official norm; in practice, allocation depended on availability. Some divisions in the east received 08/15s only in 1918. But even in small numbers the 08/15 made a difference, vitally enabling the new tactics of "resist, bend, snap back." It could be moved and concealed in the face of an attack: a near-ideal shell hole weapon. Its water cooling and 250-round belt enabled continued fire in an emergency, as opposed to the usual short bursts. And in a counterattack the 08/15s could keep pace with the infantry, providing direct fire support while the grenadiers and assault teams got close enough to do their work.

With doctrine and weapons increasingly reflecting mutually-supporting fire and movement by small groups, organization changed as well. German companies during 1917 reorganized into building blocks. Depending on unit strength they might have seven or eight men apiece, or they might have four or five. A strong platoon could consist of three squads of riflemen and grenadiers, two of 08/15s. A weak one would organize around its guns, whose official crew was five, with the extra riflemen expected to protect and support them. As long as the light machine guns could be kept in action the German infantry platoon was a self-sustained combat unit, able to defend or attack and in either case exact a high price from any but the best opponent—if the men matched their tools and tactics.[30]

War is a traumatic experience, to which individuals are unable to adjust through normal cognitive processes. In other words, individual trauma is a general consequence of warfare. At the same time, warfare's radically different circumstances challenge the formation of alternate coping systems. Arguably more than in any war before or since, the Great War's dominant environment of material mass and personal immobility generated an essentially permanent sense of helplessness, of disempowerment.[31] In response, during 1917 a new, distinctive archetype of the German infantryman emerged. A blend of warrior and technician, he had assimilated the conditions of the modern battlefield and transcended its physical and psychological limits. A man of controlled will power and calculated nerve, he understood war as the ultimate manifestation of modern life and found fulfillment in his mastery of war's demands. His image was epitomized in the writing of Ernst Jünger and the art of Otto Dix; the "asphalt man," cut off alike from natural and constructed environments, a cigarette in his mouth, a potato-masher in his belt, cradling one of the new submachine guns with the ease of familiarity. His home was the front line and his family the men of his squad. Against war's tangible horror he balanced the existential pleasures of war's demands and sacrifices—the more meaningless the better.[32]

Like most archetypes, this one was in good part a construction, fully developed only after 1918. It was also an exception, an individualized response—and not necessarily an ideal. The "normal" (if such an adjective can be applied) response to Great War trauma tended towards the collective, the comprehensive, and the contextual.[33] Its definitive manifestation was another postwar construction: the myth of "trench comradeship" (*Grabenkameradschaft*): the military version of the kaiser's civic truce that bound those who served and endured into a fellowship sealed by blood. It might also be described as secured by accents. In contrast to France, which in 1915 abandoned the practice of assigning men from certain districts to particular regiments, and to Britain, where one for one replacement of casualties for the many locally recruited battalions was militarily impossible and socially dysfunctional, Germany's depot system during most of the war was more or less able to replenish depleted regiments with men from the same or neighboring provinces and regions, who had some basics in common—more or less, and frequently less. Front-line comradeship, during the war and afterward, was widely and fundamentally challenged by veterans as an ideal seldom realized and easily disrupted. Middle-class memoirists recorded victimization and exclusion by men of alleged inferior education and lower social standing. Socialists described persecution by militaristic officers and NCOs. Jews described their identity as setting them apart. Still others suffered from being "Wackes" from Alsace-Lorraine, and therefore regarded as potential slackers and deserters.[34]

Nevertheless, everyday life, that of the combat arms in particular, generated the development of small groups based on proximity, affinity, and experience. In that context the group represented what order and security there was to be had. Essentially it was a survival mechanism, for a man alone on the Western Front was a dead man or a madman. But its roots, general and specific, ran deeper. Social psychologists identify affective involvement, goal involvement, and ego involvement as primary motivators for group loyalty. Membership provides a "basis for the individual's need for self-protection and self-transcendence."[35] Applied to the German Army of World War I, small-group associations thus reflected a need for security against outside aggression and required participation in behaviors and attitudes that affirmed male identity in a male environment. Nor is such participation necessarily assertive. It is manifested above all and time and again by bunching up, huddling together under fire, even when that exponentially enhances risk: "to know men not just by their faces but by their shoulders and signifying movements."[36] A holdover, perhaps, from humanity's millennia of existence as prey before the species learned how to be predators?

Small-group membership could also in a sense institutionalize trauma by morphing individual vulnerability into collective strength. By facing and acknowledging weakness, of any kind, the individual could reverse his trauma, redefine and reinvent himself. Erich Maria Remarque offers two overlooked examples in All Quiet on the Western Front. One involves a replacement who soils himself during a bombardment. A veteran tells him that many another man has filled his pants the first time; just throw them away. The second involves Corporal Himmelstoss, the brutal drill instructor who finds himself at the front. Initially attempting to enforce training-camp standards, he eventually brings in a badly wounded man that, significantly, the novel's narrator has left behind as a hopeless case: front-line comradeship developing in most unlikely soil.

German Romanticism has been described as enabling the inversion of trauma through memory: repeating and reconceptualizing traumatic events to enable their reversal. One immediate postwar study concluded that only religious beliefs and memories of home and family were more significant than "social emotions" as support in situations of extreme stress.

The dead, for example, were remembered and commemorated. Photographs and correspondence affirm the pains German soldiers took decorating and maintaining grave sites[37]—something of a contrast to the British, whose direct connection to the dead usually ended with their burial, and the French, whose apparently casual treatment of their dead was often remarked by British and Germans constrained to deal with decomposed corpses in fragments of blue coats and red trousers from the war's early months.

An enduring sense of bereavement combined with survivor's guilt to nurture a sense, strongest in the war's early months, that only victory could requite the losses endured. Over time, and clearly by the end of 1916, that was joined by, or evolved into, comprehensive weariness: physical and emotional fatigue that reflected the recurring strains of the front and the enduring nature of the war. Human contact at almost any level was a near-universal anodyne. Far more than their British and French counterparts, German relationship groups functioned as substitute families, often with complex delineation of roles. Nurturing functions that civil society assigned to women were assumed by men supporting men. Patriarchs, uncles, and mentors, reliable older brothers and scallywag younger ones, feature regularly in front-line memoirs and fictions. The career of Adolf Hitler indicates there could be room as well for eccentric cousins.

The reasons for this pattern remain unclear. It might be interpreted as incorporating attractive or familiar features of the homeland's culture. *Geborgenheit*, the security and comfort nurtured by familiarity even if ephemeral; the fraternal style of the prewar youth movement; patriarchy, with its comprehensive sense of order and place—all made contributions. Arguably as well, the German Army's extended relationship networks reflected the weakness of alternatives. The German regiment was never a focus of emotion and identity in the manner of a British battalion. In contrast to the French, German soldiers were not fighting on their home ground, and so lacked both the *poilu*'s spectrum of direct connections to peacetime life and his existential sense of fighting for home and homeland.[38]

Whatever their origins, the evolving dynamics of the German Army's primary affinitive groups were highly congruent with the new weapons, tactics, and doctrines. Their institutionalization was facilitated in October 1916 when Ludendorff ordered each army on the Western Front to form its own assault battalion. That continued a process that had begun earlier in the year, but the *ad hoc* formation of assault detachments and the proposal to convert Jäger battalions had two problems. One was providing replacements. The other was the risk of stripping regiments of their most experienced and aggressive men. The fifteen battalions authorized by Ludendorff were assigned a dual mission. They were primarily to act as training institutions. Officers and men were rotated in for limited periods, became part of the small, complex combat teams of riflemen, light and heavy machine guns, trench mortars, and flamethrowers, then returned to their parent regiments to serve as instructors and examples. The battalions also executed trench raids, participated in limited attacks—and not least were used to disrupt the "live and let live" conditions that began as occasional fraternizations and in quiet sectors increasingly developed into mutual agreements of convenience, acceptable when not welcome to units from both sides rotated in to recover from an active front and rebuild for the next bloodletting. Propaganda declared Frenchmen were not comrades; Englishmen were paid hirelings; and Germans were too trustful, too easily forgiving. Front rumor had German guns firing short rounds to disrupt "unauthorized understandings." Storm troop deployment gave line regiments a harsher choice: either sustain an acceptable level of hostile activity during their trench tours, or risk having a detachment of storm troopers completely disrupt the settled condition and then disappear to the rear while the *Frontschweine* ("Front Hogs") suffered the consequences.[39]

IV

Ludendorff had consistently insisted that the Siegfried Line and its theoretical counterparts were only precautionary measures, economy of force initiatives. On January 25, 1917, at a briefing at Cambrai, Hermann von Kuhl, who had followed Rupprecht of Bavaria as his chief of staff when the prince rose to army group command, declared the time for implementation had come. The Allies were sure to attack so consistently and with such massive force that Germany could not afford to waste any of its already overextended resources in offensive initiatives. Instead the line must be shortened, drastically shortened, even though the Siegfried project was still incomplete. Rupprecht affirmed Kuhl's position when on January 28 he stated the trenches in his sector could not be held against a renewed Allied offensive. Ludendorff, gratified to have his own opinion confirmed, calculated that a general retreat to the Siegfried Line would buy two months before the Allies could lurch forward—and two months as well for the Hindenburg Program to find its footing. Operation *Alberich* was authorized on February 9. The withdrawal was conducted between March 16 and 19. It was arguably the German Army's most successful initiative on the Western Front since 1914. It saved over forty miles of front and enabled moving thirteen divisions into reserve. Surprise was complete. So was Allied shock as their vanguards pushed carefully across twenty-five miles of empty devastation towards a looming network of concrete dugouts, fortified trenches, and prepared artillery positions—none of which influenced their offensive plans for 1917.[40]

Those were focused initially on the jaunty assurances of Robert Nivelle, who had replaced Pétain as French commander in chief in December 1916. He presented a plan for a massive two-pronged attack, the British around Ypres and an Anglo-French attack south of Arras and along the Chemin des Dames: a neglected sector offering corresponding prospects for the kind of decisive breakthrough projected for the Somme in the previous year, only this time with the French Army doing the heavy lifting. "Victory is certain," Nivelle declared. A week-long preparatory barrage, then a million men closely following a rolling barrage along a forty-mile front, bypassing strong points, aiming for the German rear: the war would be decided in a matter of days.[41]

The BEF was to set this triumph's stage by a series of secondary attacks around Arras. These began on April 9 when the Canadian Corps signaled its emergence as the finest fighting instrument on the Western Front by capturing Vimy Ridge. For arguably the first time on a large scale, the Germans were not merely outfought. They were outsoldiered by extensive preparation, sophisticated tactics, and better than competent command from platoons to corps.[42] Vimy was a harbinger—but it came to be understood as a one-off. From a German front-line perspective, the main attack was initially a shock. On a front of over ten miles the British advanced as far as four miles and beyond in only six days. Tanks, even deployed in small numbers, had been disproportionally effective, as had low-flying aircraft. Total casualties were over 23,000. Ominously, 16,000 were listed as "missing," and the unusually episodic reports from the front suggested that as casualties mounted and ammunition ran low, morale might be the next thing to crack.

Instead, the Germans turned the offensive into a Somme manqué. Reaction evaluation began even as the situation was deteriorating. The immediate conclusion was that some front-line formations had been worn down by the three-week British barrage, ineffectively countered by German artillery both outgunned and poorly handled. Of more significance, the forward positions, in accordance with the new doctrine of flexibility, were thinly held. First lines had been correspondingly easily broken by Western Front standards. In consequence, second and third positions were often surprised, overrun or left fighting for their own lives before they could mount the local counterattacks needed to buy time for reserves to intervene. Finally, the half-dozen divisions in reserve were held too far back to perform the support and counterattack missions essential to the new tactics of defense in depth. The result was too often the worst of both forward and flexible defensive systems, and the advantages of neither.[43]

Ludendorff responded on April 11 by reassigning Fritz von Lossberg as chief of staff to the hard-hammered Sixth Army—with, predictably, *Vollmacht*: authorized to issue orders in the commanding general's name, he took hold with characteristic vigor and no arguments. He replaced most of the hard-hammered front-line divisions and ordered the relieving formations to offer only token resistance when the British came again before falling back to new positions. In accordance with the manuals issued at the turn of the year, these were to be based not on trenches but strong points: shell holes surrounded by barbed wire. The guns were to avoid fixed positions, using terrain as cover and keeping their ability to move. When the British barrage passed, the infantry was to counterattack in coordinated depth from the new front line to reserves now deployed within striking distance, supported by the heaviest fire the guns could produce.[44]

The system was simple enough in outline, and devastating when it worked. For example, at Monchy-le Preux on April 14 the 1st Newfoundland Battalion, which had been eviscerated on the first day of the Somme, crossed high ground east of the village and disappeared, enmeshed in a web of company-scale counterattacks that cost it 487 casualties out of the 597 men who went into action. Further south around Bullecourt, the British were wrong-footed by having to advance through the *Alberich* demolitions, then ran into a German division whose most recent assignment had been as a demonstration unit specializing in defensive tactics. The result was a catastrophe comprehensive even by trench warfare standards.[45]

The challenge for the Germans involved systematic, coordinated, large-scale execution of a still-unfamiliar defensive doctrine. Here they benefitted from British exhaustion, disorganization, and casualties. Victory *never* came cheaply on the Western Front. It was April 23 when the BEF's offensive resumed, and by then a revitalized Sixth Army was able to take effective tactical control of the battlefield. Defining engagements were around Gavrelle and Oppy, where initial British gains were enmeshed in shell holes and limited by counterattacks. Fighting tailed off in May as British attention shifted north towards Messines and Passchendaele. Advances across a mile and a half of nothing in particular on a front of eighteen miles had cost 170,000 British, Australian, and Canadian casualties—twice the German number. It was a vindication of Lossberg's theories on defense in depth and a case study of the German Army's continuing, indeed increasing, ability to adjust from the back foot.

But there were two material straws in the wind, both overlooked while drawing the more encouraging tactical balances. An improved version of the Albatros fighter, the D III, had entered service in December 1916. With its teething troubles resolved, it emerged in spring 1917 as the dominant air superiority fighter on the Western Front, making the initial reputations of most of the new generation of German aces including Manfred von Richthofen. Concentrated in the Arras sector, the German fighter squadrons accounted for most of the 250 British aircraft shot down in "Bloody April,"[46] a third of the British force in the sector. But the German success did not prevent the Royal

Flying Corps (RFC) from flying the reconnaissance and observation missions essential to the effective use of artillery. Like its counterpart ground operations, the air arm's achievement was defensive. And it depended even more on a technical superiority likely to prove temporary.

No less significant were the conclusions drawn from the experience of fighting tanks. The evidence seemed clear: giving the infantry enough armor-piercing ammunition and small trench guns would "literally mean the end of tank attacks. We have recognized their weak points and know where they are vulnerable."[47] In other words, there seemed no particular need to give high priority to resolving the constant quarreling in the first months of 1917 between the High Command and the tank design committee over such details as the shape and the protection of a weapons system still at drawing-board status, much less addressing the no less fundamental question of what level of increasingly scarce resources should be devoted to the project.

The primary strategic purpose of the Arras offensive had been to enable the French offensive on the Aisne and in Champagne. Instead it underwrote a far greater catastrophe. "Violence, brutality, and speed" remained the watchwords of a "*décision à la hussarde,*" a cavalryman's gamble defying Nivelle's background as an artilleryman. His primary tactical objective was the fifty-mile long Chemin des Dames ridge in the heart of the "Lousy Champagne." His strategic goal was to break the German Army's spine. He deployed two armies along a twenty-five mile front, with thirty-three divisions between them, including some of the best of the French assault troops. A third army was in reserve, to develop the expected victory. This mass of men was supported by 5,350 guns. During the course of the battle, slightly over a month, they would fire over eleven million rounds. One hundred twenty tanks were to accompany the infantry, their first appearance in a French order of battle.

It would have been difficult to choose a less promising sector for a war-winning attack. The terrain enabled most of the German positions to be placed on reverse slopes and dead ground. Its western half was a kaleidoscopic five or six miles worth of broken and boggy ground. The ridge had been a quarry site for centuries, and was honeycombed with caves and tunnels needing only a little work to become excellent shelter sites. The offensive's buildup, gun positions, airfields, supply dumps, and rail lines proliferated to degrees impossible for the airmen to overlook. As early as February, the Germans secured a preliminary attack directive. During the next month prisoners provided a rich fund of documents and codes, carried contrary to orders. The capstone of French security failure came on April 7 with the capture of a map giving deployments and objectives. The Chemin des Dames had been one of the quietest sectors on the Western Front, a rest area for convalescent divisions. Defense in depth was a theoretical concept, until February. By the time the French barrage began on April 8, the Germans had sixteen divisions holding the front, fourteen more available in reserve, 200 batteries of heavy guns alone, and a spare army headquarters ready to step in and share command responsibility if needed.[48]

The French artillery preparation was handicapped by bad weather that hindered ground observation and interrupted ammunition resupply. German air superiority restricted aerial reconnaissance. One Bavarian battalion commander described his men as "passing the time singing good old soldiers' songs"[49]—though there was more praying than singing in other shelters! The Germans not only knew the date of the attack, April 16, but the projected time, reported to all forward units during the night. When the French left their trenches at 6 am, the machine gunners were waiting for them. Rain and sleet had turned the ground to a sponge. The Senegalese battalions, in whom much faith had been placed as assault troops, were demoralized and immobilized by the near-freezing cold. Of the 121 tanks engaged, eighty-one were knocked out, mostly by the artillery. Thirty-five of them burned when unprotected cans of gasoline, fastened externally to enable refueling, instead caught fire. Compounding that particular horror, the cans were attached near the tanks' doors, turning them into roasting ovens.[50]

The French gained ground—in places. The Germans were shaken—in places. None of their accounts describe anything but hard, close-quarters fighting. But the French had achieved nothing resembling a breakthrough. By April 20 it was clear to everyone involved on both sides that Nivelle's "brutal and continuous" assault had produced nothing but another of the Western Front's broken-backed slaughter pens. During May the offensive degenerated into a near-random sequence of local attacks and counterattacks with marginal meaning even on tactical levels. And on April 29 came the first recorded case of a French regiment refusing to enter the trenches for an attack.[51]

Despite desperate French efforts to keep their secret, the German High Command had little difficulty obtaining a clear and comprehensive sense of the rampant disaffection across the trench line. Exploiting it was another matter. Over seventy divisions had been used to check the Nivelle offensive—and that in the context of continued British pressure around Arras. There simply were no fresh troops left. Stocks of artillery ammunition were dangerously low. To cap the operational situation the British were—again all too obviously—preparing for a major initiative in Flanders. Finally, the German Army had just spent months reconfiguring itself as a defensive instrument. To shift gears on the fly was a sufficiently high risk that it never emerged as an option. Instead, the Germans concentrated on evaluating the reasons why they had been able to turn the Allied spring offensive into a spectacular joint failure.

On the Chemin des Dames front alone, French casualties totaled over 270,000; German numbers were a hundred thousand fewer. The High Command's overall conclusion was that flexible defense needed no more than fine-tuning—as a defensive system. Problems remained: positioning of reserves at all levels, adjusting the timing and the force of counterattacks; coordinating artillery support in a fluid battle zone. Command, from squad to division and upward, depended more than ever on initiative and intuition—on a "fingertip feeling" (*Fingerspitzengefühl*) that could be cultivated but not inculcated by training or experience alone, and whose loss was potentially even more serious than the fighting spirit so often described as bled away at Verdun and on the Somme. In strategic terms, moreover, the Germans may finally have won a major battle of attrition, but it was a defensive battle. It had bought time and nothing more—but time for what? And the British were on the verge of offering an uncomfortable answer.

IV

On June 7, 1917, over 450 tons of high explosives packed into nineteen mines blew up under the forward positions of the Fourth German Army along Messines Ridge. Planning dated back to September 1915. Surprise was complete. The RFC controlled the air and collected payback for Black April as a new family of fighters took the measure of the suddenly-obsolescent Albatros. On the ground, almost three weeks of bombardment wore down the defenders to a point where "careful watchfulness ... gave way to complete indifference,"[52] which produced limited resistance. By mid-morning the British—including a high proportion of Anzacs—held the crest of the ridge. They maintained their positions against disorganized counterattacks. Further exploitation was less successful, in good part due to the German artillery, which accounted for an increasing percentage of British casualties.

Messines was obviously a one-off, impossible to replicate because of its terrain specificity. In any case, the time frame required would have brought the Allies to the Rhine sometime in the Twenty-First Century. That said, Messines is generally and legitimately counted as a tactical success for the BEF: the significant forward movement of a learning curve that effectively applied the combined-arms fire and movement tactics that had emerged on the Somme and at Arras.[53] The operation's effect on morale alone was sufficient to confirm the Germans, from the High Command to the rifle companies, in a reactive mode: watch, wait, and evaluate; respond to the next Allied initiative.

That initiative was expected in the Ypres sector. It had been quiet since 1916, and was the only one remaining in the British area of operations with a potential strategic objective: the Flanders U-boat bases. The High Command's immediate initiative was a near-predictable personnel transfer. On July 12 Lossberg was assigned as chief of staff to the Fourth Army, responsible for holding the threatened zone. Lossberg was determined to make the Flanders defense system the best in the West. He had seven weeks to do it before the first British bombardment began. His new commander, Sixt von Arnim, had worked with Lossberg on the Somme and gave him a free hand. Two years of make-or-break assignments had diminished neither his insight nor his energy. And he had a solid base with which to work.[54]

The High Command had planned no offensives in Flanders: First and Second Ypres remained vivid memories. The sector was defensively configured: the German position consisted essentially of four lines about two miles apart, based on concrete bunkers sited above ground because of the high water table. In dry weather, Lossberg noted, the ground surface was firm and gave a certain edge to the attacker. Rain transformed it to a swamp, and shifted the advantage significantly to the defense. And rain could reasonably be expected in a Flanders autumn. He correspondingly rejected Kuhl's recommendation of a local withdrawal: the Flanders region lacked operational, let alone strategic depth. Instead he organized a defense based on holding the front line as the only practical tactical option in the face of an overwhelming British artillery superiority that made orderly withdrawal impossible even on small scales. But the fight would be conducted on the principles of elastic defense: layered organization, flexible response, and close cooperation among all arms. And the *Eingreif* divisions would be held close enough behind the front, ten to fifteen miles, that the initial defenders could expect effective counterattacks before being completely overrun.

Kuhl thought Lossberg's approach too schematic. Rupprecht favored a local withdrawal to throw the British off balance. Ludendorff balked at providing the reinforcement necessary to provide Lossberg's quota of *Eingreif* divisions. Lossberg, however, held his ground in conferences as firmly as he expected it to be held in combat. The men in the front sectors suffered increasingly under air attacks, gas shelling that poisoned the air four miles into the German positions, lack of sleep, insufficient food and constant over-exertion. But when the British attack began on July 31, Rupprecht decided, "I can face this offensive in confidence because ... never before have we deployed ... such strong reserve forces which have been so well trained in their role."[55]

In the first days' fighting, the Allies (a French army was operating on the left flank) made reasonable gains: up to almost two miles—except on the vital Gheluvelt Plateau. Enough German blockhouses and machine-gun positions survived the two-week preliminary bombardment to slow the attack and buy time for the *Eingreif* divisions to intervene effectively. The price was nevertheless high. A senior staff officer at OHL said that "whole divisions burn out to slag within a few hours. In some zones two defensive lines had been overrun and a third threatened before the counterattacks hit home. Even then a good few of them were thwarted by cratered ground and Allied artillery."

On August 1, Lossow's over-the thumbs-calculation trumped those of the BEF's meteorologists. The weather broke, and broke "exceptionally ... and unexpectedly bad,"[56] the worst in seventy-five years. Heavy rains, little sun and less wind meant the ground indeed turned into a swamp. Successive British attacks drowned in Flanders muck and their own blood. The defenders breathed a collective sigh of relief. Their casualties were no bagatelle: between June 1 and August 19 Army Group Rupprecht lost over 85,000 officers and men. The average loss for a division during two weeks was between 1,500 and 2,000. But on the Somme it had been double the higher number. Small wonder that at OHL troop morale seemed "much better than last year."[57] Nor was this mere rear-echelon fustian. "The men have stuck to it remarkably well," noted a company commander writing home.[58] The divisions deployed to Flanders, particularly the *Eingreif* formations, had been briefed and trained in their roles, benefitting from the lessons learned on the Somme and at Arras. A recurring, unexpected "fog and friction" problem of flexible defense involved the mixing and re-sorting of units and individuals among front-line units, their reserves, and the *Eingreif* divisions. On the whole, however, the German system appeared to be succeeding.

That changed in mid-August as the BEF switched generals and techniques, moving from attempted breakthrough to "bite and hold" limited advances of a thousand yards at a time, on narrower fronts, with artillery support a German survivor called "incomparably worse" than Verdun.[59] On September 20, the British not only advanced an average of 1,500 yards along the Menin Road. They also virtually annihilated the forward companies, and in the next days threw back all but one of the increasingly desperate counterattacks by *Eingreif* divisions deployed too far to the rear, disorganized by disrupted communications, and mercilessly hammered by the British artillery as they sought to move into position.

The single successful operation was limited in results and almost insulting in its isolation. Higher headquarters declared the defenders could "look back with pride on their achievements" and proclaimed that "troops and commanders performed to the highest standard."[60] On September 30, the Fourth Army published its real reactions. The British infantry, Lossberg and his colleagues declared, seemed to be advancing to a predetermined point, pre-calculated with their artillery, then waiting for and seeing off equally predictable counterattacks. Given the limited ground available in the Flanders sector for long-term withdrawals, a situation exacerbated by the need to maintain the U-boat bases at Zeebrugge and Ostend, the recommended response was to take lessons from 1916. Build up the front lines, with as many as eight machine guns every 250 yards, and "fight decisively for every piece of ground."[61] The *Eingreif* divisions were to strike preemptively in order to force the commitment of larger numbers of infantry into prospective killing zones.

Tested on October 4 around Broodseinde, the revised tactics proved disastrous. The forward positions were virtually annihilated: "the few remaining men [were] overwhelmed, bayoneted, bludgeoned ... and robbed."[62] To men under the well-coordinated British artillery and machine-gun fire, "no power of the devil could create anything more violent. Against this work of man hell itself would seem feeble."[63] Counterattacks were slowed, then halted, and generally resumed only with the familiar balance of heavy losses for limited results. On October 7, the Fourth Army returned to a policy of holding front lines lightly and establishing main battle zones behind them.

This reversion had little effect in the first half of October. The weather contributed as much as tactics and fighting power to the defense, slowing attacking infantry and diminishing the effect of artillery, particularly in the pillboxes and bunkers that stood out like concrete islands in the sea of mire. The front-line divisions were so worn down by rain, mud, and cold that there was little difference in wastage levels between major periods of fighting and "routine" duty. German casualties totaled 35,000 in the first ten days of the month. By November the average strength of a German battalion was 640 men. The shortage of numbers was however compensated for by an increase in fire power. One regiment received no fewer than two dozen additional light machine guns before entering the line; its forward battalion could call on no fewer than forty-nine heavy machine guns as well. The German Army was not equipping its men as much as it was manning its equipment.[64]

And that balance was becoming ever more precarious. On October 11, the Fourth Army declared tactical effectiveness could best be maintained by constant mutual relief of ground-holding divisions by *Eingreif* divisions. By then the difference between the two categories was becoming minuscule. Nor was this merely a matter of numbers. In Rupprecht's words, "the fighting ability of our troops is reducing all the time." Assignment to Flanders "flashed round the regiment like news of a death—everybody knew the fateful hour was upon them."[65] By mid-October Rupprecht was considering a comprehensive withdrawal to conserve men and materiel, whatever the consequences for the submarine service. Ludendorff, declared the Bavarian prince, was predicting victory in two weeks—"but what has led him to this optimistic assessment is beyond my comprehension."[66]

As the month waned, the weather got worse and the British kept coming. Interrogation reports noted that prisoners "made a good impression ... Morale among the men was said to be good."[67] In "filthy weather and a largely featureless swamp," the Germans were forced back a yard at a time. A regimental medical officer reported: "As a result of the immense physical effort, lack of sleep and constant mental strain, all the officers and men exhibit the signs of utter exhaustion."[68] The commander of one of the *Eingreif* divisions, hardly a sentimental or romantic man, unburdened himself to his diary:

> This mass murder here on the Flanders front is appalling. One is accustomed to much in this terrible war. But here the waste of men goes far beyond the concepts of other fronts, including Verdun. The procedure seems like an uncaring factory with a blast furnace, to burn new divisions to slag with a loss of 2,000–3,000 men in a short time ... With the heroism and endurance a single six-day battle demands and receives here, one could make an entire Serbian or Rumanian campaign. Inferno.[69]

The Canadian Corps captured Passchendaele village on November 6. Thinly-manned counterattacks were ineffective. Communications and morale alike broke down. In one sector, retreating men were not only threatened by their own officers, they were strafed by their own aircraft. In the end the High Command decided to abandon efforts to recapture another pulverized village. For their part, the British shut down the Ypres offensive on November 10. Within ten days the front was quiet enough that a corps headquarters complained, "Recently the standard of saluting by officers ... leaves a great deal to be desired."[70]

The price of that admonition was 217,000 German casualties since July 21. The U-boat bases were safe—but the U-boat offensive was stagnating. The French Army had recovered sufficiently to mount a limited operation at

Malmaison in late October that combined infantry, artillery, tanks, and aircraft to capture the heights of Chemin des Dames at a tenth of the price vainly paid by Nivelle.[71] At OHL the question loomed ever larger: "What now?"

V

Grand strategy as a term and concept is a product of the twentieth century. As Williamson Murray says, it has no precise definition. It is affected by a state's geography, history, government, and leadership. It incorporates political and moral, economic, social, and military realities. B. H. Liddell-Hart described grand strategy's purpose as coordinating and directing a nation's total resources towards the objectives of national policy. Hew Strachan offers a warning that grand strategy so defined tends to seek goals "more visionary and aspirational than pragmatic and immediate"—in other words, to neglect contingency. Murray takes that point further, asserting that grand strategy can only be understood in historical contexts that emphasize the ambiguities and uncertainties influencing specific policies and decisions.[72]

In the context of those descriptions, German grand strategy is frequently and legitimately called a contradiction in terms.[73] Grand strategy's formulation requires a certain detachment, intellectual, structural, even physical: Athens, Rome, the France of Louis XIV, America during the Cold War. Specifically in the Great War, German grand strategy was to win the first battle, then win the next one—a fundamental denial of millennia of evidence suggesting grand strategy can only be developed in a climate of the *longue durée*. The decision for war in 1914 and the Hindenburg Program of 1916 bookend an approach that foreshadowed, if it did not determine, disaster.

And yet, examining the Hindenburg–Ludendorff team's decisions in a comprehensive context, it is possible to suggest the outline of a grand strategy—a strategy that its proponents may not even have developed consciously, like the novice language student who has been speaking prose all his life without knowing it. The reconfiguration of Germany's army and war effort during 1916 was implemented on four interrelated levels: tactically, with the overhauling of doctrine, organization, and armament;

operationally, with the drastic shortening of the Western Front and the shift to a defensive mode; strategically, with the focusing of the economy on direct, comprehensive support of the war; and grand strategically, as Hindenburg and Ludendorff sought to develop Germany's base in two contexts. One was maritime: the introduction of unrestricted submarine warfare. This was arguably the only policy since the Navy's emergence as a rival for resources and influence, on which the two services enthusiastically agreed. Ludendorff's support of that initiative surprised even Admiral von Tirpitz.[74] But the focus of base development, the sphere in which the army could exercise not merely a dominant but a decisive influence, was in the Reich's decades-long-neglected back yard.

German interactions with Russia began in a narrowly military context. Initially the German Empire expected a short war, and the German Army was committed to maintaining war's autonomy. In a Russian context that required controlling civilian behavior and securing civilian cooperation—on a temporary, *ad hoc* basis. But as the war endured, the German high command sought to exploit occupied Russia's resources, first in order to make the eastern theater self-sufficient, then to support the Second Reich's war effort. Success depended on securing Russian cooperation and Russian participation. This in turn required long-term pacification, to be achieved in three ways. First was intimidation: overwhelming force, to be applied only as necessary but always obviously present. Second was administration: the restructuring of public institutions disordered by the tectonic disruptions and displacements that were a consequence of the military events of 1914–15. Third was the civilizing mission: introducing modernity to a society whose comprehensive "backwardness" was from the beginning an emotional and intellectual challenge to its occupiers.[75]

German soldiers harbored an obsessive and unsubstantiated fear of partisans in the war's early weeks. The initial result, replicating that in Belgium and France, was a random pattern of more or less brutal reprisals against civilians guilty of nothing but being in the way. That behavior did not become a pattern. In personal terms, the locals who remained to tend their fields and shops were usually the kinds of people determined to mind their own affairs, to a point of being assertively inoffensive. German soldiers, themselves overwhelmingly civilians in uniform, tended to pay for most of what—and whom—they took. And in sharp contrast to Russians, Germans as a rule responded to orders even when drinking or lusting.

The Germans, however, needed to secure systematically their communications and supply lines. Under international law, the Germans were also responsible for public order and safety in territory under their control. The difficulties of implementing these imperatives were enhanced by the complex linguistic and cultural patterns of the occupied Eastern territories, and further exacerbated by the Russian policy of evacuating civilians when the army retreated. In consequence the Germans often found themselves forming administrations entirely from scratch, without even the structure of minor officials, postmen, firemen, and clerks, that their counterparts had to work with in Belgium and northern France.[76]

The German Army had nothing resembling a civil affairs department. Expecting a short war, the army's organization was front-loaded, and its rear echelons focused on the conduct of operations rather than administration. The German Army had a heritage and an ethos of paternalism, the consequence of its self-assumed position as "the school of the nation." From its lower echelons and among its marginal figures emerged men of insight, flexibility, and common sense—one in particular. Hans Hartwig von Beseler retired as a general in 1910 after a successful second-tier career. Recalled in 1914 to command a reserve corps, again successfully, he was appointed governor-general of Poland in 1915. He had no direct knowledge of Poland, but brought to his post an open, cultivated mind—and few illusions. Fear, he noted privately, was the best ultimate guarantor of Polish–German cooperation. Twenty-first Century experience suggests Beseler had a point in any context of nation-building. But fear was a last resort. Beseler quickly decided Germany was best advised to sponsor a recreated Polish state. It would be a constitutional monarchy, a client in foreign and military matters but domestically selfgoverning and culturally autonomous. To that end Besler established a Polish-centered educational system, a network of autonomous local governments, even the beginnings of an army. Under German guidance, he argued, Poles would develop viable public institutions and gain practice in responsible self-rule during the war, and achieve full autonomy afterwards.

Beseler's occupation regime had its ups and downs. Poles protested and resisted the imprisonment of overenthusiastic nationalists, the pressure to provide workers for Germany, and the continued exploitation of Poland's subsistence economy for the Second Reich's war. On the other hand, the disintegration of Russia significantly diminished the obvious long-term alternatives. Beseler's Poland might have remained like Plato's Republic, "a thing laid up in heaven," but the occupation regime sustained its stability until well into 1918.[77]

That it progressed no further reflected in good part its increasing absorption into Germany's developing grand strategic design. Beseler possessed significant autonomy. He reported directly to Berlin. As German control moved further east, however, the Baltic region, Lithuania and Courland, and White Russia came under the direct control of High Command East—which meant Erich Ludendorff. Convinced that Germany must retain the Baltic lands, by October 1915 he was advocating their colonization by German emigrants. His personal Social Darwinist xenophobia was structured even at this relatively early date by his concern for Germany's resource imbalance in the current war, and his growing conviction that in the future Germany could rely for its security only on itself. While anything but original, both ideas resonated among political figures disillusioned by the ephemerality of Germany's overseas empire and the inactivity of Germany's navy. Considered in the context of other continental expansionist projects—Russia towards Galicia for example, or the Ottoman Empire regarding its Armenian subjects—the German vision was in principle neither exceptional nor genocidal. In practice, however, "Ober Ost" was a military state administered by army officers and experts in uniform for the duration. Its guiding principle was an order of June 7, 1916 stating that "the interests of the army and the German Reich always precede the interests of the occupied territory." Its underlying *mentalité* was an early variant of settler colonialism.[78]

Wherever they went in the East, and in whatever capacities, Germans of all ranks were frequently, indeed one might say universally, shocked by their first experiences, visual and olfactory, of Poles, Russian, and Jews—perhaps, above all, Jews, whose poverty lacked even the limited picturesqueness associated with the gentile countryside. If Yiddish had moved far enough from its German roots that it was no longer a cognate language, many Jews could at least make themselves understood in German. Some German Jewish soldiers—and some non-Jews as well —came to admire the "authenticity" of a Jewish life lived by Jews who neither questioned nor justified their identity. Arnold Zweig emerged a committed Zionist. Victor Klemperer on the other hand found his eventually misplaced identity as a German visiting a Talmud school in Vilna. What he called the "repellent fanaticism" of that environment convinced Klemperer: "I did not belong to these people even if one proved my blood relation to them a hundred times over. I thanked my creator that I was a German."[79]

As the front stabilized, the German Army initiated what amounted to a civilizing campaign behind its lines. This reflected an arguably distinctive German work ethic, and a belief, common in most armies, that planned activity is inherently of the good. Since the Thirty Years' War, European armies had paid increasing attention to at least surface cleanliness: what might be called preventive sanitation. One officer put the matter bluntly. It was, he said, a question of "soap. Only when the population has learned to wash themselves can we think of political measures." Wherever the Germans went, they scoured. Usually the cleanups began in general-access public spaces, markets and railway stations. Work details cleaned streets, disinfected schools and bathhouses, established public toilets. School children, then whole communities, were deloused and bathed, in mass processes more effective than polite.

German behavior is easy to describe dismissively, as a bourgeois/Freudian obsession, or symbolically, as prefiguring other kinds of cleansing.[80] German authorities took little account, for example, of the strong nudity taboos of eastern Jewish communities, or of historically conditioned concern for the safety of women in the immediate hands of any conqueror. On the other hand, German health officials faced varying degrees of indifference and antagonism from individuals and communities for whom generations of Tsarist rule had made a bad joke of the concept, "I'm from the government. I'm here to help you."

There was more to German hygiene, however, than principled uplifting— or oppression. Russian defeats and retreats had resulted in a near-breakdown of public welfare and utility systems that were none too elaborate to begin with. An already-overworked Tsarist administration was unable to manage the masses of evacuated civilians. Refugees who were cold and hungry stole food and fuel. Refugees with no access to toilet facilities polluted water. Refugees with no opportunity to wash became lousy. With lice came disease. Typhoid and cholera were joined in 1915 by a typhus epidemic almost medieval in its scope and its consequences.

The links between these approaches to World War II policies describing Jewish ghettos as quarantine areas, and World War II propaganda equating lice with death, scarcely requires elaboration. Also worth emphasizing, however, is the widespread conviction among the German medical and administrative personnel engaged in the antityphus campaign of World War I and similar efforts that they were doing good—albeit good *de haut en bas*—for people unable to care appropriately for themselves.[81]

The question of Germany's ultimate responsibility for the situation by invading Russia in the first place emerged only among particular centers of advanced social consciousness, like the army newspapers published in the larger cities. Infrastructure development in Ober Ost was structurally limited and military oriented. The regional command included far more bureaucrats than economists, agronomists, or anyone else capable of building as opposed to administering. Building permanent airfields near the front, reconstructing and expanding the regional railway network, and developing Libau into a major port and base did little to win hearts and minds. Efforts to produce loyal German clients through education and persuasion regularly unraveled. The Germans imposed a system of control beyond anything existing or imagined in European administrations. It was accompanied by synergized comprehensive structures of taxation, food requisitioning, and forced labor—the latter eventually employed people away from their homes, on short rations and under brutal discipline.[82] As plans failed and goals went unmet, "native" fecklessness and inferiority made handy scapegoats for paper-shufflers. Verbal abuse and physical violence indeed became increasingly standard operating procedure at all levels and in all situations throughout Ober Ost. Arguably this was part of a pattern of control consciously built around brute force. Certainly it reflected the pragmatism of the schoolmaster, the drill instructor, and the ganger: a blow or an insult makes an example and saves time.

Frequently overlooked as a more or less subliminal influence on German behavior was the sense of alienation induced by the Russian experience. To men who prior to 1914 had seldom been beyond the sound of their church bells or factory whistles, Russia was foreboding. In German forests the trees seemed to stand to attention. Russian forests were uncultivated, tangles of old trees that seemed impervious to human influence and suggested to German romantics that "forest" meant something quite different east of the Vistula. Even in towns, one felt a sense of infinitely open horizons.[83]

A suggestion might perhaps be made that the German emphasis on cleanliness and enlightenment was a successor to the fires made by primitive man to provide a focus against the night. Whatever its motives, repression provoked resistance and discouraged cooperation. An occupying force spread thin and increasingly drawn down to provide replacements for the fighting fronts began experiencing the wisdom of the aphorism that it is possible to do anything with bayonets except sit on them. That experience, however, did not prove a learning experience, especially because Russia seemed all too far from being finished as a combatant.

German intelligence accurately noted Russia's promise to replicate its performance of 1916 with another major offensive, and its concentration of over sixty divisions to underwrite the guarantee. By then, however, the government of Tsar Nicholas had sacrificed any legitimacy it once possessed. A revolution supported by both moderates and radicals overthrew the Empire in March 1917. The new provisional government then sought to affirm its alliance *bona fides* by beginning its own major offensive in June. That collapsed in a matter of days, and the army along with it. The Central Powers counterattacked, then pursued, but sheer exhaustion and lack of supplies put an end to the advance by the end of the year.[84] The provisional Kerensky government* in place since July was finished as well by the autumn. A Bolshevik movement, energized in part by exiled revolutionaries the German government allowed to reenter Russia in a sealed train, seized power in November. That "trainload of plague germs" was the second time Germany

---

* The Kerensky Government was the name commonly used for the Russian Provisional Government that replaced the Tsar and whose Minister-President from July to November 1917 was the moderate Socialist Alexander Kerensky.

had resorted to chemical or biological warfare. Ypres had been a tactical initiative without decisive results. Vladimir Lenin's voyage home, a near-random dice throw, turned out to be a wildly successful grand strategic initiative. And Erich Ludendorff may well have been the most surprised man in the Second Reich.

Totally involved in the operational grapple on the Western Front, he had refused to transfer even minimal forces eastward during the summer. Then on November 26 the near-inconceivable happened. The new Bolshevik government opened contact with the Central Powers for the purpose of determining their interest in discussing peace. On December 3 Ludendorff halted offensive operations against Russia. On December 5 a ten-day cease-fire was agreed upon. On December 22 negotiations began in Brest-Litovsk.[85]

Germany had gone to war in good part from fear of Russia, and had fought the war in good part to break Russia's real power potential and end Russia's existential threat. A Central European customs union, new thrones in the Baltic states and Poland, colonization of lands vacated by wartime migrations: these and similar grandiose projects had increasingly become the stuff of memoranda and working papers at Germany's highest levels. At seventh and last they had also been the stuff of dreams—until now. At a crown council held in February 1918, the discourse reflected a metastasized developed consciousness of the East as a source of power—perhaps, indeed, the mythic successor to the US as a "land of limitless possibilities." William II discussed Russia's partition into four lesser empires. Hindenburg asserted that he needed the Baltic States for the maneuvering of his left wing in the next war. Ludendorff suggested annexations ranging as far as the Caspian Sea.[86] It was perhaps appropriate that the meeting took place at a sanatorium—the dialogue at Bad Homburg matched for absurd abstractions anything held on Thomas Mann's Magic Mountain in his classic 1924 novel of the same name. Its setting is a remote sanatorium in the Swiss Alps, and its structure a series of abstract analyses of life and its meanings—all completely remote from the "real" world of the flatlands. The institution might have been a model for Bad Homburg.

At this stage of the war, the German Empire still had the option of seeking a negotiated victory by offering to end the U-boat campaign and withdrawing from its conquests in the west. That would put the burden on the Allies to seek the bargaining table or risk continuation of what by now seemed an endless bloodletting. The failure to consider such a policy seriously had much to do with the failure of the U-boat campaign: tactically in terms of its inability to cut Britain's oceanic lifelines and strategically its enabling of America's comprehensive entry into the war in April 1917.

A certain amount of "we always *told* you the Navy was a waste of resources" underwrote the Hindenburg–Ludendorff s team's corresponding compulsion to think, however uncomfortably, more or less systematically in grand strategic terms.

Domestically, in the context of the Russian revolution, material hardship, political gridlock, and disagreement over war aims fostered radical opposition. If military production had gradually increased in 1917, that owed more to the relatively moderate, relatively compromising approach of Wilhelm Gröner than to either the Hindenburg Program's methods of force and control, or to its vision of redefining Germany's moral base in a wartime configuration. In particular the Auxiliary Labor Law and its penumbral manifestations succeeded only in radicalizing an already strained work force. Beginning in April, strikes proliferated and metastasized.[87] And while America's immediate military power and long-term military potential were subjects of ridicule in Berlin's uniformed community, even the massive *ad hoc* gains of resources and territory accompanying Russia's debacle seemed insufficient by themselves to assure Germany's long-term future against an emerging coalition of the world's two greatest maritime powers and a France that stubbornly refused to behave logically and sue for peace.[88]

The summer of 1917 was the summer of Germany's discontent. But did it portend a deeper crisis of legitimacy? Gröner, who had been the Hindenburg Program's linchpin, became its scapegoat for failing to prevent strikes, for criticizing profiteering industrialists, and for demanding the extension of price controls. The business community denounced him as too easy on the workers. The unions cooperated with him, but at arm's length. The generals regarded him as the next thing to a defeatist. His dismissal was a foregone conclusion. Dismissing Gröner, exiling him to a divisional command, were palliatives. The time had come to consolidate and stabilize Germany's position by the means the ruling dyad understood as both familiar and optimal: armed force, specifically land power. And Ludendorff's economy of force policy in the East had fortuitously provided what seemed the final element in a long-elusive victory won and fought on basic German terms by core German strengths: tactics and operations.

Germany's 1917 offensives in Russia had been opportunistic, practically random—except in one sector. Max Hoffman, the Eastern Front's chief of staff and *de facto* commander (Hindenburg's replacement Prince Leopold of Bavaria was no figurehead, but he did not challenge Hoffman's insights) was convinced that capture of the Baltic port of Riga would crush what remained of Russian military morale, open the way for a direct advance, and compel the provisional government to seek peace on any terms the Central Powers offered. But the defense system around Riga and south along the Dvina River was the strongest in Russia. Ludendorff had made clear that the Reich had no resources available for a battle of attrition on the Western Front model. That made an economy of force operation essential. The region's logistic system was able to support such an operation. But was it militarily feasible?[89]

During 1916/17 the German Army had successfully introduced in the West potentially significant innovations in the category of infantry assault. To date, however, they had been applied on limited scales, with no systematic evidence that their principles could be expanded to cover division and army levels of operation. A crucial element, moreover, was still lacking. On the Western Front artillery on both sides had increasingly devolved during 1917 towards "a blunt instrument for the indiscriminate hammering of real estate."[90] "Destructive firepower had become like an addictive drug."[91] In the process, the German artillery had not only lost the superiority it enjoyed in 1914. It was also being overpowered, forced onto the defensive, by the sheer mass of Allied guns and shells—a mass even a successful Hindenburg Program could not hope to match directly.

An alternative approach had emerged in Russia—an approach inspired by another of the relatively low-ranking, relatively obscure officers who sustained Germany's army as an instrument of war. Georg Heinrich Bruchmüller was retired for medical reasons in 1913 as a lieutenant-colonel after a thoroughly unremarkable career in the foot artillery. Recalled on the outbreak of war, assigned as artillery commander in an obscure war-raised division, he established enough credibility to be trusted with thirty batteries in a brilliantly successful corps-level attack against superior numbers at Lake Naroch in 1916. At this mid-stage of the war the German Army had no systematic experience in artillery fire control above division level. Bruchmüller demonstrated the potential of centralization and systematization convincingly in a half-dozen subsequent engagements, personally controlling the unheard-of number of 134 batteries of all calibers for a single counterattack during the Kerensky Offensive in July 1917, the last Russian offensive of the war. He introduced a major procedural innovation as well. Before the war artillery had been regarded, and regarded itself, as a supporting arm. Bruchmüller shifted the paradigm not merely to a combined-arms approach, but to one recognizing that the Great War was essentially a gunners' war. He conducted "artillery lectures:" briefing and consulting the commanders and staff officers of the infantry his guns would be supporting, and when feasible incorporating their ideas into the final fire plan. The infantrymen, who too often considered themselves let down by the gunners, responded affirmatively, then enthusiastically.[92]

Bruchmüller's achievements were recognized with the *Pour le Mérite*, only one of four awarded to senior artillery commanders during the war. By then Bruchmüller's reputation was so high that when Max Hoffman ordered him north to command the Eighth Army's artillery for the projected attack on Riga, he was sent via Berlin and his presence at Eighth Army headquarters was kept secret to avoid alarming the Russians.

Oskar von Hutier was new to army command, but had made his reputation since 1914 as a first-rate field general with an ability to sustain mobile operations insofar as that was possible between 1914 and 1918. He welcomed Bruchmüller enthusiastically. He was even more enthusiastic at Hoffman's promise of every gun that could be spared anywhere in Russia, and by the High Command's provision of a half-dozen additional infantry divisions, almost doubling his strength. The attacking divisions were given two weeks to train; artillery and infantry officers were jointly and systematically briefed. Hutier planned to make his initial assault across the Dvina with small combined-arms units organized along storm troop lines, synergized with a hurricane bombardment personally organized and controlled by Bruchmüller. Over 500 trench mortars would prevent the Russians from occupying their forward positions. The light artillery would concentrate on the Russian second line and their communications trenches, isolating the battle zone with a mixture of gas shells and high explosives; the heavy pieces were given specific targets. In addition to the mortars, Bruchmüller controlled over 600 guns on a front of five and a half miles. Six hundred fifty thousand rounds of ammunition were stockpiled in the battery positions.

Each of the three assault divisions was also assigned three infantry contact planes, well enough armored to survive at low altitudes, responsible for keeping track of and reporting the ground troops' positions and situations; and a squadron of six of the light ground-attack planes that had proved increasingly valuable in the West to hit gun positions, disrupt counterattacks, and break morale. Add in an observation squadron for each division to spot new targets and adjust old ranges for the artillery, and the German infantry was in a situation significantly different than its predecessors had faced two years earlier at Verdun.

In the West, artillery preparation for an operation like the Dvina crossing would take days at best. At Riga the time allocated was five hours and ten minutes. German air supremacy had enabled systematic photography of the projected battle zone. The Eighth Army had prepared detailed maps showing Russian defensive positions and strong points, command posts—even telephone lines. The preparation was correspondingly intense and correspondingly violent. In a little over five hours the guns alone fired over 560 rounds—almost 500 per barrel. Over a quarter of the total was gas, the highest proportion fired in the war to date, and a reflection of Bruchmüller's recognition that gas shells addressed arguably the major problem conventional artillery preparation created for the infantry: the blast effect that by mid-1916 all too literally redefined assault zones beyond recognition and beyond passage.

Riga was the first test of a fundamental alternative: preparation as neutralization. Bruchmüller's intention was to fix the Russian infantry and artillery in their positions, cross the river, and overwhelm the enemy in a crushing side attack. For one of the few times in the war, everything went according to plan in the crucial sector. The assault teams rowed across the watery no man's land of the Dvina, 300 to 400 yards wide. The mortars fixed the Russian defenders in place; most surrendered or ran as the storm troops closed in, hardly needing to employ their flamethrowers or try out their small-group tactics. Responding promptly and smoothly to signal flares, the artillery segued into a rolling barrage. The German assault wave pushed through the Russian second line; pioneers threw pontoon bridges across the river; and before noon a full-scale combined arms crossing was under way.

On the flanking sectors, progress was not quite as smooth. One regiment was even pinned for a time in its own trenches by Russian artillery. But with the river line well and truly breached, the Russians retreated *en masse* and in panic. By nightfall six German divisions were across the river and moving forward. A Latvian brigade bought time at a price of 50 percent casualties, but by September 3 Riga was well in German hands and the Eighth Army was stretching out in a pursuit that gained thirty miles, which Max Hoffman said could have continued on through the Baltic States. Instead it ended abruptly when the High Command closed down the offensive as a good will gesture to the Bolsheviks.

As a consolation prize Hutier was awarded the *Pour le Mérite*, and his name entered military history as the author of a tactical system that restored mobility to Great War battlefields and came close to tipping the conflict in Germany's favor. In fact contemporary German records make no mention of a new tactical style, let alone crediting Hutier—or, more appropriately, Bruchmüller.[93] It is also legitimate to assert that the German attack was made against a prototypical obliging enemy, a demoralized army looking for any excuse to abandon the field. Bruce Gudmundsson appropriately suggests that Riga was a model at operational rather than tactical levels: surprise, concentration, and penetration were its real hallmarks. James Corum notes that the Germans took a similar approach to the October 1917 invasion of the Baltic Islands, paying even more attention to integrating and coordinating air power with ground operations.[94]

The ultimate lesson of Riga is that the German Army's nervous system was still highly functional: its senior officers were comprehensively aware of lessons learned on other fronts and willing to apply them in different contexts. And that was specifically true of Erich Ludendorff.

CHAPTER VI

CLIMAX AND
DENOUEMENT

Beginning in October 1917, the German High Command began systematically considering the project of an offensive on the Western Front in the coming spring. On the most basic level this was seen as a preemptive strike, forestalling and disrupting an expected Allied repetition of 1917's massive assaults. Given the continued large-scale arrival of American troops, even should they prove little more than cannon fodder, sustaining 1917's defensive posture appeared unsustainable in the long—even the medium—duration.

--- I ---

Ludendorff from the beginning specifically argued for a counterattack against the BEF in Flanders. If the Germans had no room in that sector to move in a strategic context, neither did the British. Properly prepared and executed, chances were good that an all-out attack could drive the British back against the Channel, split the Allied armies beyond recovery, and finally decide the war in Germany's favor. As so often with German Great War planning, the problem lay in implementation: deploying and employing sufficient force to achieve the objective. Two unexpected events reinforced optimism and persuaded critics. One was in Italy. Beginning on October 24, a joint German–Austrian offensive overpowered the poorly deployed Italian Second Army. The Fourteenth Army, the German contingent, in particular made extensive initial gains at low cost, taking advantage of bad weather, making extensive use of gas bombardment, and above all making use of storm troop tactics on regimental and divisional scales. The Alpenkorps in particular, and its attached Württemberg Mountain Battalion (WMB), demonstrated a combination of flanking maneuvers and lightning attacks that fractured Italian morale as much through confusion as through combat. In four days, elements of the WGB, never more than 500 strong, crossed around twelve miles of Italian positions, ascended 8,000 feet and descended 3,000, destroyed five Italian regiments and captured some 8,000 prisoners. Their commander, a young major named Erwin Rommel, would apply the lessons learned in Italy's mountains in a later and greater war.

Even more impressive were the successes of non-specialist divisions in applying storm troop tactics and storm troop technology on large scales. The 12th Division was part of the active army and enjoyed a good reputation; the 200th Division was a wartime creation composed of Jäger battalions, and Allied intelligence in 1917 regarded it as one of the best in the German Army. Both systematically applied infiltration techniques, probing for and exploiting weak spots, and supported them with a panoply of light machine guns, grenades, mortars and flamethrowers to keep pace with the elite mountaineers. By November 10 the Italians has suffered 40,000 battle casualties—and lost over a quarter-million prisoners, by no means all of them, it must be noted, to the Germans. The men of the Central Powers had advanced over fifty miles before exhausting their resources and energy. If this could be achieved with only the seven divisions deployed for Caporetto, what might be done with seventy or more, even on the Western Front? The Fourteenth Army, renumbered the Seventeenth but with the same command and staff, was transferred north to help set an example.[1]

The second welcome harbinger was Cambrai. That battle began with a British attack on November 20. Operationally it was aimed at breaking into the Siegfried Line, disrupting German supply lines, and even, perhaps, hopefully, finally sending cavalry through "the G in gap" into the German rear. Pragmatically Cambrai was understood as a "tank raid," to test the potential of armored fighting vehicles used in large numbers in a limited area by surprise, without the extensive artillery preparation characteristic of major offensives since 1915. The Cambrai region was chosen because it had been quiet enough for long enough that the ground was at least relatively firm, smooth, and dry. The sector was thinly held by around a half-dozen divisions with limited air and artillery support and low stocks of ammunition. The formations were usually, moreover, recovering in the relative calm of the "Flanders sanatorium" from a tour at Third Ypres. They were likely to put disproportionate trust in the passive defenses they occupied, and to expect any major British initiatives to be heralded by the usual preliminary bombardment. It was a corresponding shock when at 7:20 am a thousand guns opened on the German forward positions and almost 400 tanks rolled forward nearly simultaneously, supported by what seemed an endless number of aircraft attacking everything they could see or suspect.[2]

Unlike on the Somme and at Passchendaele the tanks worked together, flattening wire entanglements, bypassing strong points, crossing trenches and clearing them as the infantry mopped up those survivors who were unable or unwilling to run once the barrage lifted to target reserve positions and rear areas. The tanks seemed unstoppable, and often were. "We felt betrayed and sold out," declared one survivor of his personal "life or death race."[3] Hand grenades and small arms proved futile, as did small improvised counterattacks. "We were simply powerless against the tanks, especially because we had no training or experience in countering them," reported a regimental history in a typical mixture of explanation and justification.[4]

In spite of the initial shock, the Germans, as usual, recovered at squad and company level to take a toll of both the armor and its supporting infantry, which increasingly lost—or abandoned—contact with tanks that drew fire like magnets. Along Flesquières Ridge at midday the gunners of the 108th Field Artillery claimed forty-nine tanks knocked out over open sights, with twelve credited to a single battery. Like aerial victories, such numbers were usually exaggerated, a consequence of adrenaline rather than mendacity.

The issue is further obscured by the long-running postwar debate as to whether a single gunner did most of the tank killing, and whether that gunner was an officer or an enlisted man—the subtext being as much an issue of social class and military hierarchy as of marksmanship and courage. More significant is the fact that the commander of the 54th Division, to which the 108th belonged, had since November 1916 responded to the appearance of tanks on the battlefield by emphasizing training his gunners to hit moving targets over open sights. The initiative prized and cultivated in mission tactics could be applied as well to mission training. General Oskar von Watter underwrote his particular military hobbyhorse with diagrams, models, even life-sized moving targets pulled by horses; and the 108th's gunners had had what amounted to live-target practice against French Scheiders on the Chemin des Dames. The division's officers and the division's infantry observed and participated in the artillery exercises, and also practiced close-quarters defense against tanks. The 54th Division was arguably the most capable in the entire German Army to meet a large-scale tank attack. And on November 20, the 54th was by sheer chance athwart the main British axis of advance. An example of the importance of contingency in war—or proof that Bellona has a sense of humor?[5]

In any case, there can be no doubt of the effect of German guns across the front as the weather cleared. British figures give forty-three tanks bogging down, seventy-one more breaking down, and sixty-five destroyed by "enemy action," mostly close-range artillery fire. But nor can there be any question that by late afternoon most of the gun positions had run out of ammunition and were being overrun. By day's end the British had advanced up to five miles on a ten-mile front, an overall gain greater than in three months at Third Ypres.

The Germans were still trying to understand what happened and how to respond. Rupprecht described the situation as "considerably worse than might have been expected from a reading of the afternoon reports."[6] The weather turned nasty during the night: the familiar autumn witches' brew of cold, rain, and high wind. But the German infantry—how many times has this sentence been repeated—rallied, held, and even managed successful local counterattacks. Army Group and Second Army, the directly responsible headquarters, began funneling in reinforcements, a battalion at a time when nothing larger was available. The British lack of reserves to develop the first day's success was compounded by the unexpectedly heavy loss of tanks. Those remaining were checked and mated by machine guns and light trench mortars, horse-mobile field pieces, and freshly deployed truck-mounted antiaircraft guns, the mobility of which in the well-developed road network enabled them to shift from one crisis point to another before the British could respond. The tanks' numbers were fewer, the terrain less favorable, the German countermeasures more effective. As their casualties mounted across the sector, the offensive stalled at Bourlon village, Bourlon Wood and Bourlon Ridge in the face of strong German reinforcements. "We throw in everything we have," said a German corps commander,[7] particularly the 3rd Division of the Prussian Guard, whose presence stiffened spines as much as lines.

The British command responded by assuming the defensive in what had by then become just another of the Western Front's salients, this one about seven miles by six. The Germans' thoughts turned to counterattack—on an unprecedented scale. As early as the offensive's Day One, Rupprecht was informed that his army group would have sufficient resources in position to mount its own offensive in a week. Ludendorff was sufficiently concerned to harass Rupprecht with a barrage of questions on what the Bavarian crown prince considered "totally inessential matters." But he also provided four fresh divisions from GHQ reserve. Kuhl responded by noting that "in all the battles we have never been able to mount a good counter-attack."[8] Rupprecht and Ludendorff both accepted the idea of hitting the newly formed salient simultaneously from north and south, with everything that could be brought to bear. Rupprecht emphasized the requirement of preparation in the German Army's first counteroffensive, as opposed to a counterattack. Ludendorff stressed the need for haste in what he saw as a general crisis in the Western Front's northern half. He was concerned, indeed, to the point of making a personal appearance in the Cambrai sector and directly ordering the Second Army to attack on November 30.

Rupprecht was not best pleased at being bypassed. It was, however, difficult to argue with results. The code name in one sector was *Sturmflut* ("tidal wave"). For once the designation was appropriate. Fifteen divisions were directly committed to the attack, with nine more available as needed. Over 1,200 guns were in support. Tactics reflected immediate experience. As at Riga the artillery preparation was of short duration, an hour at most, and made heavy use of gas. As at Caporetto, the infantry was ordered to bypass wooded and built-up areas, leaving their neutralization to the artillery. Keeping contact with flanking formations was not to be allowed "to lead to the situation where one division awaits the advance of its neighbors."[9] Most attacks were spearheaded by storm troopers. The Second Army's storm battalion, the converted 3rd Jäger, was under strength, having sent half its men to Italy. As a result, most of that mission burden fell on divisional and regimental assault units, *ad hoc* companies and platoons. There had been too little time to refresh collectively any individual skills inculcated in divisional training centers. But with the advantage of comprehensive operational and tactical surprise, and cooperative weather, the initial attack hit the British forward positions with what seemed like the end of the world.

"Today we are doing the drumming,"[10] repeatedly declared a gunner officer. German enthusiasm should not be overstated, but after being on the receiving/defending end since the Somme, a spirit of payback was noticeable. The initial attack followed a trench raid model of shock and awe, hit and run—only this time the running was forward in pursuit rather than back to the German lines. The assault teams almost immediately overran the front-line positions and pushed forward. The follow-up waves dealt with surviving strong points and holdouts, taking them at a rush when possible and when not, then resorting to maneuver. By 9 am three British divisions had been overrun, five villages recaptured, and British troops were fleeing incontinently and in large numbers. On the other hand German assault units had become badly mixed up and suffered heavy losses in the junior officers and NCOs who set the pace and the example. Loss of drive and loss of focus were frequent results. Nor did the British collapse in the kind of collective panic characteristic of Riga and Caporetto. Pockets of resistance endured. Tank-supported counterattacks recovered some of the morning's losses. Stiff upper lips were plentiful on both sides that day. "The success," in Rupprecht's words, "is nowhere near as great as we might have expected."[11] It was nevertheless impressive enough for an improvised operation. Two British division commanders narrowly escaped capture. At the end of the first day alone another 9,000 lower ranks were prisoners of war. By the time the offensive ended on December 6, the Germans had retaken about three-quarters of the ground lost on the first day, and made some inroads into the original British positions as well. Perhaps the best indicator of the scale of the German achievement, however, is the questions it generated about the competence of the BEF's higher command. A series of inquiries resulted in a purge of Haig's staff and left Sir Douglas himself sufficiently vulnerable at least to consider a compromise peace.[12]

In evaluating Cambrai, the Germans focused—predictably—on operational factors. The question was whether the army was able as currently structured to conduct mobile warfare for a long term on a large scale. Rupprecht was given credit for his insistence on preparation. In the future, major offensive commanders at all levels would require time to evaluate their missions, the terrain, and the opposing defenses. Plans and boundaries must both be developed and understood; initiative could not degenerate into randomness.

Preparation must also include a need to reduce preliminary human exertion. A trench raid or a limited local counterattack could be sustained on adrenaline, but nothing larger. For extended offensive operations, formations should be in their assembly areas two full days before the attack. On November 30 too many of the front-line troops had been on the move for several days, had struggled through traffic and mud to reach their final positions, and were worn out before ever crossing their start lines.

In that context, logistics, not a usual German preoccupation, was a primary concern. Enough men had gone into action so hungry that advances had been delayed by luxuriously supplied dugouts and quartermaster stores. English cigarettes and English footwear also proved particularly distracting. Nor was nourishment a specifically human consideration. Fodder was also scarce. Ill-fed animals were vulnerable to collapse when worked as hard and as unpredictably as mobile operations required. Not only did horse-drawn convoys obstruct road networks inevitably limited relative to the size of an offensive, but teams had to be increased to get the same draught power. The Allied blockade had shut off the importation of horses. Replacing them with motor transport raised a new spectrum of problems involving equally diminished resources like rubber and gasoline. Finally, what could best be done with specialized trench warfare materiel, much of which had been developed with minimal concern for weight? Even the 08/15 light machine gun was heavy, bulky, and complicated—to a point where bounties were paid for captured Lewis guns.[13] Was it preferable to reduce the number of these indispensable weapons carried into action? Was it worth assigning carts and light wagons to assault units for the transport of grenades, flares, and ammunition, at the risk of slowing the advance?[14]

And what of the tanks? The Cambrai battlefield provided the first opportunity to study them at close range in large numbers, and to evaluate the options when confronting them in force. The results were ambiguous. Even in the context of offensive operations, the Second Army's commander declared, Germany lacked the resources to introduce a weapons system that would lose more than a third of its strength whenever committed to battle.[15] At Cambrai, the tanks had been deployed in near-optimal conditions: on favorable terrain, with the advantage of surprise, in conditions of light and weather that concealed their movements, and not least against opponents that—with the notable exception of the 54th Division—were essentially unprepared to face them. The high rate of destruction and disabling under those conditions still made tanks at seventh and last a luxury item the Allies could afford and the Germans could not. The High Command was less sanguine. It secured the tank program top priority for steel and iron, and increased the production target by over a third. The final number agreed on was, however, only thirty-eight tanks in all—hardly a declaration of increased faith in that particular piece of war machinery.[16]

Cambrai's major material contribution was in the air. During 1917 a high proportion of German aerial resources had been devoted to a bomber offensive against England the results of which had been visually spectacular and emotionally disruptive but strategically inconsequential. Over the Western Front, as on the ground, operations had been essentially defensive: maintaining a balance against increasingly aggressive, increasingly competent, increasingly well-equipped Allied opposition. One manifestation of this was the creation in 1917 of *Schutzstaffeln* (escort squadrons) to support the increasingly hard-pressed observation aircraft. Their success in that role was sufficiently limited that they were omitted from the June Amerika Program of air force expansion. On the other hand, during 1917 the British in particular put increasing emphasis on ground-attack operations. Primarily carried out by fighters, their effect was sufficient to inspire emulation. Ground attack increasingly became the escort squadrons' major mission—in good part because German fighters were considered, not least by themselves, to be too valuable in the air-combat role to be routinely risked and expended at low levels. A new generation of Halberstadt and Hannover CLs proved rugged and maneuverable, formidable adversaries best compared to the British Bristol F2b despite their different roles.

Beginning in August, the CLs made their mark in the Ypres salient, attacking forward positions and artillery batteries in small numbers with enough success that the Germans concentrated seven six-plane squadrons for their Cambrai counterattack. Against British troops who had never experienced such attacks in force they were sufficiently effective that British generals credited them with a major role in the initial German breakthrough. The effect was as much psychological as physical, against men who had been left in the line too long. But the sight of entire British battalions breaking and running for any length of time for any reason was unusual, not to say rare. Even the first use of gas had not produced that result. Might twice or three time as many CLs be a down-market counterpart of tanks? Might next time they keep their targets moving backwards long enough for a break-in to become a breakthrough?[17]

Another alternative existed—at least in theory. America's entry into the war and Woodrow Wilson's call for "peace without victory" had struck chords in the Reichstag. Political opinion, however, remained polarized between advocates of compromise and supporters of a "Hindenburg peace:" all or nothing. The generals threatened resignation if Bethmann-Hollweg was not replaced. His successor, Georg Michaelis, was little more than the hard-liners' mouthpiece until forced out of office in his turn and replaced by an even less consequential bureaucrat, Georg von Hertling. The Papal Peace Note of August 1, 1917, calling for an immediate armistice, reduction of armaments, freedom of the seas, and arbitration of international disputes, was not exactly ignored in Germany. Instead it became a political football, ultimately deflated by Ludendorff's intransigent insistence that Germany's future security depended on retaining its key conquests—Belgium in particular. But as political and social polarization not only continued but expanded to levels which raised the question of general constitutional reform, negotiation seemed a promising alternative to disintegration even in some military circles. The High Command's liaison officer to the Foreign Ministry prepared a detailed proposal for a peace initiative, and negotiated its provisions with Wilson's delegate to the Hague. Ludendorff's refusal to budge on the Belgian question made the peace prospect moot, as Hindenburg advised the kaiser that only victory in the West would secure the political and economic power Germany needed.[18] It may also be observed that by this time France and Britain were working towards a peace of victory, not compromise. The difference was they had, just barely, the price—if they were willing to pay it.

The ultimate irony came on March 3, 1918. After a series of *opera bouffe* episodes involving unilateral cessation of hostilities by one party and their unilateral resumption by the other, Russia's Bolsheviks agreed to a peace that stripped the country of a third of its population, most of its raw materials, and the majority of its industrial capacity, to the benefit of the Central Powers. The reaction in Germany was ecstatic, that in OHL no less so. Not only were the terms a down payment on Germany's future security; not only did Russian grain and meat seem a guarantee against another hungry winter; but Brest-Litovsk seemed to justify Ludendorff's acumen in the fields of strategy and policy. The military party, that is to say, by then Erich Ludendorff, finally and virtually by default had a free hand to win the war on its terms.

II

Despite the ongoing *ad hoc*, problem-solving nature of the Hindenburg Program, Germany was not objectively short of the tools of victory: small arms, cannon, aircraft, and ammunition. The army had compensated effectively for inferior resources with competent management. Behind the lines was another story. The shortage of horses was chronic and increasing. Trucks were relatively few in number—around 30,000. More of them were running on iron tires due to a shortage of rubber. The railroads so vital in transferring divisions across Europe and shifting reserves to crisis points were feeling the effects of overuse and lack of down time for equipment maintenance and track repair.

Manpower was an even more complex and less soluble problem. Statistics indicate that the German Army was as efficient at killing men as it was in using material. Even including Austria-Hungary in the calculations, the Central Powers have been credited with inflicting three deaths in battle for every two they suffered.[19] But mathematics also indicated Germany was nearing the end of its human resources. Prewar conscription bore more heavily on rural areas and small towns, partly for political reasons and partly because it was an article of faith that countrymen were better suited to war's physical and psychological demands than poorly developed, highly strung urban dwellers. Rural communities thus bore a higher proportion of the casualties and were less able to replace them. The effectiveness of units recruited in rural Germany declined as the sense of bearing a disproportionate share of the war effort increased. Farmers in uniform seem to have suffered particularly, certainly overtly, from homesickness, especially at planting and harvest times. Though the system of territorial replacement was never abandoned, in general it became difficult to maintain the links between units in the field and depots from their corps district. As battalions and companies became increasingly heterogeneous, underlying social and cultural bonds grew correspondingly frayed.[20]

Over a million men more or less fit for field service still remained working in war industries. But the only way they could be made available in any number was to introduce compulsory labor for women—a social and political impossibility given the growing domestic discontent. Another million men deployed across eastern Europe were also becoming increasingly available as Russia's implosion continued. But many of them were in their late thirties and older: hardly storm troop material, dubious even as trench-holders.[21]

Nor could the East be drawn down indefinitely, even in the circumstances of a peace of conquest with the Bolsheviks. The large-scale transfer of troops from the East that began in mid-1917 posed a broad spectrum of morale issues. Between November 1, 1917 and the end of May 1918, the German Army transferred over fifty divisions (the exact number remains uncertain) from Russia to the West. The statistic is impressive, but the difference in fighting power between most of these formations and even a below-average

Western Front division was substantial and noticeable. The Russian front had long since been stripped of every man willing to fight or who could reasonably be made to fight. Many of the rest had made themselves more or less at home. Constant, often friendly—not to say intimate—contact with the civil population made it difficult to screen them from antiwar propaganda, or from the everyday example of uniformed Russians simply going home. When these ostensible combat divisions were ordered West, their rank and file shouted antiwar slogans from troop trains. They decorated cars with graffiti like "slaughter cattle for William and Sons." They disappeared in increasing numbers whenever troop trains paused anywhere in Germany. A common response when upbraided was some version of "What are you going to do, Herr Leutnant? Send me to the Western Front?"[22]

Numbers, moreover, were the lesser aspect of the army's fundamental problem. Were the men who must use the hardware up to the demands of an all-out, decisive offensive? In the homeland's depots and training centers, as deferments and exemptions grew increasingly difficult for men of military age to obtain, freshly caught heroes who obeyed the rules and answered their call-up notices were increasingly likely to feel victimized. Activists and strikers drafted as punishment brought with them their organizing skills and a festering sense of grievance. This combination was at best unpromising material for cadres often themselves physically or emotionally scarred and wishing only to see out the war in relative peace and quiet. Other front-line veterans rotated home as a reward for survival regarded their older charges as fat-cat draft dodgers, and delighted in making their lives as unpleasant as possible. The schoolmaster in *All Quiet on the Western Front*, conscripted in the war's later stages and systematically tormented by one of the students he had cajoled into volunteering in 1914, is presented as receiving no more than his just deserts. Such attitudes and practices were, however, not calculated to produce willing and effective soldiers. By 1917 a third of the draft intake was men over thirty-five, sufficiently used to being family heads that in particular they responded poorly to officers young enough to be their sons who were perceived as acting like spoiled brats, rank-proud and fumble-brained.[23]

Combat units' profiles changed significantly in another way after 1916. In contrast to the war's first half, their replacements grew increasingly younger.

Trench war's physical and emotional demands favored youth. Their elders were more likely to have skills useful in the economy or connections taking them out of the trenches. The existence of whole classes of eighteen- and nineteen-year-olds invited induction ahead of the peacetime age of twenty, rather than a repeated comb-out of older age groups. In 1917–18 up to a quarter of the German Army was under twenty-one. That meant rifle companies in particular contained fewer and fewer men with established civilian backgrounds. The 238th Infantry Division, for example, was formed in March 1917, part of the last "wave" of divisions organized during the war. Half its men were either transfers from the front or recovered wounded. Neither provenance was likely to produce either warriors or mentors to inspire the division's other half, most of them drawn from the class born in 1898, who by this time had few illusions about what awaited them in the trenches.[24] Many as well had enjoyed unprecedented freedom in an environment of absent fathers, preoccupied mothers, and high wages. The generational rebellion of the prewar youth movement correspondingly reemerged as a growing tension between the young-adult privates and the older men, especially the NCOs.

The consequences of these tensions were noticeable, but should not be exaggerated. Beginning in the first half of 1917, desertion rates doubled and tripled. But the absolute numbers, while difficult to calculate exactly, remained small, in good part because there were few safe places to go. The Dutch and Swiss borders were closely patrolled. Nor was it exactly easy for anyone not a career criminal to disappear into a wartime Germany where arguably the most familiar official request was "papers please."

Only 4,200 cases of desertion were prosecuted in 1917. Disaffection also took overt form in some formations. To call these outbreaks mutinies is, however, to overstate their duration and their intentions. Incidents of "collective indiscipline" involved disobedience and refusal of duty on small scales for brief periods. They did not lead to the comprehensive "remobilization" based on the renegotiation of "working conditions" Leonard Smith describes as taking place on the French side of the line. Instead they were addressed *ad hoc*. Company officers and senior NCOs scrounged extra rations, extra leaves and extra liquor to palliate what they considered—and hoped—were temporary aberrations. They also wondered what to do next time. And there were more and more next times.

Almost from the beginning of the war, the military justice system had taken account of the radical changes in battlefield conditions and the radical increase in battlefield demands. Officers grew increasingly aware of the negative effects of a disciplinary system based on repression and coercion. Determination and good will were more than ever vital to combat effectiveness in an environment of transcendent violence and transcendent tensions. Nor was "fragging" entirely a product of the Vietnam War: accidents could easily happen at the front, and questioning could be minimal.

The result was a series of reforms in the judicial system that took increasing account of practices and circumstances in imposing sentences for offenses like unauthorized absence and disobedience of orders. In April 1916, the Reichstag demanded approval of a law reducing minimum sentences for offenses committed in the field. The military authorities for their part recognized that it made no sense to retain draconian punishments military courts were reluctant to impose. In April 1917 a new legal code further altered penalties for many common offenses. Judicial flexibility was significantly enhanced, giving courts more authority to consider circumstances. The minimum sentence of ten years for disobedience in the face of the enemy, a concept sufficiently elastic to invite command abuse, was suspended. Desertion no longer carried a mandatory capital sentence. Far more popular with the rank and file was abolition of the German counterpart of Britain's Field Punishment Number One: tying the offender to a fence, a tree, or a wheel for a certain time each day. Frequently and casually imposed, it was also considered degrading.

The army, in short, modified its laws in the same spirit of flexibility it applied to its tactics. Nor is it an exaggeration to say that the German military system, composed of citizens and existing in a state of law, was personally and institutionally capable of showing common sense and mercy. Almost 8,000 soldiers were tried for desertion during the war. Forty-nine were sentenced to death. Eighteen were actually executed. German military courts imposed a total of 150 capital sentences for all offences. Forty-eight were carried out. Mathematically this amounted to only two-thirds of the annual prewar average of nineteen executions imposed by the civil authority. Whatever one's positions on capital punishment and military discipline, these numbers by themselves were unlikely to exercise either a punitive or a deterrent effect in the context of a total war.[25]

Systems, however, depend on people. The German Army consistently refused to expand its permanent officer corps—around 30,000 strong after the authorized increase of 1913— in proportion to its increased size. Like so many other aspects of the Second Reich at war, the motives behind the policy defy familiar one-dimensional explanation: in this case caste prejudice.[26] Often overlooked was the economic factor. Someday the war would end, but a regular commission was a permanent fiscal responsibility on a military budget that never seemed sufficient for the country's needs. Considered in a professional context, the principle "no officer rather than a bad officer" was not a mere smokescreen for excluding social or political undesirables. Regiments were allowed to nominate enlisted men with combat experience for officer training courses—eight, then twelve weeks for an active commission, less and more random for prospective reservists. To a degree far greater than any of its counterparts, the German Army regarded even a junior officer's responsibilities as involving more than providing effective combat leadership. Paternalism, taking a consequent interest in the men under one's command, had been a key element since the Wars of Liberation. "Never-resting care for the welfare of his men is … the rewarding privilege of the officer," stated the prewar *Felddienst-Ordnung*: "It is not enough that one orders, [it] is the way in which one orders."[27] Administration, being able to keep pace with the military bureaucracy's never-ending demands for paperwork in triplicate, was as much part of the commissioning package as looking after the men—and the horses.

All this meant that more than an elementary education was required for commissioning, and also that a degree of *Bildung*, cultivation or social awareness, was equally necessary. Initially those standards differed little from those in peacetime.

They were reduced and broadened as the war demanded more shoulder-straps. Similarly, though for practical purposes the officer candidate pool remained restricted to the middle classes that provided the bulk of the army's reserve officers before the war, the definition of "middle class" became increasingly flexible, not to say ascriptive. The training courses, however, continued to emphasize leading from the front and looking after the men. The touchstone was the same: power conveys responsibility. In contrast to peacetime practice, the point was developed more in the contexts of military pragmatism than of caste. Vertical, mission-oriented links were a more immediate condition of effectiveness (and survival) than horizontal, social ones.

Candidates who passed the courses and absorbed their subtexts were reassigned to the front, usually as platoon sergeants and often to their original regiments—on the principle that a man who could not lead and command where he had served was not fit to hold a commission. If they performed well they were commissioned in the reserve or Landwehr.

By 1918 there were over 225,000 of them in the kaiser's army. And the closer one came to the front the less likely there was to be any practical distinctions made as to whether a company officer's commission was in the active army, the reserves, or the Landwehr—except by rank-dazzled, self-impressed newbies who usually learned better in a hurry.

Those whose educational or social backgrounds—far more often the former than the latter—made them ineligible for the officer training courses were made *Offizierstellvertreter* (deputy officers) or *Feldwebelleutnants* (sergeant-lieutenants). These rank titles, combined with the image of the officer corps as socially restricted, have usually been interpreted as designating a lower species of officer. In fact, rather than being—or considered—more or less a caste-based insult, these appointments were considered a means of increasing the status and authority of the best of the NCOs. A reasonable comparison would be to the contemporary French *adjutant* (a rank not an appointment), or the US Army's present-day warrant officer. They were usually no less welcome in a constant context of empty spaces. A German infantry battalion in 1914 had about two dozen officers, but by late 1917 there might be as few as seven: a captain commanding the battalion with a lieutenant as his adjutant, lieutenants or warrant officers commanding the rifle companies, and platoons led by warrant officers or more often by NCOs, *Vizefeldwebels* (staff sergeants) or sergeants.

One of the reforms immediately initiated by Hindenburg and Ludendorff in 1916 was a stern injunction against unofficial and unsanctioned "disciplinary excesses:" verbal or physical mistreatment of subordinates. Unlike many of its counterparts, this one seems to have been generally honored more in the observation than in the breach. In particular, the active officers from the prewar army were a major part of the army's "culture of competence" in 1914–15: generally respected, often admired, and frequently emulated for their knowledge, understanding, and courage. They were also a diminishing asset. Almost 20 percent of those serving in 1914 were killed in the first fifteen months. That was a statistic calculated to induce survivor's syndrome among those who remained. Any doubt new regiments needed experienced officers had been removed by the debacles in front of Ypres. Many staff posts created by high-intensity industrial war were sufficiently specialized that they could not be assumed by reservists or wartime commissions. By 1918 two-thirds of the staffs of corps headquarters were composed of peacetime regulars. In the front lines they were correspondingly scarce, and proportionately missed.

Given the life expectancy of a junior officer in a front-line unit, not a few of the officers, whatever their provenance, adopted an attitude blending *carpe diem* with *gaudeamus igitur*, performing their duty in the trenches and gun positions but taking whatever pleasures they could out of the line. Paternalism was also eroded, less spectacularly but certainly significantly, by the administrative tasks the limited number of officers imposed on commanders whenever a unit was out of the line. Filling out forms left little time for human contact on any level, even with the assistance of an efficient *Feldwebel*.

The combination of changes in age distributions and command structures combined with the changes in weapon and tactics discussed in previous chapters to produce an informal metamorphosis in small-group front-line dynamics. World War I has frequently been described in terms of a factory. In the shell holes and the trenches of 1917, however, the German Army began developing what might be called an artisanal approach to modern war. The front line increasingly came to resemble a workshop, with groups of craftsmen combining to complete a job in the most effective way. Existential warriors might be welcome, in the way a crossbreed wolf may be in a pack of feral dogs—but only when their personal energies fuelled the small collective military enterprises that were the result of storm troop methods applied by surrogate families. The peacetime army's NCO was a man set apart from the rank and file. He was a professional soldier; they were temporary ones. He was their instructor, not their mentor—and certainly not their comrade. By 1917, however, few of these men remained in the rifle companies. Their places had been filled by reservists and wartime conscripts promoted in the field. With company officers and senior NCOs few and busy, more and more responsibility fell to this new breed of junior leaders. They were usually trusted by their subordinates as capable and experienced veterans who had proven brave, intelligent, and lucky. That trust, however, was anything but absolute. Group relations were close; group discipline was internal. Corporals and sergeants tended to exercise command by consensus. They tested attitudes rather than risk giving orders that would be disregarded or disobeyed—an approach facilitated because they were in constant, comprehensive contact with their small group. Everyone, in other words, was dependent, however involuntarily, on everyone else in his artisan collective and correspondingly constrained to do his own best whether as rifleman, machine gunner, grenadier, or squad leader. They were tactically formidable, able to stand a lot of killing—but were nevertheless citizen soldiers beginning to ask awkward questions.

The German Army of 1914, like the society that sustained it, was accustomed to living well. That officers enjoyed certain privileges was understandable and acceptable to the rank and file—as long as the stew contained meat and the coffee was hot; as long as a man off duty could enjoy a decent smoke, a glass of beer, and a shot of schnapps. As life's good things, from bread to toilet paper, became scarcer and coarser, the everyday inequalities of a caste/class-based society, once taken more or less for granted even by Social Democrats, became less and less bearable. As early as the spring of 1916 the army was suffering from increasingly endemic food shortages. The official caloric content of soldiers' daily rations, 3,100 in 1914, decreased to 2,500 by the winter of 1917. Palatability declined even more sharply as turnips were substituted for potatoes and bread rations were reduced and adulterated. The foci of complaints were more personal than institutional. "The system" was vilified in the abstract. Concrete denunciations addressed the officers' alleged privileges: better food and more of it; superior living conditions; higher pay unjustified by higher performance. Even the limited privileges of NCOs came under fire. Words like *Ungerechtigkeit* (injustice) and *Misstände* (maladministration) appeared on an increasing number of latrine walls—and in letters home, on leave trains and in railway stations, anywhere men from different units came together to exchange gossip without being overheard.[28]

The army responded with palliatives: seeking to ensure food was distributed fairly, warning officers to be unobtrusive about their better circumstances. Systematic reforms like adjusting pay and encouraging officers to eat with the men were rejected as reducing necessary separation between leaders and led. Alexander Watson makes a more decisive point by asserting that the problem was structural as opposed to institutional. Halfway through the war, Germany could not meet systematically the perceived basic needs of its soldiers.[29]

Another set of grievances involved the increasing dichotomy between front and rear. The French were on home ground; the British were allies; their behaviors behind the lines were correspondingly restricted. In France and Belgium, Poland and Russia, the Germans were conquerors. As much to the point, the concept of "rear echelon" was alien to an army that, expecting to win the war in a matter of weeks, put most of its men into combat formations and wound up detaching them as necessary. As late as the summer of 1918 a single infantry battalion had over 10 per cent of its nominal strength assigned to duty somewhere in the rear.[30] Improvisation favors opportunists. Few companies did not have men luckier, more egocentric, or less scrupulous than their former comrades who had not wangled a post sorting mail or guarding supplies in some remote village. Few regiments did not have officers on what amounted to permanent detachment supervising detached rank and file. Some, officers and enlisted, worked hard at jobs they considered necessary and honorable. Their absence from the trenches was temporary. Soon, they told each other and themselves, they would request transfer to the front. They may even have occasionally believed it. Others made good livings from military administration in time-honored fashions: skimming off the top, cooking the books, dealing with civilian black markets, pimping, or just keeping a low profile. Comb-outs and courts-martial were infrequent; dog did not eat dog. The hope that peace would not break out too quickly was common, if not universal.

Far from being out of sight, out of mind, these *Etappenhengsten* (rear echelon studs) were all too visible to any front-line division rotated for retraining, reinforcement, and recreation. As early as 1916 idealists, realists, and cynics alike spoke of two armies: one in the trenches and one fighting the war in the bars and brothels of the occupied zones.[31] Dislike of the rear echelon, defined as anywhere behind the definer, is a universal constant of war-making, embracing those who stood in the rear ranks of a Hoplite phalanx or a Viking shield wall. The mistrust, not to say hatred, ran particularly deep in a German Army whose articulate elements stressed the importance of what is now called "authenticity." A man was in the line or he was not: thesis/ antithesis. In the midst of the carnage at Verdun, a staff officer addressed a shivering rifleman: "You're freezing? Only jerkoffs, drunks, and horndogs freeze. Which one are you?"[32] The one-sided interchange might have been an attempt at raw soldiers' humor. It might even have been so taken—if the speaker was understood as sharing the same miserable conditions. Instead, remembered and repeated at a half-century's distance, it symbolized the growing dichotomy not merely between front and rear, line and staff, but between the two halves of the German Empire: those who commanded and those who obeyed.

III

The first conference on the details of the last German offensive was held on November 11, 1917—a date offering another proof of Bellona's sardonic sense of humor.[33] Its conclusions were that the attack must come early, before American troops tipped the balance permanently. The attack must force Britain out of the war. Most ominously, the attack would be a one-off. Initially Ludendorff, at Kuhl's urging, seriously considered a double blow incorporating a second major attack in the north, against the Ypres salient. This was sidetracked and downgraded because the High Command's general consensus was that German resources could not support a second try except as a limited-force diversion. In short, Ludendorff proposed to play *va banque*: all or nothing, with the Empire's destiny as a wager. No one at the conference seemed to remember that Moltke the Elder had been a passionate whist player, a master at calculating the odds of that cerebral pastime. But now the game was baccarat.

In the second planning conference held on December 27, the army groups were instructed to prepare a spectrum of operations covering almost the entire front, for an offensive sometime in March. Ten days later, Ludendorff informed Kuhl that the attack would in fact be against the British—not, apparently a particular surprise—and would be the direct responsibility of Kuhl and Rupprecht. Detailed planning began immediately. The final high-level conference took place on January 21, when Rupprecht, Crown Prince William, and their chiefs of staff urged setting specific military objectives. Ludendorff replied that in Russia, he and Hindenburg set an initial objective, then decided where to go next and things worked out quite well, thank you very much. It was here Ludendorff made the comment that ever since has defined the March offensive: "We talk too much about operations and too little about tactics."[34]

Aphoristically reduced to some version of "punch a hole and see what develops," Ludendorff's statement has invited description by the present author as the strategic insight of a regimental commander. That was an egregious oversimplification. On one level it is worth noting that *Vernichtungsschlacht* (battle of annihilation) in a German context has a moral as well as a material dimension. It involved breaking wills as well as destroying armies. It meant creating a situation where even if a war's outcome was critical to the loser, the stakes now exceeded his readiness to meet them.[35] In that context it can be suggested, though the idea's full development is outside this work's scope, that Germany by 1918 had so much in the game that it was easy—arguably necessary—to believe the Allies were not, *could* not, be as deeply committed.

Far more significant, however, is an insight developed by David Foley. He points out that the prewar German Army had recognized two forms of warfare: *Bewegungskrieg* (war of motion) and *Stellungskrieg* (war of position). It was *Bewegungskrieg* that brought about *Vernichtungssieg* (victory of annihilation) by maneuvering the enemy into an unfavorable position—usually by means of flanking operations—and then outfighting him so that his will to continue collapsed.[36] From Königgrätz to Sedan that formula had produced victories of the kind Germany vitally needed.

Ludendorff may well have identified inappropriately with Schlieffen, the elder Moltke, and perhaps even Frederick the Great. But he was no fool. What worked in Russia in 1915 had significantly limited applicability on the Western Front in 1918. The German Army needed top to bottom overhauling. It had not mounted a major offensive in the West since Verdun—and that was hardly a suitable model for a campaign of movement. Even more fundamentally, the junior-ranking staff officers who had contributed so much to the army's successful adaptations to the trenches had been formed by *Stellungskrieg*— a war of steps and processes, executed in systems applied by armies inappropriately trained and unimaginatively commanded at all levels. Now in a matter of weeks they had to reconfigure themselves to the plans and concepts demanded by a war of movement. A human factor was present as well. Beginning in November, Kuhl, Lossow, and Georg Wetzell, OHL's director of operations and in high favor since the success of the Caporetto offensive that he had urged, submitted detailed position papers offering various proposals for the grand offensive's timing, location, and objectives. Each reflected the author's previous experiences and current responsibilities. All were comfort-zone exercises, having in common—predictably—an operational focus, emphasizing places and methods at the expense of considering strategic objectives even in the limited context of operational frameworks. This invites interpretation as one more case study in a German way of war focused inward and downward as opposed to upward and outward. An alternate perspective is that these three staff officers might have been craftsmen, technicians of war, but they also understood that Ludendorff's perspective and Germany's resources combined for a situation in which if the army could not do what it was historically and institutionally oriented to do—that is, to win the first battle, then the second one, then the third—strategic and grand-strategic insight, no matter how brilliant, would make little difference to the end result.

In particular, Kuhl and Lossberg agreed Britain was the preferable target. The Allies had neither a unified command nor a central reserve. In terms of numbers the BEF was weaker than the French. In terms of ground it had no strategic depth. Wetzell, Crown Prince William, and William's chief of staff supported a French alternative. But in defeat the French army retained the option of retreating south, behind the Loire. Never mentioned, moreover, but always present was the memory of Verdun, where the French nut had proven unexpectedly uncrackable. Losing twice in the same lottery was not an option.

The die, then, was cast. Rupprecht confided to his diary that success was to be hoped for but could not be guaranteed: "with the force available it will be very difficult."[37] But Rupprecht and his staff were war-hardened professionals and began immediately to improve the odds. They worked in the context of a High Command decision that was a final, major, and necessary step into crisis. About fifty of the army's 240-odd divisions were categorized as "attack divisions," developments of 1917's *Eingreif* divisions. They were intended for offensives as opposed to counterattacks. The remaining divisions were defined as "position troops," considered useful at best for consolidating gains, more likely to spend the rest of the war holding trenches. By this time these divisions were largely undisturbed at their loss of status. But their replacements included increasing numbers of the less fit and the more disaffected. Commanders complained of men with still open stomach wounds, or such poorly healed head wounds they could not wear helmets. Already short commons grew even shorter. At this stage of the war the difference between assault divisions and the other kind was understood and conceded on both sides of the line. But only the German Army institutionalized it—not only for tactical reasons, but also because Germany's human and material resources were insufficient to sustain surface homogeneity, or at least its illusion.

Assault divisions had first priority for replacements, weapons and supplies—including anaesthetics and antiseptics, whose increasing shortages were reducing the practice of medicine in some field hospitals to near-Napoleonic levels. Supporting units, particularly pioneers and signalmen, were restored to table of organization standards. Battalion officers, captains and majors, were sent on month-long training courses structured to improve both professional competence and physical fitness often eroded by a year's trench warfare. The divisions designated for the offensive's first wave were even brought up to strength in horses, albeit by the one-time expedient of grounding over a dozen of the divisions left in the East.

The price of all this attention was the certainty of being in the forefront of an offensive the coming of which was foretold and discussed in every tavern and brothel in the war zone. It also meant a winter of extended training in assault tactics as practiced at Riga, Cambrai, and Caporetto.[38] The principles were presented on New Year's Day 1918—not necessarily by coincidence. *Der*

Angriff im Stellungskrieg (The Attack in Position Warfare) was less a source of fresh insight than a compendium of doctrine developed during 1917, filtered through recent experience and summarized in aphorisms and exhortations.[39] The infantry must depend on its own skill and courage. No amount of support from other arms could relieve the foot soldier from his ultimate responsibility and his ultimate honor: closing with the enemy. That was best accomplished by initiative focused on maintaining speed and sustained by organization in depth. The first assault wave would identify positions and weak spots for the second wave, which would push through the vulnerable points. The third wave, reinforced with trench mortars and light artillery, provided fire support and widened the gaps cut by the second wave. Instead of worrying about securing flanks and maintaining contact, instead of securing an objective and awaiting relief, the leading units were to keep going as long as possible. The rest of the formation was responsible for mopping up bypassed positions, reinforcing the attack, and sustaining its momentum. The French called these "Hutier tactics," after General Oskar von Hutier, the victor of Riga. Somewhat like Blitzkrieg in a later war, the name stuck despite the fact that the Germans never used it.[40] "Infiltration tactics" is more technical and somewhat closer to the mark, when one incorporates the coda that these tactics were based on small combat groups rather than stealthy individuals. Their defining, indeed their essential, characteristic, reflected that fact. Even leadership was secondary; speed, success, and survival depended on the team remaining effective when the sergeant or corporal went down.

The assault battalions had two key roles projected in the offensive's plans.[41] First was transmitting their methods and attitudes on a larger scale and in a smaller time frame than previously attempted or projected. In particular Jäger-Sturm-Bataillon 3, which had a reputation for developing and refining assault squad tactics, conducted courses for the divisions of the Second Army that were designated to make the main attack. Inevitably these involved as much observation as practice, but the experience gained in elastic defense tactics during the past year generated a high learning curve. The men who went forward in the assault waves had a reasonable idea of what they were supposed and expected to do. Even the assault divisions' ranks were, however, by now full of men in their thirties, whose courage and steadfastness exceeded their energy and flexibility. Their instructors believed execution might well be a different story.

That led to the storm battalion's second role: participation. By March 1918 each Sturmbataillon had received a battery of "infantry guns," usually light field pieces modified for direct support over open sights. The rifle companies' firepower and shock effect also benefitted from the introduction of the first true submachine guns. Though available only in limited numbers, the Bergmann Machine Pistol 18/1 proved devastatingly effective in trench fighting and similar close-quarters combat.

Bataillon 3 recommended that the assault battalion assigned to each army should provide a "storm group" to every company in an attacking division's first wave. That, however, was impossible in terms of numbers. With a few extra squads for particularly difficult objectives, a battalion could cover only two of an army's divisions. The rest would have to provide assault squads from their own resources. The result was three ghosts at the planning feast. Could storm troop tactics be sufficiently generalized and sufficiently sustained to enable an operational offensive? Would the casualties be kept low enough to maintain the assault divisions' combat effectiveness—to say nothing of the storm battalions, whose ranks were impossible to replenish in a hurry? And should the first two answers be negative, what were the chances of position divisions stepping into the breach? The official answer was to keep the assaulting divisions advancing as long as possible—up to five miles in one rush. It was not infiltration of which plans and orders spoke, but rather surprise, speed, and flexibility—the basic principles of *Bewegungskrieg*. If second-line divisions had to be deployed on Day One, then the offensive had failed. Their mission was to sustain momentum, not restore it.

Putting to rest the ghosts demanded limiting the direct pressure on the assault divisions' infantry by providing as much institutional support, direct and indirect, as possible.[42] More than any German general of the Twentieth Century, organization was Ludendorff's forte. In that context, logistics played a role uniquely important in German operational planning—a fact meriting its presentation at the head of the operation's "to do" list instead of its usual position bringing up the rear. The major paradigm shift involved front-loading the offensive: shock, awe, and follow-through. That in turn meant converting its logistics from a pull to a push system. In a pull system, the using units request what they need. A push system means supplies are sent forward systematically without the need for specific requisitions. The latter system is usually considered as less economical, but better suited to mobile operations. The German logisticians recognized that movement forward in all aspects was the key to sustaining the offensive. That meant keeping roads clear. It meant moving gravel forward to repair wear and damage. It meant filling craters to create routes across ground torn up by years of shelling. It meant establishing and enforcing route priorities— thereby giving the military police something to do other than roust drunks and check passes in behind-the-lines safety. It meant capturing and restoring narrow-gauge railways behind Allied lines, and eventually main lines as well. Sixty construction companies and forty-eight labor companies were available for those purposes. Again, two fundamental questions remained. Would the supply services, after three and a half years of regular schedules and limited scope, after repeated combing out of their younger, fitter, men, be able to sustain long-term long-distance effort? And given the wastage inevitable in a push system, would the country and the rear areas be able to keep the boxcars, trucks, and wagons loaded?

A second approach to improving the German odds involved surprise. At this stage of the war, it was clear that strategic surprise for an operation on this scale was impossible. The operational level was another story. Even the attacking armies' headquarters were not informed of the decision for an offensive until February 8. Ten days later OHL began circulating plans for secondary offensives and follow-up attacks. These were both deceptions designed to mislead French and British intelligence and outlines for responding to situations and opportunities as they might develop. Institutionally the High Command created an elaborate internal security system of selected officers with broad authority to enforce secrecy. Daylight movement was forbidden. Neither orders nor information were made available to forward units—a lesson learned from the French Nivelle offensive. Personal mail was rigidly controlled. Unloading trains took place as far behind the lines as possible. Vehicle movement cross-country was restricted to avoid leaving visible tracks. Air units were concentrated beyond the range of Allied reconnaissance, the planes infiltrated in small numbers and hidden in barns and under tents originally designed to shelter horses.

A third way of stacking the deck involved information. The new doctrine of limited, intensive artillery preparation without preregistration made maps and photographs essential. Gun positions, strong points, and headquarters needed to be precisely located; there was literally no time to correct mistakes. The infantry too needed maps more than ever. The overriding need for surprise made it too risky to increase the conventional method of ground reconnaissance: raiding and patrolling. That threw increased responsibility on the air force. The observation squadrons fulfilled their missions with remarkable effectiveness. The artillery batteries had their photographic intelligence; the infantry companies had maps detailed enough to show individual deep shell craters.

Often overlooked but no less significant was the Luftstreitkräfte's ability to complete the necessary missions without a massive increase in sorties. That in turn owed much to the fighter squadrons. By this time they were operating in more or less *ad hoc Gruppen*, with three permanent four-squadron *Geschwader* (wings). Short of planes, lacking experienced pilots and qualified leaders after the past year's losses, facing superior aircraft as the technical pendulum swung in the Allies' favor, the single-seater airmen nevertheless maintained the balance over the offensive's designated sectors, frustrating British observation planes and screening their own just well enough to avert exposure from above—all without unduly alarming their aerial opposite numbers or BEF headquarters.[43]

But it would be on the ground that the decision would be reached—and that would depend on the artillery. Bruchmüller had been transferred west with Hutier. Their headquarters, redesignated Eighteenth Army, had a key assignment in the offensive, and its execution depended on solving two artillery-related problems. One was general. Long, diffuse artillery preparations failed to destroy enemy defenses comprehensively. They sacrificed strategic, operational, and tactical surprise, and they created more obstacles for the infantry than they cleared. Bruchmüller responded by substituting neutralization for destruction. He concluded that force and intensity, not duration, determined a bombardment's effectiveness. He organized artillery by mission as opposed to gun type: infantry support, counter-battery fire, long-range work against flanks and lines of communication, and precision targeting of crucial objectives like headquarters and bridges. Preparation consisted of three phases: ten to thirty minutes concentrating on command and communication centers; an hour and a half to two and half hours of counterbattery; two hours focused on infantry targets and on keeping the guns neutralized. This was followed by the infantry assault, synergized with (not supported by) a creeping barrage of gas and high explosives, with the ground troops following close enough to suffer a percentage of friendly fire casualties—the price of silenced enemy machine guns.

The completed fire plan was an artilleryman's symphony, with the structural flexibility of a jazz combo. But its maximum effect depended on addressing the second problem: target acquisition. Standard operating procedure involved registering a battery's guns by firing at a target, then adjusting settings. This took time and made the battery itself a target for, naturally, counter-battery fire. During 1917, the artilleries of all the Western Front combatants had begun acquiring targets by sound and flash methods and adjusting fire by calculations based on weather conditions and the wear of individual gun barrels. Unobserved fire, predicted fire, was both efficient and effective. It also required the abandonment of rough and ready pragmatism in favor of abstract mathematics. German artillerymen were correspondingly dubious about slide-rule gunnery, resisting its full-scale imposition. Initially they regarded Bruchmüller somewhat askance, as an outsider from a secondary theater who had faced only second-rate opposition—until his system proved beyond doubt in March 1918 that theoretical calculation prefigured practical success.[44]

Artillery was not the exclusive source of the "shock and awe" on which the 1918 offensive so heavily depended. In the aftermath of Cambrai the newly redesignated *Schlachtstaffeln* were increased to thirty-eight six-plane squadrons. Twenty-seven of them were directly assigned to the three armies spearheading the March offensive. *Schlachtstaffel* doctrine emphasized following precise, predetermined orders designed to keep them in close contact with the ground troops they were supporting. The usual primary targets were infantry formations, artillery positions, and anything involving horses. The usual tactics were based on mass low-level attacks, as many as four squadrons in succession, at between 150 and 200 feet. Their effect has been described by

British sources as depending on surprise rather than firepower, being more moral than anything else, and diminishing with time and exposure.[45] But these judgments are also retrospective. Distracting attention, keeping heads down, disrupting counterattacks, and panicking horses proved no mean contributions to the first stages of just about every German attack in March and April. In that sense the durable, hard-hitting CLs effectively prefigured the impact of their Stuka successors in 1939 and 1940.

IV

The German attack on March 21, 1918 struck an obliging enemy, as much as that was possible after over three years of close-gripped war. The BEF had recently expanded its front as a gesture of support to the French at the same time it was constrained by manpower considerations to reduce its infantry strength by one-quarter. The high command recognized the result was inability to undertake major independent offensive operations in at least the first half of 1918. After having ignored defensive doctrine for most of the war, the decision to imitate the Germans—literally, by consulting captured manuals, was not an inherently bad idea. Neither was the resulting adoption of the principle of defense in depth. The British lacked the time and resources to construct a comprehensive physical framework for in-depth defense. They lacked the reserves to mount the systemic counterattacks essential to the German doctrine, and deployed those they had too far behind the front to intervene quickly. Four years of emphasis on holding ground as a primary indication of a unit's quality had inculcated a focus, a rigidity alien to the German system—a rigidity inviting exploitation by storm troop tactics. At unit level BEF training, command, and cohesion alike had in no way recovered from the military traumas of 1917. In short, given its opposition the most remarkable feature of the initial German offensive was not its impressive success, but the limited nature of that success.[46]

On March 21, Operation *Michael* was unleashed. Three German armies, a total of sixty-seven divisions, went forward on an eighty-mile front. The artillery fired almost three and a quarter million rounds, a third of them gas.

The infantry went in at 9:40 am. By mid-afternoon all that remained intact of a front line projected to hold out on its own for two days were fifteen or twenty isolated strong points. As the fog lifted, their garrisons had all day to observe the steady, relentless German progress into and beyond what had been optimistically designated the battle zone. Contrary to long-established Western Front precedent, the British positions were bypassed, ignored, as though they were not worth the trouble to finish off. Eventually the Germans sent in a message: some variant of refusal to surrender being answered by a full-scale, close-range barrage from artillery and trench mortars. Sometimes the defenders were able to see the guns moving into position and experience a few ranging rounds. With the front seemingly torn open beyond restoration, with no counterattacks developing and no relief forces in sight, further resistance could easily seem an obvious and pointless waste of life.[47]

In a single day, the Germans had cracked open an established position for a total gain of a hundred square miles—triple the British gains during the whole of Third Ypres.

From a closer perspective, results were significantly uneven. The Eighteenth Army on the left set the tone for the mythmakers and history books. Thanks in good part to Bruchmüller's artillery tactics comprehensively applied, and to the work of its 5th Sturmbataillon, Rohr's originals, the Eighteenth Army broke into the British battle zone all across its front while needing to commit only two reserve divisions out of fourteen. In the center, the Second Army achieved less while committing fourteen of its nineteen divisions. The Seventeenth Army on the offensive's right flank was almost five miles short of its objectives, and that had required sixteen of its eighteen divisions. Both the Second and the Seventeenth Armies had taken heavy casualties, particularly in their *Sturmbataillonen* and attack divisions. Ludendorff reinforced success, sending a half-dozen more divisions to Hutier's sector and supporting Army Group Crown Prince when it urged him to let the Eighteenth Army keep going south, as opposed to the original intention of shifting its axis of advance westward to support the Second Army on its right.

That last sentence contains a significant and overlooked clue to the loss of focus so often ascribed to Ludendorff's handling of the campaign in the next few days. The three armies committed to *Michael* were under two higher commands. The Second and Seventeenth Armies answered to Rupprecht's army group; the Eighteenth Army was under Army Group Crown Prince William. That division not only added an extra, complicating link to the chain of command, but the army group commanders were both scions of long established royal houses with a long-standing rivalry. The crown princes were military rivals as well. So were their respective, and highly capable, chiefs of staff. The competition was not as intense as, for example, that between George Patton and Bernard Montgomery a quarter century later. But for dynastic reasons as well as military ones, each sought recognition as the battle captain who secured Germany's future and returned the bumptious plebeian Ludendorff to the subordinate status his heritage merited. Ludendorff, no fool in such matters, was correspondingly wary of choosing either of them as *Michael's* field commander. His subsequent explanation that a single CO would make it difficult for the High Command—read Ludendorff—to offer suggestions and recommendations to subordinate formations without appearing to interfere in the chain of command is unconvincing to say the least. The non-royal Generalität offered no obvious third prospect with the status and force of character to overshadow royals who were both just capable enough that neither could be readily sidetracked even at this vital stage of the war.[48] And that was only the political aspect of the issue. In a war of movement involving mass armies, it was not the job of the supreme commander to manage his subordinate commands directly. Nor was it even possible, given Great War movement technology. In the Wars of Unification, Moltke the Elder had applied the approach of *Auftragstaktik* to *Auftragsoperationen*, giving his army commanders space and time to execute their missions. It did not always work optimally, or even well—Karl von Steinmetz in 1870 was a shining example. But its lessons had in good part sunk in the morass of trench warfare. Ludendorff's ultimate aim was to achieve a breakthrough and develop the resulting weak spots into a mobile campaign. Two attack sectors offered twice the opportunities—a prefiguration of Dwight Eisenhower's broad front strategy a quarter century later. But did Ludendorff have the strategic insight, the strength of character, and the low cunning to drive his high-born, high-spirited, half-broken horses in a team for a common purpose?

By March 23, the Germans had made a breach in the Allied line over forty miles deep—a breach deep enough that a secret weapon, a specially designed gun with an eighty-mile range, was able to open fire on Paris. The BEF had lost over 200,000 killed and wounded, almost 100,000 prisoners. The German emperor and the German public were appropriately ecstatic. The reeling British, moreover, were retreating extrinsically, opening a promising gap between their Third and Fifth Armies to complement the gap already developing between the BEF and the French on their left. Ludendorff responded flexibly and decisively—in his own mind, at least. He had always regarded *Michael* as a first step, followed by a synergized series of "shock and awe" attacks by locally superior forces: punch a hole and see what develops. He understood that he was running against two time clocks. The first measured the dates of American troops' arrival in France. The second counted the days until German replacement depots emptied. Plans to mobilize another 600,000 men as a one-time emergency effort in 1919 were little more than a paper exercise.[49] And the quartermaster-general took no time to read reports from the front that even at *Michael*'s early stage, infantry worn out and suffering heavy losses were depending more and more on the artillery to shoot them forward. Otherwise they failed to advance. Position divisions were left in the line with no hope of the reliefs necessary to rest and refit, to the point where total collapse of their powers of resistance threatened in some of them. Second-guessers have said ever since that was the time to shift to the defensive. Instead, Ludendorff ordered the Second and the Eighteenth Armies to shift west-southwest with the intention of further separating the Allies and drawing French reserves onto a new killing ground. The Seventeenth Army would swing northwest and cooperate with the Sixth Army in the Flanders sector to drive the British back to the Channel and into the sea.

In the context of *Bewegungskrieg*, Ludendorff's plan was a staff-college prize contender. At the front it was a high-risk option. The operational fist was becoming an open-fingered outstretched hand. The teeth of a shark were morphing into the tentacles of an octopus. That did not necessarily make the new course an exercise in futility. The lines on High Command maps definitely looked impressive: a tide inexorably spreading out across the heart of France. In the field, the three attacking armies advanced twenty miles in three days.

Tactics *can* influence policy. A German victory depended heavily on splitting the Allies militarily and politically, and even the stiffest of British upper lips were beginning to quiver. Pétain's chief of staff was openly describing the war as lost and recommending making peace as soon as possible. The appointment—finally—of an Allied commander in chief on March 26 seemed a barely relevant desperation move: nobody confused Ferdinand Foch with Napoleon Bonaparte. By that time, as open-warfare conditions developed in the British sector, a communications system designed for the measured pace of the trenches was starting to fray—a serious problem when accurate and timely information was vital and its absence invited order, counterorder, disorder. German forward units were reoccupying most of the old Somme battlefield. Albert fell, appropriately, to elements of the Second Army. The vital rail and road hub of Amiens, poorly defended, seemed within reach and probably was: at least a British officer prisoner told Rupprecht its capture "would have been easy ... what did we have facing [you]"?[50]

And then everything began unraveling at once. French reinforcements shored up Amiens as a BEF recovering from its initial shock stopped the Second Army in its tracks north and east of the city. The Eighteenth Army successfully widened the breach between the French and British Armies by its advance southeast, but its direction was by then extrinsic enough to remove it operationally and tactically from the fighting around Arras, at least in the judgment of Crown Prince William's headquarters. Ludendorff had originally planned for a secondary offensive by Rupprecht's army group, Operation *Mars*, to develop *Michael* on its left flank. Now he launched it on March 28 to restore the offensive's momentum. The artillery preparation lacked Bruchmüller's flair and his attention to detail. The infantry went forward in huddled masses, with almost no sign of the infiltration tactics of a week earlier. The British defense, stiffened by Guardsmen and Australians, was resolute and effective. Ludendorff cancelled *Mars* before its first day ended. And the vultures began circling High Command headquarters.

The general consensus among the staff officers of *Michael*'s three armies was that the offensive had shot its bolt. Agreement on the principal reason was also consensual: the High Command, specifically Erich Ludendorff, had no sense of direction, no goal beyond tactical success, however ephemeral.

Rupprecht described OHL as living "from hand to mouth."[51] Lossberg, still with the Fourth Army in Flanders, called the High Command's staff system rigid and arrogant.[52] Ludendorff supported that evaluation when he dismissed the questioning of the offensive's stalling by some of his staff officers as "croaking" and asked if they wanted him to make peace at any price because of a setback.[53] On March 30, the offensive resumed and went nowhere. On March 31 Ludendorff ordered a general—and, *nota bene*, a temporary—shift to the defensive.

The March 31 stand-down marked the real, if not the official, end of *Michael*, and the military, though not the territorial, climax of the March offensive. There were still plans to be made, attacks to be launched, and ground to be gained—but not immediately. Not around Arras and Amiens, nor in the French sector, where Hutier's advance was consistently blocked by successful local counterattacks. A series of small-scale, heroically named attacks intended to revitalize *Michael* only dulled further the operation's cutting edge. On April 5 Ludendorff announced *Michael* was being discontinued—again temporarily. He might have done better to take his own sarcastic advice about seeking peace. When the German offensive resumed, it would be with different configurations, revised objectives, and diminished— perhaps fatally diminished—prospects.

Ludendorff blamed "the supply situation" for his decision to shut down *Michael*. Current military and academic evaluations focus instead on Ludendorff's flawed planning; David Zabecki offers a comprehensive and persuasive checklist. He describes a lack of a clearly defined objective leading to an over-emphasis on the tactical level, an opportunism that dissipated already-limited German strength and encouraged the pursuit of opportunities that turned to mirages.[54] It must also be remembered that *Vernichtigungsschlacht's* moral effect remained limited. The Allied armies quickly responded to and recovered from the initial shock expected to shatter their equilibrium in the context of Ludendorff's grand plan. But it is also reasonable from the perspective of this book to evaluate the relationship between the German Army of 1918 and the expectations it carried into the March offensive.

To begin at the macro level, between March 21 and April 10 the Second, Seventeenth, and Eighteenth Armies suffered an official total of 239,000 casualties, roughly evenly divided among them. In any war, campaign, or battle, even modern high-tech versions, losses are disproportionately concentrated in the infantry. So are the consequences. In a week or ten days some divisions lost as many as a hundred officers, overwhelmingly the captains and lieutenants who commanded at company level. Assault-group tactics exacted a high price as well in junior NCOs. Casualties in the *Sturmbataillonen* were even heavier and essentially irreplaceable. These units were accustomed to performing a specific mission, then being withdrawn. Continued front-line service amounted to a breach of one of the informal contracts between soldiers and armies.[55] They also depended for replacements on drafts and volunteers that were no longer forthcoming from divisions that had no storm troop-qualified men, or any men at all, to spare. A German attack division in May gave its average battalion strength at 560, about two-thirds of the authorized number. The attached machine-gun battalion had only enough men to crew a dozen guns rather than its norm of thirty-six. The report gave the reason as the division's nearly uninterrupted six weeks of front-line engagement. It noted further that the lack of normal reliefs and rest periods meant no time to wash bodies and clothes. The result was general and enduring lousiness, with corresponding negative prospects for health and morale. This and similar reports, along with individual soldiers' letters and diaries, suggest that of themselves the sudden, drastic changes in expectations and requirements caused by extended commitment, constant marching, and the different random risks of open warfare could be as disconcerting as the nature of the changes. Customs and habits of the trenches died hard—sometimes harder than men.

Personnel problems were further exacerbated by the same gains of territory that earned the March offensive its recognition as a tactical success. Every mile of occupied ground expanded the area to be held. Apart from any resulting overextension, the relative absence of the kinds of developed defenses considered necessary after three years of trench warfare was discomfiting in units where few men remained with any experience of open warfare 1914-style. Attempts to replace these losses warm body for warm body foundered on the emptiness of homeland depots. By April, once the recovered wounded and the comb-outs had been tallied, the monthly gap was still 70,000. The nineteen-year-olds of the class of 1899 were almost all at the front—for what they might be worth in terms of their training and fitness, which had been a serious question months earlier. The next class of 1900 included over 300,000 eighteen-year-olds, but it would be the second half of the year before they could be shoveled into the pipeline. Trolling the war industries for fit men once more risked disrupting a barely stable balance of domestic power groups. And looming over everything else was a metastasizing influenza epidemic that thrived on crowds, dirt, and debility. The army provided all three. At the front and in the depots, initial symptoms seemed innocuous to an already strained medical system: coughs and fevers were near-universal consequences of German winters, wet trenches, and damp clothing. But as the March offensive progressed, increasing numbers of men went down with more serious versions of "Flanders flu." The connections between the epidemic's spread and the demands and privations of a near-continuous offensive are tenuous: correlation does not demonstrate causation. But by mid-July the number of sick reached a million; Ludendorff was complaining that his subordinates were using influenza as a general-purpose explanation for failure; and a second wave of the epidemic was on the way.[56]

The end result of all this was an unexpectedly rapid dulling of the army's fighting edge. Storm battalions, some like the 5th down to almost half strength, were pulled out of the line and put to training newcomers from Russia. Designated trench divisions were slotted into the front line as attack divisions bled out, which helps explain the British judgment that within days German attacks seemed periodically to be reverting to the mass frontal tactics of 1914. But the war's strains were not one sided. The Allies too felt their effects. French manpower was so reduced that the army was replacing a metropolitan regiment with a North African one in an increasing number of its divisions—a reason, in passing, why they were so willing to accept the American black regiments General Pershing did not want. French public and political morale was faltering to a point where the British ambassador suggested the possibility of civil war. Across the Channel, at the turn of the year the situation seemed so dire that the government was withholding replacements lest they too be squandered in another futile offensive to nowhere. It was not exhaustion that lamed the German Army of the March offensive. It was expectations.

These began at the institutional level. The German Army of 1918 is best understood as a force optimized for defense and counterattack in limited contexts that was suddenly required to shift its focus to offense and exploitation in an operationally open-ended situation. Its tools were limited. In terms of assault, the tanks available were an afterthought, with neither the numbers nor the tactical principles to supplement the infantry and artillery, let alone complement them. In terms of exploitation, the cavalry had either been left in Russia for internal security purposes or long since dismounted and converted to infantry. And cavalry, for all its often-delineated shortcomings, was still the only arm capable of expanding success beyond the immediate battlefield. British officers down to battalion level frequently described the German lack of it as helping to sustain fragile morale in retreating troops after March 21. In concrete terms, on the other hand, the BEF's horsemen played a useful, albeit overlooked, role in the war's final victorious months. Some cavalry, in other words, was better than nothing at all.[57] Armored cars, which proved so useful to the French cavalry, were completely absent from the German order of battle. Nor did the Germans have the trucks and other vehicles to improvise motorized forces on even the small scale of the Canadian Corps' Motor Machine-Gun Brigade, or the motorized machine-gun battalion organic to every division of the American Expeditionary Force. Nor could German artillery, whose guns by 1918 were optimized for firepower rather than mobility, and whose horses were generally in poor condition, keep consistent pace with the advance once the initial attacks were completed. And in turn the artillery was outrunning its ammunition supply to a point where in one corps the battery allocation had been reduced by half.

That left the March offensive's development up to the infantry. Many German officers ascribed the slowing of the advance to logistic and moral failings. The supply columns, according to this interpretation, were unable to deliver rations systematically. Hungry men turned to the vast British supply dumps they had just overrun and fell victim to luxuries for months unobtainable on their side of the front. Officers not only lost control of their subordinates but were themselves overwhelmed by British material superiority: everything seemed made out of material in short supply behind their own lines.[58]

The implication that German defeat was enabled by the effects of captured bully beef and pinned on poorly motivated, poorly disciplined troops fitted nicely into postwar right-wing mythology. Nor was the direct impact of British abundance on behavior and morale entirely a construction. The same cannot be said for the postwar scapegoating of the supply system. The quartermasters were stretched to their limits—not least because of the heavy losses in overworked horses that in the first place were often animals deemed too debilitated to be reassigned to the artillery or the pioneers. Over 18,000 of them died in the offensive's first ten days. Shortages were correspondingly frequent—but one of the negative characteristics of a "push" system in any case is a propensity for not meeting the using units' specific needs. It was easier for postwar German critics, especially generals, to blame logistics than to acknowledge the devastating effect of loss on a structure unable to compensate and adapt to the requirements of even a limited war of movement.

Ludendorff's second intention had been a second major offensive in Flanders to disrupt further a BEF he expected to be badly, if not terminally, weakened after *Michael*. Lack of disposable strength put Operation *George* on the shelf and earned it rechristening as *Georgette*. It was not abandoned, however, and with *Michael* bogged down Ludendorff ordered its implementation on April 9. Bruchmüller, brought in as artillery commander, grumbled that no one seemed appropriately cognizant of either the available guns or the characteristics of the terrain.[59] The Sixth Army's offensives along the Lys achieved enough initial success for Haig to issue his "backs to the wall" order on April 11. But the successes were in Great War terms: local victories followed by neither breakthrough nor breakout, at the price of absorbing more scarce reserves and creating another narrow salient difficult to defend economically.

―――――――――― V ――――――――――

Time, will, and resources alike were running thin. The next large-scale plan came from William's army group. Operation *Blücher* proposed a three-army attack along the Chemin des Dames: another frontal offensive, this one across the same terrain that had contributed so heavily to the French debacle in 1917.

Ludendorff nevertheless approved as a means of drawing French reserves from a British front that he still expected to rupture decisively somehow at some future time. Mounting *Blücher* required the transference of significant infantry and artillery from Rupprecht's army group. Even then German strength was insufficient to replicate March 21 with a single coordinated attack. Results would have to be sought in a sequential series of attacks. That meant in essence using the same resources again and again, shifting their positions rather than relieving them to rest and prepare for the next round. *Blücher* succeeded in replicating *Michael* in the secrecy of its preparations—aided, according to some accounts, by the nightly croaking of thousands of frogs in the marshes and on the river banks. Thirty-nine divisions, two-thirds of them assault formations, were available. If the number of guns was fewer than optimal, Bruchmüller was in charge of them and supplemented tube artillery with over twelve hundred trench mortars. The Allies were taken by surprise when the German barrage, three million painstakingly coordinated and devastatingly effective rounds, opened on May 27. To make matters worse, the French sector commander insisted in front-loading his positions, at the rate of one division per five miles of front-line trenches. Finally, the initial weight of the attack fell on four British divisions badly mauled in the earlier fighting and sandwiched into this quiet sector to recover.[60]

Tactically the attack was a virtuoso performance, even compared to *Michael*. Planning and serendipity enabled the Germans to advance as much as fourteen miles on the first day—the war's largest single-day ground gain on any front. As the offensive attack continued to progress, Ludendorff applied the by now shopworn principle of following up tactical success with a set of operational objectives as vague as they proved ephemeral. He wrote of threatening Paris. Instead, *Blücher* devolved into an offensive to nowhere in particular as Allied reserves shored up the line and exhausted, disgruntled Germans found solace in captured supply dumps and their stores of liquor. Material results were impressive: 127,000 Allied casualties including 50,000 prisoners; 600 guns; an advance of almost forty miles in four days. But the vital northern French railway network was still uncut, its centers uncaptured. *Blücher* and its subsidiary operations had cost over a hundred thousand Germans dead, wounded, missing—replaceable in neither numbers nor quality. And a new player was making an appearance: the American Expeditionary Force (AEF).

The improvised American Army had the obvious and predictable shortcomings: inadequate training, ineffective equipment, inappropriate doctrine, inefficient officers, inflexible organizations, inexperienced men. Two further factors exacerbated the Yanks' initial difficulties. One was the strained relations between the Americans and their war-experienced mentors, the French in particular. A sense of saving the day at the last minute reinforced frequent dismissal of the *poilus* as burned out, prone to panic and reluctant to fight. In fact, as German casualty lists attested, the French remained on the whole first-rate combatants, skilled alike in minor tactics and larger combined-arms operations, making up in craft what they had sacrificed in élan. The confidence of inexperience limited the Americans' ability to benefit systematically by observing their veteran allies. And that inexperience was red meat to the Germans who faced them.

In the "little war" of patrols, raids, and small-scale attacks that characterized the Americans' early tours on the front line, the Germans consistently set the pace in battlecraft, initiative, and effective courage. The Americans were more than willing to fight. They simply did not know how, even against the third- and fourth-rate German divisions holding down the relatively quiet sectors that were the AEF's test beds. The AEF's higher commands and staffs were no less caught up in the higher mechanics of combat and logistics on scales heretofore unimagined at West Point or Leavenworth. The divisions were on their own. From Seicheprey and Château-Thierry through Belleau Wood to Soissons, Americans learned by experience, observation—and sometimes pure serendipity. Their learning curves could be steep, but too often the lessons learned were in a context of two steps forward, one sideways, one back. Their tactical deficiencies remained: poor cohesion and worse liaison, ill-defined objectives, misplaced initiatives. Their casualty rates were swingeing—on the scale of 1914–15. Too many officers in too many positions were still not up to their jobs. Tactical cooperation with the French was, if anything, growing worse. Nevertheless, the doughboys passed their first tests with credit, given where they had begun eighteen months earlier. They would play significant roles in checking the final German offensive and the resulting Allied counterattacks.[61]

That, however, lay in the future. Present reality was Ludendorff's reaction to the huge salient *Blücher* had created. Almost forty miles across, over sixty miles long, difficult to defend and more difficult to supply, it offered a stark choice as either a magnet for a major Allied counteroffensive or a springboard for another German attack. An initial effort in early June failed for the first time in months to achieve anything worthwhile tactically, to say nothing of operationally. The Allies were increasingly able to cope with storm troop tactics. The storm troop principle of infiltration, bypassing strong points in the way water seeks the easiest path, led to a downward focus that negatively complemented Ludendorff's strategic principle of "punching a hole and seeing what happened." In both cases there were no objectives—just processes, ultimately leading nowhere in particular. The result, as casualties mounted and reinforcements dwindled, was the reduction of assault divisions and storm battalions to isolated combat teams that could be frustrated, destroyed—or stopped in their tracks.

At command level, Ludendorff's next operational decision was easily made: an attack towards the Marne, with the initial objective of—finally—capturing the railroad hub of Reims, and with Paris on the horizon as a prospect. There were more or less vague thoughts at OHL about using this offensive as a preliminary to a final, decisive blow against the BEF in Flanders. But what the Allies called the Second Battle of the Marne had first priority. If this was not an all-or-nothing effort, it was as close as the German Army could come. Forty-eight divisions, 900 aircraft, 6,300 guns, and Georg Bruchmüller were committed to the attack that began on July 15. This time the initial successes were limited, the offensive was stymied, and a series of well-coordinated Allied counterattacks retook almost all the ground lost during *Blücher*.[62] Lossberg, a supreme realist and sufficiently junior to escape the predictable consequences, set the war's "precise" turning point as July 18: the first day of the final Allied offensive on the Western Front.[63] There might be errors and misunderstandings along the way, but from that date the Allies never looked back and the Germans always fought on the back foot, ever closer to home.

English-speaking historians remain prone to give the palm of decisive victory to the BEF's attack on August 8, "the black day of the German Army" according to Ludendorff. It is more accurate to credit the empirical British with developing the first modern combined-arms team: a doctrinal, institutional, and technological synergy among infantry, artillery, tanks, and air power, coordinated by radio systems. The artillery sealed the flanks of an attack, conducted counter-battery fire against German gun positions, and provided an initial creeping barrage. Within the "artillery zone" the tanks sought targets of opportunity while the infantry probed for soft spots, each supporting the other as needed. Aircraft provided reconnaissance, artillery observation, and, increasingly, ground support: by August 1918 the Tank Corps had an RAF (Royal Air Force) squadron attached.[64]

The complex interaction of these arms could not be controlled in any modern sense with the communication technology of 1918. Radios, still bulky and unreliable, were impractical below brigade level. Above all, even in the war's final stages, technique and technology could not significantly reduce casualties. The Third Republic had the doctrine and possessed the tools for modern combat. French staff officers proclaiming "the battle of 1919 will be a battle of aviation and tanks" were, however, less expressing principled conversion to high-tech war than recognizing that their army had finally run out of men. By the time of the Armistice, "the emptiness of the battlefield" was more than just a metaphor in French sectors. The Americans were still chewing their way through the Argonne Forest on what amounted to a rifle-and-bayonet basis, suffering in under seven weeks the largest number killed of any battle in America's history. They learned as they died, impressing the Germans with a fighting spirit long since eroded in their own ranks.[65] But the AEF was still a long way from being able to implement smoothly the "semi-managed" battle, with attacks only able to move forward in a lurching progress that grew steadier with practice. It is similarly appropriate to speak of a "semi-mobile" battle, with men, vehicles, and firepower pushing back the German front as opposed to rupturing it. The initial gains of August 8 were in a sense deceptive. Neither the tactics nor the technology of 1918 was quite up to breaching even improvised defensive positions at acceptable cost. What they could do was maintain a steady pressure that compelled an eroding army to fall back steadily, never giving it time to recover.

Relative to its opponents, moreover, the German Army was demodernizing. The Fokker D-VII had acquired a reputation as the best fighter on the front, but the *Jagdstaffeln* were being whittled down by growing Allied numbers and increased Allied skill. A new generation of French and British air superiority fighters was coming from the factories to the front. Manfred von Richthofen had been killed on April 21, probably by ground fire. By mid-August his famous Fighter Wing 1 had been consolidated into a single squadron due to its heavy losses, the first of several times it would similarly be bled white. In May and June alone the Luftstreitkräfte used twice the amount of fuel that reached the front, and subsequent introduction of rationing limited some fighter squadrons to ten sorties a day. Whether a unit was fighter, attack, or observation, old hands carried the main burden and were making fatigue-related mistakes that too often proved fatal, even with the episodic introduction of parachutes in the war's final stages. On the ground, the few tanks available achieved nothing in particular. Their numbers were too limited. Their technical shortcomings were too many. The overhanging chassis was vulnerable even to slight obstacles and irregularities. In operational contexts, officers of other arms had no serious idea of what tanks should or could do. Nor, indeed, did the tankers themselves. Armor doctrine, insofar as it existed, emphasized maintaining close contact with the infantry, using surprise when possible, avoiding rough or heavily shelled terrain. On one occasion a single cannon-armed A7V prevailed against no fewer than seven British Whippets carrying only machine guns. On another, the tanks encountered a river reported as fordable that in fact proved too deep to cross. On a third an *Abteilung* of A7Vs drove into an artillery position and was constrained to beat a hasty retreat. It was a far cry from June 1940.

More prosaically, artillery horses were dying in their traces by the score, limiting when not crippling the guns' mobility, increasing the problem of providing effective fire support in what was becoming increasingly a war of movement. The deeper penetrations Allied tactics and technology enabled not only left more front-line units isolated, but made retreat an increasingly high-risk option. The result was a growing number of "ordered surrenders." Three hundred forty thousand German soldiers surrendered between July 18 and November 11, 1918. These were mostly group capitulations, organized by company officers or senior NCOs, often brokered in part or accompanied by providing detailed information on a sector's defenses and strong points as a good will gesture and to avert any later misunderstandings. It was a long way from August 1914.[66]

The Germans' fighting retreat was predictably tenacious and predictably skillful. They inflicted more casualties than they suffered. But in David Zabecki's words, "they were truly burned out."[67] Hunger, influenza, typhus, and traumatic stress shredded the ranks at the front and in the rear. By default it was becoming an infantryman's war that the infantry could not sustain indefinitely. Over 400,000 more men were dead or wounded. More ominously, almost 350,000 were counted as prisoners or missing. By early October an army corps with seven divisions in its order of battle was reporting its infantry strength at less than 5,000 men—less than 10 per cent of authorized tables of organization.[68] One regiment could count only 200 men. Another mustered 120, organized in four companies instead of the regulation twelve. Units with such low strengths fell far below the critical mass necessary to sustain cohesion as a combat force. Battalions and companies depended increasingly and disproportionally on the remaining *alte Hasen* and the *Korsettenstangen*, the "old hares" and the "corset stays"— the machine gunners in particular—that the front's artisan groups continued to produce. But as summer gave way to autumn the combat effectiveness of these groups eroded in favor of their survival aspects. Getting home alive became a primary objective of the *Korporalschaften* that in the course had become *Kameradschaften* as well as *Kampfgemeinschaften*.[69] Wilhelm Deist describes the result as a "camouflaged strike," with the "proletariat" of the war machine downing tools in a Marxist model of behavior.[70] One might refer as well to Robert Darnton's model of pre-industrial protest: challenging a system by defying its norms. Even before the army fell back towards its own frontiers, its rear areas contained increasing numbers of men who had drifted away from the front war. The will to enforce more than the minimum forms of discipline eroded, less from fear of a bullet in the back than a sense that it no longer mattered.

The German Army did win final victory—over its own government. Since August Ludendorff's behavior had grown increasingly erratic. He blamed the continuing sequence of defeat on the failures of subordinates. He insisted deserters be executed out of hand and officers enforce orders with handguns.

He had not, however, entirely lost touch with reality. On October 1 he presented a general review of the military situation. The war, he declared, was lost. The only way to save the army from disaster was for the government to request an immediate armistice. His auditors broke into fits of sobbing as the quartermaster-general finally confirmed the long-standing aphorism that "Prussia was an army with a country." Two days later, Prince Max von Baden became chancellor. His first official act was to request an armistice on the basis of Woodrow Wilson's call for "peace without victory." He received a dusty answer. Wilson demanded that any terms make German resumption of hostilities militarily impossible. He insisted on refusing to negotiate with the emperor and the generals. The protests of Ludendorff and Hindenburg amounted to spitting into the wind. William's last imperial act was to replace Ludendorff as first quartermaster-general with Wilhelm Gröner. It would be Gröner the problem-solver who would negotiate William's abdication as the Second Reich collapsed into mutiny and disorder in a matter of days. It would be Gröner who silenced the fire-eaters demanding an all or nothing end game on German soil. And it would be Gröner who arranged the compromise with an embryonic republican government that committed the army, what might remain of it, to maintain law and order if the republic restricted revolution to the political sphere.[71]

Those, however, are stories for another time and another book. The generals' rebellion that deposed the emperor and the domestic revolution that ended the monarchical order are alike remarkable for the limited influence they exercised on the army as an institution.[72] Conscript national armies are held together by a complex interface between front and home, military system and civil society, incorporating varying combinations of compulsion, patriotism, and ideology. Underlying all of them, however, is an implied contract between the soldier and the system. When the nature or the conduct of a particular conflict breaks that contract, soldiers are likely to respond negatively. To speak of a "strike" is to minimize the emotional factors, especially the sense of betrayal that accompanies the process. One might be better advised to talk of alienated affection. By November 1918, the German High Command could count no more than a dozen or so of its divisions as able and willing to fight anyone. Its storm troop battalions were increasingly used as headquarters guards. Far from being "stabbed in the back," the German Army was beaten in the field, beaten to a degree sufficient to break its social contract and erode its cohesion.

For the most part, the desires of the disaffected soldiers were expressed in the counterpart to a joke common among American GIs in World War II. A suitably edited version is "when I get home, I'm going to do three things. First I'll have a beer. Then I'll make love to my wife. Then I'll take off my pack." Such a mind-set may not make revolutions, but it can halt wars. The Imperial German Army ended its existence with a collective sigh of relief.

CODA

The most familiar wrap-up for a book on this subject deals with the soldiers' ambiguous returns home. The vignettes emerge almost of themselves. Chancellor Friedrich Ebert welcomes the "unconquered heroes" parading one last time down Berlin's Unter den Linden. Ideologues and restless spirits go off to fight Bolshevism in the east or join paramilitary *Freikorps* closer to home. Men who had become soldiers, but were once students, clerks, husbands and fathers, seek to find, in Erich Maria Remarque's words, "the way back." An aimless private first class recovering from hysterical blindness drifts aimlessly around a near-deserted Munich barracks until recruited almost by default to spy on radical political groups. Junior officers like Erwin Rommel, no less at loose ends, weigh the prospects of remaining in a Versailles-attenuated Reichswehr.

The list can be multiplied indefinitely. Yet perhaps the best last word on the German Army in the Great War comes from its most forgotten front. In East Africa, Paul von Lettow-Vorbeck formally surrendered on November 25, 1918. He had brilliantly conducted a campaign whose inconsequence relative to its costs exceeded in percentage terms anything the war had to offer. It produced no victories and no defeats—only exploitation and suffering for the African populations of a half-dozen colonies whose European masters justified imperial rule with promises of security. In the end it was sustained on both sides of the sharp end by Africans. A hundred fifty Germans grounded arms at Abercron. The rest were Africans: 1,500 carriers, around 1,000 miscellaneous camp followers, over 400 women—

and 1,100 of the askaris who from the beginning had been the hard core and the backbone of Lettow's undefeated army.

They came in under the German flag with bayonets fixed, and became the stuff of postwar German legend: soldiers of an alien race faithful to their cause and to "Bwana Lettow" until the end, and thereby giving the lie to Allied myths of Hun barbarity and affirming the Germans as model colonizers. Subsequent research has predictably eviscerated this narrative. Michelle Moyd has definitively established the askaris' search for status as "big men," seeking wealth and power through military service that served their own interests as much as those of the government of German East Africa. Askaris were agents of colonialism: constables, tax collectors, and executioners in a relationship of clientage and contract based heavily on "everyday and extraordinary violence." Their willingness to fight for colonial goals was nevertheless limited. Desertion rates spiraled during the campaign; the askaris who surrendered with Lettow most probably stayed with him because of a rational calculation—albeit a mistaken one—that it best served their interests.[1]

This is a convincing argument. Yet it is no less true that German askaris were well fed and well equipped relative to the theater of war and to their enemies. In a region seething with dysentery, typhoid, malaria, and a spectrum of other diseases, the askaris were healthy. The German medical service was expert in treating malaria and innovative in the medical adaptation of plants. German officers and African NCOs were strict in enforcing tropical hygiene and camp sanitation. The askari "campaign communities" of women, children, and low-status noncombatants were sustained even at the price of operational efficiency when feeding them grew difficult. And not least, arguably even primarily, Paul von Lettow-Vorbeck won his battles consistently, and with consistently low casualties.[2]

With a bit of imagination, Lettow and his askaris can be considered as a microcosm of Imperial Germany's ideal of a military institution: comprehensively structured, institutionally supportive, accepted by its members, and victorious in combat. But there is another comparison, less flattering but no less valid. Both Lettow's askaris and the kaiser's army, in the final analysis, existed not to serve state and society but to sustain themselves regardless of those matrices. Efficient on their own terms in what Goethe's Mephisto calls the "lesser world" of tactics and operations, they were ultimately ineffective in the wider contexts that legitimated armed forces. By 1918 both the askaris and the front-hogs were cogs in self-referencing institutions reacting to their own internal dynamics. Whether in East Africa or on the Western Front, it proved a recipe for defeat and dissolution.

NOTES

CHAPTER I: PORTENTS AND PRELIMINARIES

[1] Fritz Stern, "Money, Morals, and the Pillars of Society," in *The Failure of Illiberalism. Essays on the Political Culture of Modern Germany* (New York: Knopf, 1972), pp. 26–57.

[2] Wolfgang J. Mommsen, "A Delaying Compromise: the Division of Authority in the German Constitution of 1871," in *Imperial Germany 1867–1918*, tr. R. Deveson (London: Arnold, 1995), pp. 20–40.

[3] Christine G. Kruger, *"Sind wir denn nicht Brüder?" Deutsche Juden im nationalen Krieg, 1870/71* (Paderborn: Schöningh, 2006).

[4] Margaret Lavina Anderson, *Practicing Democracy. Elections and Political Culture in Imperial Germany* (Princeton: Princeton University Press, 2000).

[5] Alon Confino, "Localities of a Nation: Celebrating Sedan Day in the German Empire," *Tel Aviver Jahrbuch für Deutsche Geschichte*, 26 (1997), 61–74.

[6] Roger Chickering, "'Casting Their Gaze More Broadly': Women's Patriotic Activism in Imperial Germany," *Past and Present*, 118 (1988), 156–185; and Ann Taylor Allen, *Feminism and Motherhood in Germany, 1800–1914* (New Brunswick, NJ: Rutgers, 1991).

[7] The everyday circumstances of military life in Imperial Germany have been relatively neglected: Daniel Kim, *Soldatenleben in Württemberg, 1871–1914* (Paderborn: Schöningh, 2008), is a welcome exception and a model case study. Frank Bucholz, Joe Robinson, and Janet Robinson, *The Great War Dawning. Germany and its Army at the Start of World War* I (Vienna: Verlag Militaria, 2013), pp.197–207, is a good introduction in English.

[8] Peter Stearns, *Lives of Labor: Work in a Maturing Industrial Society* (New York: Holmes and Meier, 1975), remains useful here.

[9] Michael Schmid, *Der Eiserne Kanzler und die Generäle Deutsche Rüstungspolitik in der Ära Bismarck (1871–1890)* (Paderborn: Schöning, 2002).

[10] Holger Herwig, "Germany," in *Decisions for War, 1914–1917*, ed. R. Hamilton and H. Herwig (Cambridge: Cambridge University Press, 2004), pp. 70–91, is a good introduction to a fiendishly complicated subject.

[11] Holger Afflerbach, *Erich von Falkenhayn. Politisches Denken und Militärischen Handeln im Kaiserreich* (Munich: Oldenbourg, 1994), pp. 147–171.

[12] Jack Dukes, "Militarism and Arms Policy Revisited: The Origins of the German Army Law of 1913," in *Another Germany: A Reconsideration of the Imperial Era*, ed. J. Dukes, J. Remak (Boulder, Co.: Westview, 1988), pp. 19–40.

[13] Stig Förster, "Militär und staatsbürgerlich Partizipation. Die Allgemeine Wehrpflicht im Deutschen Kaiserreich, 1871–1914," in *Die Wehrpflicht: Entstehung, Erscheinungsformen und politisch-militärische Wirkung*, ed. R. G. Förster (Berlin: De Gruyter, 1994), pp. 55–70, is a brief overview of the system and its implications.

[14] Stig Förster, "Der deutsche Generalstab und der Illusion des kurzen Krieges," *Militärgeschichtliche Mitteilungen* 54 (1995), 61–93, remains the most economical statement of this familiar thesis.

[15] Cf. Stig Förster, *Vor dem Sprung ins Dunkle. Die Militärische Debatte über den Krieg der Zukunft* (Paderborn: Schöningh, 2015); and Antulio Echevarria, *After Clausewitz. German Military Thinkers before the Great War* (Lawrence, Ks: Kansas University Press, 2000).

[16] Stig Förster, *Der doppelte Militärismus. Die deutsche Heeresrüstungspolitik zwischen Status-Quo-Sicherung und Aggression 1890–1913* (Stuttgart: Steiner, 1985).

[17] Oliver Stein, *Die deutsche Heeresrüstungspolitik 1890–1914* (Paderborn: Schöningh, 2007); and Eric Dorn Brose, *The Kaiser's Army: The Politics of Military Technology during the Machine Age* (New York: Oxford University Press, 2001).

[18] Jehuda Wallach, *The Dogma of the Battle of Annihilation: The Theories of Clausewitz and Schlieffen and their Impact on the German Conduct of Two World Wars* (Westport, Ct.: Greenwood, 1986), remains useful on this point.

[19] The best presentation of this interpretation in English is Isobel Hull, *Absolute Destruction: Military Culture and the Practices of War in Imperial Germany* (Ithaca, NY: Cornell, 2005).

[20] Susanne Kuss, *Deutsches Militär auf koloniale Kriegsschauplatzen. Eskalation von Gewalt zu Beginn des 20. Jahrhunderts* (Berlin: Berlin Links, 2010), blazes a fresh trail on this subject.

[21] Dennis Showalter, "Information Capabilities and Nineteenth Century Military Revolutions," *Journal of Strategic Studies*, 57 (2004), 220–242.

[22] Holger Herwig, "German Intelligence," in *Knowing One's Enemies: Intelligence Assessments Before the Two World Wars*, ed. E. R. May (Princeton: Princeton University Press, 1986), pp. 62–97, is excellent on the subject.

[23] Helmuth von Moltke, *Erinnerungen-Briefe-Dokumente 1877–1916* (Stuttgart: Der Kommende Tag, 1922), p. 19 ff.; and for the refutation, H. von Staabs, *Aufmarsch nach zwei Fronten* (Berlin: Mittler, 1925).

[24] Ralf Raths, *Vom Massensturm zur Stosstrupptaktik. Die deutsche Landstreitkräfte im Spiegel von Dienstvorschriften uns Publiziztik, 1906 bis 1918* (Freiburg: Rombach, 2009), is particularly strong for the prewar era.

[25] Dennis Showalter, "Prussia, Technology, and War: Artillery from 1815 to 1914," in *Men, Machines and War*, ed. R. Haycock, Keith Neilson (Waterloo, Ontario: Wilfred Laurier University Press, 1988), pp. 128–151, surveys the artillery's development.

[26] For the prewar cavalry there is an informative overview in Bucholz, Robinson, and Robinson, *The Great War Dawning*, pp. 233–242. David Dorondo, *Riders of the Apocalypse. German Cavalry and Modern Warfare, 1870–1945* (Annapolis: Naval Institute Press, 2012), is useful for a wider context.

[27] Marco Sigg, *Der Unterführer als Feldherr im Taschenformat. Theorie und Praxis der Auftragstaktik im deutschen Heer 1869 bis 1945* (Paderborn: Schöningh, 2014), is a recent, splendid overview of the subject.

[28] Peter Stearns, *Be a Man: Males in Modern Society* (New York: Holmes & Meier, 1979).

[29] See Raths, *Massensturm*, pp. 29–33.

[30] It is both impossible and pointless to attempt presenting even a sample of the literature on this subject. In that context, Christopher Clark, *The Sleepwalkers. How Europe Went to War in 1914* (New York: Harper Collins, 2012), is as valuable for its reference apparatus as for its content.

[31] The best survey of and guide to this fraught and vexing subject is a conference proceeding: *The Schlieffen Plan. International Perspectives on the German Strategy for World War I*, ed. H. Ehlert, M. Epkenhans, and G. Gross, trans. ed. by D. Zabecki (Lexington: University Press of Kentucky, 2014).

[32] Annika Monbauer, *Helmuth von Moltke and the Origins of the First World War* (Cambridge: Cambridge University Press, 2001), is, however, remarkable for balance and insight.

[33] Michael Stürmer, *Das ruhelose Reich. Deutschland und ihre Nation 1866–1918* (Berlin: Siedler, 1983).

[34] Förster, "Illusion des kurzen Krieges," p. 92.

[35] Herwig, "Germany," p. 187.

[36] Förster, "Illusion des kurzen Krieges," p. 94.

Chapter II: Autumn of Decision

[1] On war fever's myths and realities see especially Jeffrey Verhey, *The Spirit of 1914: Militarism, Myth, and Mobilization in Germany* (Cambridge: Cambridge

University Press, 2000); and the contributions to *August 1914: Ein Volk zieht in den Krieg*, ed. Berliner Gesichtswerkstatt (Berlin: Nischen, 1989).

[2] Paul Plaut, "Psychographie des Kriegers," *Beihefte zur Zeitschrift für Angewandte Psychologie*, 21 (1920), 11 ff.

[3] Roger Chickering, *The Great War and Urban Life in German. Freiburg, 1914–1918* (Cambridge: Cambridge University Press, 2007), pp. 59–72, offers a case study.

[4] Theodor W. Fuchs, "The Readiness and Performance of German Army Reserves in 1914, with Particular Reference to the combat of the XXV Reserve Corps at Lodz, Poland," in HERO Report prepared for the Assistant Secretary of Defense, February 1980, pp. 32–36.

[5] B. Ziemann, "Fahnenflucht im deutschen Heer, 1914–1918," *Militärgeschichtliche Mitteilungen*, 55 (1996), 93–130.

[6] Dennis Showalter, "A Grand Illusion? German Reserves 1815–1914," *Scraping the Barrel. The Military Use of Substandard Manpower 1860–1960*, ed. S. Marble (New York: Fordham University Press, 2012), pp. 28–53.

[7] H. H. Hässler, *General Wilhelm Gröner and the Imperial German Army* (Madison: University of Wisconsin Press, 1962), remains the most accessible work in English. An update is badly needed.

[8] For preparation see Arden Bucholz, *Moltke, Schlieffen, and Prussian War Planning* ((New York: Berg, 1991), pp. 269–312. Implementation is presented in Bucholz, Robinson, and Robinson, pp. 291–295.

[9] For a perceptive summary of the General Staff's structure and dynamic, see *Chief of Staff. The Principal Officers Behind History's Great Commanders*, ed. D. Zabecki (Annapolis: Naval Institute Press, 2008), Vol. I, pp. 5–13.

[10] On this subject cf. two familiar standbys, F. F. Campbell, "The Bavarian Army, 1870–1918: The Constitutional and Structural Relations with the Prussian Military Establishment" (dissertation, Ohio State University, 1972); R. T. Walker, Jr., "Prusso-Württembergian Military Relations in the German Empire, 1870–1918" (dissertation, Ohio State University, 1974); and more recently J. Hoffmann, "Die sächische Armee im Deutschen Reich, 1871 bis 1918," (dissertation, University of Dresden, 2007).

[11] David Stone, *The Kaiser's Army. The German Army in World War One* (London: Conway, 2015), pp.199–236, competently surveys uniform and equipment.

[12] Buchholz, "Die Coca und ihre Anwendung bei Mängel an Nahrungsmittel für die Verpflegung der Truppen ins Feld,"*Jahrbücher für die deutsche Armee und Marine*, 2 (1872), 211–216.

[13] Terence Zuber, *Ten Days in August. The Siege of Liège 1914* (Stroud, History Press, 2014), is provocative and up to date.

[14] R. A. Doughty, "Strategy in 1914: Joffre's Own," *The Journal of Military History*, 67 (2003), 427–454.

[15] Arthur Coumbe, "Reputation of an Army: Foreign Opinion of the Bavarian Army in the Franco-German War: An Illustrative Case Study" (dissertation, University of Michigan, 1988).

[16] The best source for this often-overlooked operation is the translation of the 1929 Bavarian official history, Karl Düringer, *The First Battle of the World War: Alsace-Lorraine*, tr. and ed. by T. Zuber (Stroud: History Press, 2014). Predictably it gives the Bavarians rather the best of it, but is a useful counterweight to the far more numerous Prussocentric analyses.

[17] Holger Herwig presents this comprehensive contretemps in *The Marne 1914. The Opening of World War I and the Battle that Changed the World* (New York: Random House, 2009), p. 91.

[18] Robert C. Doughty, *Pyrrhic Victory. French Strategy and Operations in the Great War* (Harvard: Belknap, 2005), pp. 64–65

[19] The gap has been recently filled by two fine complementary monographs: Terence Zuber, *The Battle of the Frontiers: Ardennes 1914* (Stroud: Tempus 2007): and Simon House, "The Battle of the Ardennes, 22 August 1914" (dissertation, King's College, 2012), soon to be published.

[20] Pierre-Paul Lavauzelle, *L'Hecatombe des generaux* (Paris: Lavauzelle, 1980).

[21] Bucholz and the Robinsons continue their analysis of German cavalry in *Great War Dawning*, pp. 343–365; Joe Robinson, Francis Hendriks, and Janet Robinson offer a case study in *The Last Great Cavalry Charge. The Battle of the Silver Helmets. Haelen 12 August 1914* (Stroud: Fonthill, 2015).

[22] See especially Andre Bach, *Fusilées pour l'exemple* (Paris: Tallandrier, 2003); and *Justice militaire 1915–1916* (Paris: Éditions Vendémiaire, 2013).

[23] John Horne and Alan Kramer, *German Atrocities 1914. A History of Denial* (New Haven: Yale, 2001) is the standard work in any language. Jeff Lipkes, *Rehearsals: The German Army in Belgium, August 1914* (Leuven: Leuven University Press, 2007), presents German behavior as consciously proto-Nazi.

[24] John Röhl, *Wilhelm II: Into the Abyss of War and Exile, 1900–1941*, tr. S. de Belaigue, R. Bridges, 3 vols (Cambridge: Cambridge University Press, 2013), pp. 1084–1134. The final volume of his monumental trilogy is an indispensable supplement to the present work.

[25] Hans-Georg Kampe, *Nachrichtentruppe des Heeres und deutsche Reichspost. Militärisches und staatliches Nachrichtenwesen in Deutschland 1830 bis 1945* (Berlin: Meisser, 1999), pp. 170 ff., establishes 1914's communications context.

[26] Petr Schöller, *Der Fall Löwen und das Weissbuch. Eine Kritische Untersuchung die deutsche Dokumentation über die Vorgänge in Löwen vom 25. bis 28. August 1914* (Köln: Böhlauy, 1958), remains the most detailed critical analysis.

[27] Herwig describes the insouciant rejoicing in *The Marne*, p. 170.

[28] Terence Zuber is at his iconoclastic best on the BEF in *The Mons Myth: A Reassessment of the Battle* (Stroud: History Press, 2010). Adrian Gilbert, *Challenge*

of Battle. The British Army's Baptism of Fire in the First World War (Oxford: Osprey, 2015) is a state-of-the-art counterpoint.

[29] Bucholz, Robinson, and Robinson survey the logistical problems admirably in *Great War Dawning*, 330–343. Cf. Martin von Creveld, *Supplying War. Logistics from Wallenstein to Patton* (Cambridge: Cambridge University Press, 1977), pp. 114–141.

[30] See generally Annika Mombauer, "The Moltke Plan. A Modified Schlieffen Plan with Identical Aims?" in *The Schlieffen Plan*, pp. 43–66.

[31] Herwig, *The Marne 1914*, p. 200 ff. is up to date and persuasive on this prospect and its possibilities. Hermann Gackenholz, *Entscheidung in Lothringen 1914: Der Operationsplan der jüngeren Moltke und seine Durchführung auf dem linken deutschen Heeresflügel* (Berlin: Junker and Dünnhaupt, 1933), is more detailed and less pessimistic.

[32] See Dennis E. Showalter, *Tannenberg: Clash of Empires* (Hamden Ct: Archon, 1991), pp. 293–297.

[33] Herwig, *The Marne 1914*, p. 171

[34] Zuber, *Mons Myth*, p. 268.

[35] Herwig, *The Marne 1914*, pp. 222–223.

[36] Karl Helfferich, *Der Weltkrieg*, vol. 2 (Berlin: Allstein, 1919), p. 18.

[37] Düringer, *First Battle*, p.373.

[38] Herwig, *The Marne, 1914*, p. 246.

[39] The only detailed study of the Hentsch mission, its consequences and ramifications produced before the destruction of the relevant archives is Wilhelm Müller-Löbnitz, *Die Sendung des Oberstleutnants Hentsch am 6–19 September 1914. Auf Grund der Kriegsakten und persönlicher Mitteilungen* (Berlin: Mittler, 1922). Herwig, *The Marne 1914*, pp. 266–285 adds the human dimension. Bradley Meyer, "Operational Art and the German Command System in World War I" (dissertation, Ohio State University, 1988), provides a contextual framework.

[40] Heike Teckenbrock and Bernard Vogt, "Der Zwang Es nicht zu tun," in *Sexualmoral und Zeitgeist im 19. und 20. Jahrhundert*, ed. M. Salewski and A. Bagel-Bohlan (Opladen: Leske and Budrich, 1990), p. 167.

CHAPTER III: REEVALUATING

[1] Holger Afflerbach, *Falkenhayn. Politisches Denken und Militärisschen Handeln im Kaiserreich* (Munich: Oldenbourg, 1994), p. 197.

[2] Alex Watson, "The Identity and Fate of the German Volunteers, 1914–1918," *War in History*, 14 (2005), 44–74, is recent and comprehensive. Cf. also Karl von Unruh, *Langemarck: Legende und Wirklichkeit* (Koblenz: Bernard and Gräfe,

1986); and H. Kopetzky, *In den Tod, Hurra. Deutsche Jugendregimenter im Ersten Weltkrieg* (Cologne: Pahl-Rugensstein, 1981).

[3] Anonymous, *The German Army at Ypres*, ed. J. Sheldon (Barnsley: Pen & Sword, 2010), p. 99.

[4] Kopetzky, *In den Tod*, pp. 83–85.

[5] Robert T. Foley, *German Strategy and the Path to Verdun. Erich von Falkenhayn and the Development of Attrition, 1870–1916* (Cambridge: Cambridge University Press, 2005), pp. 103–104.

[6] Bernd Hüppauf, "Langemarck, Verdun and the Myth of a New Man in Germany after the First World War," *War & Society*, 6 (1988), 70–103.

[7] Ibid., 134–138

[8] Recent and comprehensive is Terri Blom Crocker, *The Christmas Truce. Myth, Memory, and the First World War* (Lexington: University Press of Kentucky, 2015).

[9] *German Soldiers in the Great War. Letters and Eyewitness Accounts*, ed. B. Ulrich and B. Ziemann, tr. C. Brocks (Barnsley: Pen & Sword, 2010), is a useful overview of the subjects discussed.

[10] Michael Neiberg, *Dance of the Furies. Europe and the Outbreak of World War I* (Harvard: Belknap, 2011), demonstrates this shift.

[11] Käthe Kollwitz, *The Diary and Letters of Käthe Kollwitz*, ed. H. Kollwitz (Chicago: Regnerey, 1955), pp. 62–63.

[12] Christoph Nübel, *Durchhalten und Überleben an der Westfront. Raum und Körper im Ersten Weltkrieg* (Paderborn: Schöningh, 2014), presents the human and physical dimensions of German trench systems in the contexts of landscape shaping and space control.

[13] The division's rehabilitation and its immediate results are presented in Sheldon, *German Army at Ypres*, pp. 205–220.

[14] James S. Corum, *The Roots of Blitzkrieg* (Lawrence: University Press of Kansas, 1992), p. 26.

[15] Rudolf Binding, *Aus dem Krieg* (Potsdam: Ruten & Löning, 1940), p. 21

[16] Hew Strachan, "Germany's Global Strategy," in *The First World War. To Arms* (Oxford: Oxford University Press, 2001), pp. 694–814.

[17] Bruce Menning, "War Planning and Initial Operations in the Russian Context," *War Planning. 1914*, ed. H. Herwig, R. Hamilton (Cambridge: Cambridge University Press, 2010), pp. 80–102, is an excellent overview.

[18] Best on this in English is John R. Schindler, *Fall of the Double Eagle. The Battle for Galicia and the Demise of Austria-Hungary* (Lincoln, Neb.: Potomac, 2015).

[19] Afflerbach, *Falkenhayn*, pp. 233–254; Foley, *German Strategy*, pp. 114 *passim*; and, older but more detailed, Karl-Heinz Janssen, *Der Kanzler und der General. Die Führungskriseum Bethmann-Hollweg und Falkenhayn 1914–1916* (Göttingen: Musterschmidt, 1967).

[20] Holger Herwig, *The First World War. Germany and Austria-Hungary, 1914–1918* (London: Arnold, 1997), pp. 130–140.

[21] Alexander Watson, "'Unheard-of Brutality': Russian Atrocities against Civilians in East Prussia, 1914–1915," *The Journal of Modern History*, 86 (2014), 780–825.

[22] Neiberg, *Dance of the Furies, passim.*

[23] Bernd Ulrich, *Die Augenzeugen. Deutsche Feldpostbriefe im Kriegs- und Nachkriegszeit 1914–1933* (Essen: Klartext, 1997).

[24] Benjamin Ziemann, *War Experiences in Rural Germany, 1914–1923*, tr. A. Skinner (Oxford: Berg, 2007), p. 161.

[25] Gerald Feldman, *Army, Industry, and Labor in Germany 1914–1918* (Princeton: Princeton University Press, 1966), pp. 97–116, describes the crisis from an administrative perspective. Chickering, *Great War and Urban Life*, pp. 160–188, gives the consumers' perspective.

[26] Avner Offer, "The Blockade of Germany and the Strategy of Starvation, 1914–1918: An Agency Perspective," in *Great War, Total War. Combat and Mobilization on the Western Front, 1914–1918*, ed. R. Chickering, S. Förster (Cambridge: Cambridge University Press, 2000), p. 177.

[27] Chickering, *Great War and Urban Life*, pp. 188–200, uses Freiburg as an example that seems to have been reasonably typical.

[28] Niall Ferguson, "How (Not) to Pay for the War: Traditional Finance and 'Total' War," in *Great War, Total War*, pp. 409–434, is a predictably perceptive and iconoclastic introduction. Gerald Feldman, *The Great Disorder: Politics, Economics, and Society in the German Inflation, 1914–1924* (New York: Oxford University Press, 1993), remains a sound, if intellectually challenging, analysis of German war financing and its consequences. Winifried Lampe, *Der Bankbetrieb in Krieg und Inflation. Deutsche Grossbanken in den Jahren 1914 bis 1923* (Stuttgart: Steiner, 2012), focuses on one of the focal points.

[29] Robert Whalen, *Bitter Wounds. German Victims of the Great War 1914–1939* (Ithaca: Cornell University Press, 1984), is a solid survey; Deborah Cohen, *The War Come Home. Disabled Veterans in Britain and Germany, 1914–1939* (Berkeley: University of California Press, 2001), offers a comparative dimension.

[30] Heather R. Perry, *Recycling the Disabled. Army, Medicine, and Modernity in WWI Germany* (New York: Manchester University Press, 2015).

[31] Otto Binswanger, *Die seelische Wirkung des Krieges* (Stuttgart: Deutsche Verlag, 1914).

[32] Wolfgang U. Eckart, "'The Most Extensive Experiment that the Imagination Can Conceive:' War, Emotional Stress, and German Medicine 1914–1918," in *Great War, Total War*, 133–149, surveys the subject; Paul Frederick Lerner, *Hysterical Men: War, Psychiatry and the Politics of Trauma in Germany 1890–1939* (Ithaca: Cornell University Press, 2003), is comprehensive.

[33] Feldman, *Army, Industry, and Labor*, p. 45 *passim.*

[34] Richard Bessel, "Mobilizing Germany for War," in *Great War, Total War*, pp. 437–452.

[35] Ernst von Wrisberg, *Heer und Heimat 1914–1918* (Leipzig: Köhler, 1921), pp. 16–17.

[36] Yves Buffetaut, "Le Grignotage, une tactique qui n'en était pas une," *Tranchées, Hors Série*, 2 (December 2011), 5–9, is a perceptive critique.

[37] Foley, *German Strategy*, pp. 157–162.

[38] L. F. Haber, *The Poisonous Cloud. Chemical Warfare in the First World War* (Oxford: Clarendon Press, 1986), by Haber's son, best contextualizes his father's work.

[39] Rudolf Binding, *A Fatalist at War*, tr. I. F. D. Morrow (Boston: Houghton Mifflin, 1929), p. 64.

[40] Albert Palazzo, *Seeking Victory on the Western Front. The British Army and Chemical Warfare in World War I* (Lincoln: University of Nebraska Press, 2000), is an outstanding overview.

[41] Christian Stachelbeck, *Militärische Effektivität im Ersten Weltkrieg. Die 11. Bayerische Infanteriedivision 1915 bis 1918* (Paderborn: Schöningh, 2010), p. 77–78.

[42] Theo Schwarzmüller, *Zwischen Kaiser und "Führer." Generalfeldmarschall August von Mackensen: eine politische Biographie* (Paderborn: Schöningh, 1995), incorporates Mackensen's military career and ability.

[43] R. L. Di Nardo, *Breakthrough: The Gorlice-Tarnow Campaign* (Santa Barbara: Praeger, 2010).

[44] For an overview see Igor Narskij, "Kriegswirklichkeit und Kriegserfahrung russischer Soldaten an der russischen Westfront, 1914/15," in *Die vergessene Front. Der Osten 1914/15. Ereignis, Wirkung, Nachwirkung*, ed. G. Gross (Paderborn: Schöningh, 2006), pp. 249–261.

[45] Joshua Sanborn, *Imperial Apocalypse. The Great War and the Destruction of the Russian Empire* (New York: Oxford University Press, 2014), p. 77.

[46] Jakob Jung, *Max von Gallwitz. General und Politiker.* (Osnabrück: Biblio, 1995).

[47] Cf. Afflerbach, *Falkenhayn*, pp. 294–305; and Volker Ullrich, "Zwischen Verhandlungsfrieden und Erschöpfungskrieg. Die Friedensfrage in der deutschen Reichsleitung Ende 1915', *Geschichte in Wissenschaft und Unterricht*, 37 (1986), 397–419. The quotation is from 403.

[48] Michael Geyer, "German Strategy in the Age of Machine Warfare, 1914–1945," in *Makers of Modern Strategy from Machiavelli to the Nuclear Age*, ed. P. Paret (Princeton: Princeton University Press, 1986), pp. 534 ff.

[49] Keith Neilson, *Strategy and Supply: The Anglo-Russian Alliance, 1914–1917* (London: Allen & Unwin, 1984), remains the best in English on the subject.

[50] Wayne C. Thompson, "The September Program. Reflections on the Evidence," *Central European History*, 11 (1978), 348–354, is a useful introduction.

[51] Richard L. Di Nardo, *Invasion. The Conquest of Serbia, 1915* (Santa Barbara: Praeger, 2015).

[52] Jack Sheldon, *The German Army on Vimy Ridge 1914–1917* (Barnsley: Pen & Sword, 2008), pp. 1–133, combines first-person accounts with a narrative overview. Doughty, *Pyrrhic Victory*, pp.153–292, covers the French side from a command perspective.

[53] Jonathan Krause, *Early Trench Tactics in the French Army: The Second Battle of Artois, May–June 1915* (Farnham: Ashgate, 2013), makes a persuasive case that the French learned more from experience than is generally acknowledged or understood.

[54] Major Kiesel, II/15th Reserve Infantry Regiment, in Jack Sheldon, *The German Army on the Western Front 1915* (Barnsley: Pen & Sword, 2012), pp. 230–231.

[55] *Militärgeschichtliches Forschungsamt, Die Militärluftfahrt bis zum Beginn des Weltkrieges, Technischer Band* (Frankfurt: Mittler, 1966), p. 91.

[56] John H. Morrow, *German Air Power in World War I* (Lincoln: University of Nebraska Press, 1982), is a comprehensive overview. Christian Kehrt, *Moderne Krieger* (Paderborn: Schöningh, 2010), is useful for its presentation of the importance of technical knowledge in the *Luftstreitkräfte*.

[57] Thomas Fegan, *The "Baby Killers:" German Air Raids on Britain in the First World War* (Barnsley: Pen & Sword, 2012).

[58] Elizabeth Greenhalgh, *Victory through Coalition: Britain and France during the First World War* (Cambridge: Cambridge University Press, 2008).

[59] Wachtmeister Franz Brückle, 6th Bavarian Reserve Field Artillery, in Sheldon, *1915*, p. 72.

[60] Quoted in Sheldon, *Vimy Ridge*, p. 85.

[61] Martin Samuels, *Command or Control? Command and Tactics in the British and German Armies, 1888–1918* (London: Cass, 1995), pp. 161–166.

[62] Sheldon, *Vimy Ridge*, p. 48 *passim*.

[63] Ibid., p. 76.

CHAPTER IV: VERDUN AND THE SOMME: END OF AN ARMY

[1] Unteroffizier Nolle, 160th Infantry, Sheldon, *Vimy Ridge*, p. 78.

[2] Bethmann's diary entry of January 7, 1916, in Janssen, *Kanzler und General*, p. 288.

[3] Egmont Zechlin, "Friedensbestrebungen und Revolutionierungsversuche im Ersten Weltkrieg," *Das Parlament*, B, May 15, 1963, 36–40.

[4] Foley, *German Strategy*, pp. 181–193, covers the military aspect; Afflerbach, *Falkenhayn*, pp. 360–403, emphasizes the strategic and policy elements.

[5] Kronprinz Wilhelm, *Meine Erinnerungen aus Deutschlands Heldenkampf* (Berlin: Mittler, 1923), p. 160.

[6] Ulrich Trumpener, "Konstantin Schmidt von Knobelsdorf," *Chief of Staff*, p. 167.

[7] Zabecki, *Chief of Staff*, Vol. I, p. 167.

[8] The body of literature on Verdun almost defies categorization. Ian Ousby, *The Road to Verdun. France, Nationalism and the First World War* (London: Jonathan Cape, 2002) tells the story smoothly. Paul Jankowski, *Verdun: The Longest Battle of the Great War* (New York: Oxford University Press, 2014); and German Werth, *Verdun. Die Schlacht und der Mythos* (Bergisch-Gladbach: Lubbe, 1979), give the respective combatants' perspectives. William F. Buckingham, *Verdun 1916: The Deadliest Battle of the First World War* (Chalford: Amberley, 2016), is operationally focused and state of the art.

[9] David Stone, *The Kaiser's Army. The German Army in World War I* (London: Conway, 2015), pp. 177–181, is a summary overview of the process.

[10] Cf. Raths, *Massensturm*, p. 27 *passim*; and Sigg, *Unterführer als Feldherr*, pp. 177–218.

[11] Friedrich Seeselburg, *Der Stellungskrieg 1914–1918* (Berlin: Mittler, 1926).

[12] Bruce Gudmundsson, *Stormtroop Tactics. Innovation in the German Army, 1914–1918* (Westport, Ct.: Praeger, 1989), pp.45–75, and Hellmuth Gruss, *Aufbau und Verwendung der deutschen Sturmbataillone im Weltkrieg* (Berlin: Junker and Dünnhaupt, 1939), pp. 28–31.

[13] Christina Holstein, *Fort Douaumont*, rev. ed. (Havertown: Pen & Sword, 2002), combines the strengths of a history and a guidebook.

[14] Doughty, *Pyrrhic Victory*, p. 271.

[15] Erich von Falkenhayn, *General Headquarters and its Critical Decisions, 1914–1916* (London: Hutchinson, 1919), p. 235.

[16] See David Zabecki, "German Artillery," in *King of Battle. Artillery in World War I*, ed. S. Marble (Leiden: Brill, 2016), pp. 115–118.

[17] Hans Linnenkohl, *Vom Einzelschuss zur Feuerwalze. Der Wettlauf zwischen Technik und Taktik im Ersten Weltkrieg* (Bonn: Bernard and Gräfe, 1996), pp. 268–274.

[18] Trumpener, "Knobelsdorf," p. 168.

[19] Neil J. Wells, *Verdun: An Integrated Defence* (Uckfield: Naval & Military Press, 2009), p. 102.

[20] Christina Holstein, *Fort Vaux* (Barnsley: Pen & Sword, 2012), does for Vaux what she does for Douaumont.

[21] Foley, *German Strategy*, p. 228.

[22] See generally Bernd Stegemann, *Die deutsche Marinepolitik 1916–1918* (Berlin: Duncker & Humblot, 1970).

[23] Foley, *German Strategy*, pp. 227–228.

[24] Jean-Clause Laparra and Pascal Hesse, *Le Sturmbataillon Rohr, 1916–1918* (Paris: Histoire et Collections, 2010), p. 23 *passim*.

[25] Gudmundsson, *Stormtroop Tactics*, pp. 67–68.

[26] Wells, *Verdun*, p. 102

[27] Pionier Harry Wasserman in Werth, *Verdun*, p. 290.

[28] Gen Adolf Wild von Hohenborn to his wife, August 5, 1916, *Wild von Hohenborn. Briefe und Tagesaufzeichnungen des preussischen Kriegsminister und Gruppenführer im Weltkrieg*, ed. H. Reicholdt, G. Granier (Boppard: Boldt, 1986), p. 79.

[29] Wells, *Verdun*, p. 102.

[30] P. C. Ettinghoffer, *Verdun, Das Grosse Gericht*, 5th edn (Wiesbaden: Limes, 1985), pp. 190–191.

[31] Ibid., p. 156.

[32] Ralph Peters, *Cain at Gettysburg* (New York: Forge, 2012).

[33] Franz Schauwecker, *Das Frontbuch. Der deutsche Seele im Weltkrieg*. 6th edn (Halle: Dieckmann, 1927), pp. 182 ff.

[34] Alois Peter, *Zeitliches und Ewiges aus dem Weltkrieg* (Passau: Passavia, 1938), p. 155.

[35] Karl Eberhardt, *Schlachtfeld Verdun. Europas Trauma*, ed. G. Werth (Berlin: Brandenburgisches Verlaghaus, 1994), p. 73.

[36] Fritz Günther, *Verdun ruft! Eine Reise in das Kampfgebiet um Verdun* (Saarbrücken: Saarbrücker Drurckerei und Verlag, 1935), pp. 12, 16.

[37] Christoph Gradmann, "Medical Service," *Brill's Encyclopedia of the First World War*, 2 vols, ed. G. Hirschfeld, G. Krumeich, O. Renz , tr. supervised J. Corum (Leiden: Brill, 2012), vol. II, pp. 716–717.

[38] Joachim Radkau, *Das Zeitaletr der Nervosität. Deutschland zwischen Bismarck und Hitler* (Munich: Hanser, 1998).

[39] Werner Beumelberg, *Douaumont* (Oldenburg: Stalling, 1926), p. 165.

[40] Erwin Zindler, *Auf Biegen und Brechen* (Leipzig: Köhler, 1929), p. 188.

[41] Kirsten Meyer, *Bildung* (Berlin: de Gruyter, 2011), is recent and comprehensive.

[42] Fritz von Unruh, *Opfergang* (Berlin: Erich Reiss Verlag, 1919), pp. 171, 198.

[43] Harry Turtledove, "Ils ne passeront pas," in *Armageddon*, ed. D. Drake, B. Mossman (New York: Baen, 1988), pp. 9–41.

[44] Ralph J. Whitehead, *The Other Side of the Wire*, Vol. I, *With the German XIV Reserve Corps on the Somme, September 1914–June 1916* (Solihull: Helion, 2009), is exhaustive on the German preparations.

[45] Sanders Marble, *"The Infantry Cannot Do with a Gun Less." The Place of the Artillery in the British Expeditionary Force, 1914–1918* (New York: Columbia, 2003), pp. 72–84, is a solid introduction.

[46] Lance Corporal James Glenn, Paul Kendall, *Somme 1916. Success and Failure on the First Day of the Somme* (Barnsley: Frontline, 2015), p. 53.

[47] Robert T. Foley, "A Case Study in Horizontal Military Innovation: The German Army, 1916–1918," *The Journal of Strategic Studies*, 35 (2012), 807.

[48] Thomas Bradbeer, *Battle for Air Supremacy over the Somme, 1 June–30 November 1916* (SI: Biblioscholar, 2012), goes beyond cockpit perspectives.

[49] Evening Report, Second Army, June 28, 1916, Jack Sheldon, *The German Army on the Somme 1914–1916* (Barnsley: Pen & Sword, 2005), p. 128.

[50] Lyn Macdonald, *Somme* (London: Joseph, 1983), p. 71.

[51] Robin Prior and Trevor Wilson, *The Somme* (New Haven: Yale, 2006), pp. 71–118.

[52] William Philpott, *Three Armies on the Somme. The First Battle of the Twentieth Century* (New York: Knopf, 2010), p. 180 *passim*.

[53] Fritz von Lossberg, *Meine Tätigkeit im Weltkrieg* (Berlin: Mittler, 1939), p. 126 *passim*.

[54] Ibid., pp. 221 ff.

[55] Second Army Order (Secret), July 3, 1916, Sheldon, *Somme*, p. 179.

[56] Sir Tom Bridges, *Alarms and Excursions* (London: Longmans Green, 1938), pp. 156–159.

[57] Walter Blöm, in Christopher Duffy, *Through German Eyes: The British and the Somme 1916* (London: Weidenfeld & Nicholson, 2006), p. 193.

[58] Col. Paul von Muhlmann, historian Lehr Infantry Regiment, Sheldon, *Somme*, pp. 186–187.

[59] Foley, "Horizontal Innovation," pp. 808–809.

[60] Ian S. Uys, *Delville Wood* (Rensburg: Uys Publishers, 1983), p. 205.

[61] Army Group Gallwitz, July 30, 1916, Sheldon, *Somme*, p. 222.

[62] Clough Williams-Ellis, Annabel Williams-Ellis, *The Tank Corps* (London, Country Life, 1919), p. 64.

[63] Captain von Steinacker, September 12, 1916, Sheldon, *Somme*, p. 289.

[64] G. S. I. Inglis, *The Kensington Battalion: Never Lost a Yard of Trench* (Barnsley: Pen & Sword, 2010), p. 157.

[65] Ernst Jünger remains the archetype. See Thomas R. Pohrkramer, "Die Verzauberung der Schlange. Krieg, Technik und Zivilizationskritik beim frühen Ernst Jünger," *Der Erste Weltkrieg. Wirkung, Wahrnehmung Analyse,* ed. W. Michalka (Munich: Piper, 1994), pp. 849–874.

[66] Lieutenant Wolfgang von Vormann, 26th Infantry, Sheldon, *Somme*, p. 222.

CHAPTER V: RECONFIGURATIONS

[1] Timothy C. Dowling, *The Brusilov Offensive* (Bloomington: Indiana University Press, 2008)

[2] Afflerbach, *Falkenhayn*, pp. 437–450, has the often petty, often sordid, details.

[3] Cf. Glen E. Torrey, *The Romanian Battlefield in World War I* (Lawrence: University Press of Kansas, 2011; and Michael B. Barrett, *Prelude to Blitzkrieg. The 1916 Austro-German Campaign in Rumania* (Bloomington: Indiana University Press, 2013).

[4] For a clear and acerbic presentation of this argument one can still do no better than Martin Kitchen, *The Silent Dictatorship: The Politics of the German High Command 1916–1918* (New York: Holmes & Meier, 1976).

[5] See for example Alexander Watson, *Ring of Steel. Germany and Austria–Hungary in World War I* (London: Penguin, 2015). The subtitle is *The People's War*; the text presents that war as waged in good part by default at higher levels.

[6] Manfred von Nebelin, *Ludendorff. Diktator im Ersten Weltkrieg* (Munich: Siedler Verlag, 2011) p. 231.

[7] The best combination of doctrinal development and the accompanying human dynamic is Timothy Lupfer, "The Dynamics of Doctrine. The Changes in German Tactical Doctrine during the First World War," Leavenworth Papers (Fort Leavenworth, US Army Command and Staff College, 1981).

[8] David R. Fine, *Jewish Integration in the German Army in the First World War* (Boston: De Gruyter, 2012), p. 95.

[9] Cf. Fine, *passim*; and more generally Michael Berger, *Eiserne Kreuz und Davidsstern. Die Geschichten Jüdischer Soldaten in Deutschen Armeen* (Berlin: Trafo, 2006) for the details.

[10] Peter C. Applebaum, *Loyal Sons: Jews in the German Army in the Great War* (Edgware: Valentine Mitchell, 2014), presents an alternate picture of systematic, institutionalized discrimination that could reach a level of persecution.

[11] Werner Angress, "The German Army's 'Judenzählung' of 1916. Genesis–Consequences–Significance," *Leo Baeck Institute Yearbook*, 23 (1978), 117–135; and the more detailed Jacob Rosenthal, *"Die Ehre des jüdischen Soldaten." Die Judenzählung in Ersten Weltkrieg und ihre Folgen* (Frankfurt: Campus, 2007).

[12] Belinda Davis, *Home Fires Burning: Food, Politics, and Everyday Life in World War I Berlin* (Chapel Hill: University of North Carolina Press, 2000), is vivid for the dynamics from below.

[13] Ulrich and Ziemann, *German Soldiers in the Great War*, p. 115.

[14] Feldman, *Army, Industry, and Labor*, p. 95.

[15] A useful summary overview is T. Hunt Tooley, "The Hindenburg Program of 1916: A Central Experiment in Wartime Planning," *Quarterly Journal of Austrian Economics*, 2 (1999).

[16] Feldman, *Army, Industry and Labor*, pp. 149–252. Cf. Robert B. Arneson, *Total Warfare and Compulsory Labor: A Study of the Military–Industrial Complex in Germany during World War I* (The Hague: Nijhoff, 1964).

[17] Watson, *Ring of Steel*, pp. 384–394; Jens Thiel, *"Menschenbassin Belgien:"*
Anwerbung, Deportation und Zwangsarbeit im Ersten Weltkrieg
(Essen: Klartext, 1997).

[18] Arneson, *Total Warfare and Compulsory Labor*. Günther Mai, *Kriegswirtschaft und*
Arbeiterbewegung in Württemberg 1914–1918 (Stuttgard: Klein-Cotta, 1983), is
regionally focused but thorough and perceptive.

[19] Feldman, *Army, Industry and Labor*, pp. 253–282.

[20] Geyer, "Machine Warfare", pp. 539 ff.

[21] For the thinking behind the Siegfried/Hindenburg Line's construction, and its
implementation, see Michael Geyer, "Retreat and Destruction," in Irina Remz,
Gerd Krumeich and Gerhard Hirschfeld (eds) *Scorched Earth: The Germans on the*
Somme (Barnsley: Pen & Sword, 2009), pp. 141–178.

[22] Nebelin, *Ludendorff*, p. 232.

[23] Larry Zuckerman, *The Rape of Belgium: The Untold Story of World War I* (New York:
New York University Press, 2004).

[24] See particularly Heather Jones, *Violence against Prisoners of War in the First World*
War (Cambridge: Cambridge University Press, 2013), pp. 127–222 *passim*.

[25] Helen McPhail, *The Long Silence: Civilian Life under the German Occupation of*
Northern France, 1914–1918 (London: I. B. Tauris, 2001), offers a far more
critical perspective.

[26] Geyer, "Retreat and Destruction," pp. 155–147. The quotation is from p. 149.

[27] The best overview of German tank development and employment is Ralf Raths,
"From the *Bremerwagen* to the A7V: German Tank Production and Armoured
Warfare, 1916–1918," in *Genesis, Employment, Aftermath. First World War Tanks*
and the New Warfare, 1900–1945, ed. A. Searle (Solihull: Helion, 2014),
pp. 80–107. Alexander Fasse, "Im Zeichen des 'Tankdrachen'. Die Kriegsführung
an der Westfront 1916–1918 im Spannungsverhältnis zwuischen Einsatz eines
neuartigen Kriegsmittels der Alliierten und deutschen Bemühungen um seine
Bekämpfung" (dissertation, Humboldt University, 2007) (available online) is
impressively definitive for the operational aspect.

[28] On this subject see particularly—and persuasively—Feldman, *Army, Industry, and*
Labor, p. 407 *passim*. Kitchen, *Silent Dictatorship*, describes it as "halfway between
the Bonapartism of Bismarck and the fascist dictatorship of Hitler" (p. 277).

[29] "Maschinengewehr 08/15" in Robert Bruce, *Machine Guns of World War I*
(London: Windrow & Green, 1997), pp. 33–45 emphasizes what it took to move
and shoot the gun under field conditions.

[30] Raths, *Massensturm*, pp. 184–189, provides the context.

[31] Mary R. Habeck, "Technology in the First World War: The View From Below," in
The Great War and the Twentieth Century, ed. J. Winter, G. Parker, M. Habeck
(New Haven: Yale University Press, 2000), pp. 99–129.

[32] Cf. Friedrich Altrichter, *Die seelischen Kräfte des Deutschen Heeres im Frieden und im Weltkrieg* (Berlin: Mittler, 1933).

[33] See definitively Alexander Watson's comparative analysis, *Enduring the Great War. Combat, Morale, and Endurance in the German and British Armies, 1914–1918* (Cambridge: Cambridge University Press, 2008).

[34] Cf. *inter alia* Thomas Kühne, *Belonging and Genocide. Hitler's Community 1918–1945* (New Haven: Yale University Press, 2010), pp. 15–28; and Bernd Ulrich, "Die umkämpfte Erinnerung. Überlegung zur Wahrnehmung des Ersten Weltkrieges in der Weimarer Republik," in *Kriegsende 1918. Ereignis, Wirkung, Nachwirkung*, ed. J. Düppler, G. Gross (Munich: Oldenbourg, 1999), pp. 367–375.

[35] See the excellent presentation of Christopher T. Goodwin, "Varied Nationalisms and Prussian Masculinity: Foundational Roles for the Stabilization of Gender Roles during the Wars of Liberation," (masters thesis, Norwich University, 2016).

[36] Ralph Peters, *Valley of the Shadow* (New York: Forge, 2015), p. 119.

[37] Watson, *Enduring the Great War*, pp. 67–68.

[38] Showalter, "German Soldiers," pp. 386. Cf. Stachelbeck, *Militärische Effektivität*, pp. 322–349; and Watson, *Enduring the Great War*, pp. 140–184.

[39] Cf. Martin Samuels, *Doctrine and Dogma. German and British Infantry Tactics in the First World War* (Westport, Ct: Greenwood, 1992), pp. 11–56; and Gudmundsson, *Stormtroop Tactics*, pp. 77–91.

[40] Geyer, "Retreat and Destruction," 144–145; Philpott, *Three Armies*, pp. 425–427.

[41] For the details see Doughty, *Pyrrhic Victory*, pp. 323–344.

[42] Jack Sheldon and Nigel Cave, *The Battle for Vimy Ridge 1917* (Barnsley: Pen & Sword, 2007) is another Pen & Sword publication combining the features of history and guidebook in an overview presented from both sides' perspectives.

[43] Summarized in Rupprecht's report of April 21, 1917, cited in Jack Sheldon, *The German Army in the Spring Offensives 1917. Arras, Aisne & Champagne* (Barnsley: Pen & Sword, 2015), p. 77.

[44] Lossberg, *Tätigkeit im Weltkrieg*, pp. 280–284.

[45] Paul Kendall, *Bullecourt 1917. Breaching the Hindenburg Line* (Stroud: History Press, 2010).

[46] Peter Hart, *Bloody April: Slaughter in the Skies over Arras, 1917* (London: Weidenfeld & Nicholson, 2005) tells the story from the RFC's perspective. Peter Kilduff, *The Red Baron Combat Wing: Jagdgeschwader Richthofen in Battle* (London: Arms & Armour, 1997), pp. 74 ff., covers the German fighters.

[47] Quoted in Kendall, *Bullecourt*, p. 97.

[48] Best summaries in English on the Nivelle offensive are Doughty, *Pyrrhic Victory*, pp. 344–335; and Elizabeth Greenhalgh, *The French Army and the First World War* (Cambridge: Cambridge University Press, 2014), pp. 182–200. David Murphy,

Breaking Point of the French Army: The Nivelle Offensive of 1917 (Barnsley: Pen & Sword, 2015), is a solid overview.

[49] Lt Col Vogel, III/25th Bavarian Reserve Regiment, in Sheldon, *Spring Offensive*, p. 129.

[50] For the fate of the French tanks see Tim Gale, *The French Army's Tank Force and Armoured Warfare in the First World War: The Artillerie Special* (Burlington, Vt: Ashgate, 2013), Chapter 2 *passim*.

[51] For the mutinies' matrices and their consequences see Leonard V. Smith, *Between Mutiny and Obedience: The French Fifth Infantry Division in World War I* (Princeton: Princeton University Press, 1994).

[52] Oberleutnant Scheele, II/Grenadier Regiment 4, in Jack Sheldon, *The German Army at Passchendaele* (Barnsley: Pen & Sword, 2007), p. 4.

[53] Ian Passingham, *Pillars of Fire: The Battle of Messines Ridge, June 1917* (Stroud: Sutton, 1998).

[54] Lossberg, *Tätigkeit im Weltkrieg*, pp. 293–295.

[55] Rupprecht, diary entry July 11, 1917, in Sheldon, *Passchendaele*, p. 91.

[56] John Hussey, "The Flanders Battleground and the Weather in 1917," in *Passchendaele in Perspective: The Third Battle of Ypres*, ed. P. Liddle (London: Leo Cooper, 1997), pp. 140–158. The quotation is from p. 149.

[57] Heinz Hagenlücke, "The German High Command," Liddle, *Passchendaele*, p. 52.

[58] Lt Josef Behm, 10/62, Sheldon, *Passchendaele*, p. 99.

[59] Lt Walsermann, 6/Reserve Infantry Regiment 92, Sheldon, *Passchendaele*, p. 176.

[60] Group Ypres Order of the Day, September 23; and Army Group Crown Prince Rupprecht, Daily Report, September 20, in Sheldon, *Passchendaele*, pp. 164–165.

[61] Fourth Army Operations Order, September 30, Sheldon, *Passchendaele*, p. 185.

[62] Reserve Lieutenant Groth, 12/77, Sheldon, *Passchendaele*, p. 199.

[63] Unteroffizier Paul Stolz, 4/Reserve Infantry Regiment 92, Sheldon, *Passchendaele*, p. 203.

[64] Sheldon, *Passchendaele*, p. 283.

[65] Vizefeldwebel Alfred Kleysrüber, 12/Reserve Infantry Regiment 223, in Sheldon, *Passchendaele*, p. 215.

[66] Diary entry, October 13, Sheldon, *Passchendaele*, p. 233.

[67] Quoted in Sheldon, *Passchendaele*, p. 251.

[68] Regimental Medical Officer, Infantry Regiment 132. Quoted in Sheldon, *Passchendaele*, p. 290.

[69] Entry of November 7, quoted in Stachelbeck, *Militärische Effektivität*, p. 223.

[70] Headquarters, IX Reserve Corps, November 20, Sheldon, *Passchendaele*, p. 309

[71] Yves Buffetaut, "La bataille de la Malmaison," and Bruni Jurkewitz, "Les chars a la Malmaison," *Tranchées, Hors Série*, 1 (June 2011), 47–52, 53–68.

[72] Williamson Murray, "Thoughts on Grand Strategy," in *The Shaping of Grand Strategy: Policy, Diplomacy and War*, ed. W. Murray, R. H. Sinnreich, R. Lacey (Cambridge: Cambridge University Press, 2011), pp. 1–33.

[73] As by the present author in *Militärgeschichtliche Mitteilungen*, 48 (1990), 65–102.

[74] Bernd Stegemann, *Die deutsche Marinepolitik, 1916–1918* (Berlin: Duncker & Humblot, 1970), covers the big picture.

[75] Dennis Showalter, "Conquest, Occupation, Exploitation: Imperial Germany and Occupied Russia," presented at the conference "Russia and the First World War," National Research University, Moscow, June 2014.

[76] Cf. Eric Lohr, *Nationalizing the Russian Empire. The Campaign against Enemy Aliens during World War I* (Cambridge, MA: Harvard University Press, 2003); Daniel Graf, "The Reign of the Generals: Military Government in Western Russia, 1914–1915" (dissertation, University of Nebraska, 1972); and Peter Gatrell, *A Whole Empire Walking: Refugees in Russia during World War I* (Bloomington: Indiana University Press, 1999), pp. 16–23.

[77] Jesse Kaufman, *Elusive Alliance. The German Occupation of Poland in World War I* (Cambridge: Harvard University Press, 2015), is comprehensive and persuasive.

[78] Cf. Aba Strazhas, *Deutsche Ostpolitik im Ersten Weltkrieg: Der Fall Ober Ost, 1915–1917* (Wiesbaden: Hamassowitz, 1993); Vejas Gabriel Liulevicius, *War Land on the Eastern Front: Culture, National Identity, and German Occupation in World War I* (Cambridge: Cambridge University Press, 2000); and *The German Myth of the East, 1800 to the Present* (Oxford: Oxford University Press, 2009); and Eberhad Demm, "Das deutsche Besatzungsregime in Littauen im Ersten Weltkrieg—Generalprobe für Hitlers Ostfeldzug und Versuchslabor des totalitären Staates," in *Ostpolitik und Propaganda im Ersten Weltkrieg*, ed. E. Demm (Frankfurt: Lang, 2003), pp. 329–339.

[79] Arnold Zweig, *Das ostjüdische Antlitz* (Berlin: Welt Verlag 1920); Victor Klemperer, *Curriculum Vitae. Erinnerungen, 1881–1918*, Vol. II (Berlin: Taschenbuch, 1996), p. 684, 687. The best general treatment of this subject is Steven E. Aschheim, *Brothers and Strangers: The East European Jew in German and German Jewish Consciousness, 1800–1923* (Madison: University of Wisconsin Press, 1982), pp. 143 ff.

[80] As in Julian Wendling, *Epidemics and Genocide in Eastern Europe, 1890–1945* (Oxford: Oxford University Press, 2000), pp. 90 ff.

[81] Alfred Cornebise, *Typhus and Doughboys: The American Polish Typhus Relief Expedition, 1919–1921* (Newark, NJ: University of Delaware Press, 1982), shows there were no significant differences between authoritarian German and democratic American approaches to the disease.

[82] See particularly Christian Westerhoff's pathbreaking *Zwangsarbeit im Ersten Weltkrieg. Deutsche Arbeitskräftepolitik im besetzten Poland und Litauem 1914–1918* (Paderborn: Schöningh, 2012).

[83] On this subject generally see Jeffrey K. Wilson, "Environmental Chauvinism in the Prussian East: Forestry as a Civilizing Mission on the Eastern Frontier, 1871– 1914," *Central European History*, 41 (2008), 27–70.

[84] Stone, *Russian Army in the Great War*, pp. 272–292, is an up-to-date overview. Cf. Louise Erwin Heenan, *Russian Democracy's Fatal Blunder: The Summer Offensive of 1917* (New York: Praeger, 1987); and Tsuyoshi Hasegawa, *The February Revolution: Petrograd 1917* (Seattle: University of Washington Press, 1981).

[85] Still a standard here is John W. Wheeler-Bennett, *Brest-Litovsk, the Forgotten Peace, March 1918* (London: Macmillan, 1938). A solid and more up-to-date counterpoint is Stephen M. Horak, *The First Treaty of World War I: Ukraine's Treaty with the Central Powers of February 9, 1918* (Boulder, Co: East European Monographs, 1988).

[86] Cf. Holger H. Herwig, "Tunes of Glory at the Twilight Stage: The Bad Homburg Crown Council and the Evolution of German Statecraft, 1917/18," *German Studies Review*, 6 (1983), 53–63; and Winfried Baumgart, *Deutsche Ostpolitik 1918* (Vienna and Munich: Oldenbourg, 1966).

[87] Feldman, *Army, Industry, and Labor*, p. 336 passim.

[88] Still the most detailed and the most useful is Wolfgang Steglich, *Die Friedenspolitik der Mittelmächte, 1917–1918*, 2 vols (Wiesbaden: Steiner, 1964).

[89] For the Riga operation cf. James S. Corum, "How to Prepare for a Battle," MHQ, Autumn, 2014, 52–63; Gudmundsson, *Stormtroop Tactics*, pp. 114–121; and from the Russian perspective Stone, *Russian Army in the Great War*, pp. 292–297.

[90] David T. Zabecki, *Steel Wind. Colonel Georg Bruchmüller and the Birth of Modern Artillery* (Westport, Ct: Greenwood, 1994), p. 14.

[91] J. B. A. Bailey, *Field Artillery and Fire Power* (Annapolis: Naval Institute Press, 2004), p. 255.

[92] Zabecki, *Steel Wind*, pp. 27–30.

[93] Lazlo M. Alfoldi, "The Hutier Legend," *Parameters*, 5 (1976), 69–74.

[94] Corum, "How to Prepare," 63. Cf. Richard L. Di Nardo, "Huns with Web-Feet: Operation *Albion* 1917," *War in History*, 12 (2005), 396–417.

CHAPTER VI: CLIMAX AND DENOUEMENT

[1] The best overview of Caporetto in English is Mario Morselli, *Caporetto 1917: Victory or Defeat?* (Portland: Cass, 2001). R. and Eileen Winks, *Rommel and Caporetto* (Barnsley: Leo Cooper, 2001), focuses on the German role. For storm troop specifics see Gudmundsson, *Stormtroop Tactics*, pp. 127–137; and Friedrich Müller, *Brandenburgisch Jäger-Bataillon Nr. 3* (Oldenburg: Stalling, n.d.), pp. 76–84.

[2] Bryn Hammond, *Cambrai 1917: The Myth of the First Great Tank Battle* (London: Weidenfeld & Nicholson, 2008), is good for the British planning and the initial assault; "Practical Considerations in British Tank Operations on the Western Front, 1916–1918," in *Genesis, Employment, Aftermath*, pp. 31–56, analyzes the learning curve.

[3] Lieutenant A. Saucke, 6/Infantry Regiment 84, Jack Sheldon, *The German Army at Cambrai* (Barnsley: Pen & Sword, 2009), p. 51.

[4] Reserve Infantry Regiment 27, cited in Sheldon, *Cambrai*, p. 68.

[5] Sheldon, *Cambrai*, pp. 37–39.

[6] Diary entry, September 20, cited in Sheldon, *Cambrai*, p. 131

[7] General Otto von Moser, *Feldzugserinerungen als Brigade-, Divisionskommandeur, und als Kommandierer General*, 3rd edn rev. (Stuttgart: Belser, 1928), p. 314.

[8] Diary entry, September 23, cited in Sheldon, *Cambrai*, pp. 190–191.

[9] Orders, Group Caudry, November 28, cited in Sheldon, *Cambrai*, p. 212.

[10] Lieutenant von der Goltz, Field Artillery Regiment Nr 14, Sheldon, *Cambrai*, pp. 227–228.

[11] Diary entries, November 30, cited in Sheldon, *Cambrai*, p. 269.

[12] For this episode see J. P. Harris, *Douglas Haig and the First World War* (Cambridge: Cambridge University Press, 2008), pp. 409–421.

[13] Feldunterarzt Schweizer, III/Fusilier Regiment Nr 40, Sheldon, *Cambrai*, p. 247.

[14] See the reports of Army Group Rupprecht for December 4 and 12 in Sheldon, *Cambrai*, pp. 306–311.

[15] General der Kavallerie Georg von der Marwitz, cited in Sheldon, *Cambrai*, p. 304.

[16] Raths, "German Tank Production and Armoured Warfare," 94–95.

[17] Rick Duiven and Dan-San Abbott, *Schlachtflieger: Germany and the Art of Air-Ground Support, 1916–1918* (Afglen, PA: Schiffer, 2006).

[18] Roger Chickering, "Strategy, politics, and the search for a negotiated peace. The German Case, 1914–1918," in *The Purpose of the First World War. War Aims and Military Strategies*, ed. Holger Afflerbach (Berlin: De Gruyter Oldenbourg, 2015), pp. 112–114.

[19] Niall Ferguson, *The Pity of War* (London: Allen Lane, 1998), pp. 296 *passim*.

[20] Cf. Hermann Gauer, *Von Bauerntum, Bürgtertum, und Arbeitertum in der Armee* (Heidelberg: Schulze, 1930) and Richard Bessel, *Germany after the First World War* (Oxford: Oxford University Press, 1993), p. 8 *passim*.

[21] See the overview in David T. Zabecki, *The German 1918 Offensives. A Case Study in the Operational Art of War* (New York: Routledge, 2006), pp. 83–90.

[22] G. Fong, "The Movement of German Divisions to the Western Front, 1917–1919," *War in History*, 7 (2000), 225–235.

[23] Cf. for background Hew Strachan, "The Morale of the German Army 1917–18," in *Facing Armageddon. The First World War Experienced*, ed. H. Cecil, P. H. Liddle

(London: Leo Cooper, 1996), pp. 383–397; and Benjamin Ziemann, "Enttäusched Erwartung und kollektive Erschöpfung. Die deutschen Soldaten an der Westfront auf dem Weg zur Revolution," *Kriegsende 1918*, pp. 165–182.

[24] Martin Samuels, *Command or Control? Command, Training, and Tactics in the British and German Armies, 1888–1918* (London: Frank Cass, 1995), p. 257.

[25] Steven R. Welch, "Military Justice, 1914–1918," *International Encyclopedia of the First World War* (online) is an excellent comparative overview. Christoph Jahr, *Gewöhnliche Soldaten: Desertion und Deserteure im deutschen und britischen Heer 1914–1918* (Göttingen: Vandenhoeck & Ruprecht, 1998), is a specialized case study.

[26] The best overview is Watson, *Enduring the Great War*, 114–139. Cf. Heiger Ostertag, *Bildung, Ausbildung und Erziwhungdes Offizierkorps des deutschen Kaiserreiches 1871–1918* (Frankfurt: Lang, 1990); and Wolfgang Kruse, "Krieg und Klassenheer. Zur Revolutionierung der deutschen Armee im Ersten Weltkrieg," *Geschichte und Gesellschaft*, 22 (1996), 530–561.

[27] Kriegsministerium, *Felddienst-Ordnung* (Berlin: Mittler, 1908), pp. 9–10.

[28] See generally Martin Hobohm, "Soziale Heeresmisstände im Ersten Weltkrieg und im Reichswehr," in *Menschenführung im Heer*, ed. J. C. Allmayer-Beck (Herford: Mittler, 1982), pp. 113–138; and Hermann Kantorowicz, *Der Offiziershass im deutschen Heer* (Freiburg: Bielefelds, 1919).

[29] Watson, *Enduring the Great War*, p.129.

[30] Alfred Stengler, *Der letzte deutsche Angriff, Reims 1918, Schlachten des Weltkrieges*, 34 (Oldenburg: Stalling, 1930), p. 7.

[31] Cf. Wilhelm Deist, "Le Moral des troupes allemandes sur le front occidental la fin d'année 1916," in *Guerre et Culture, 1914–1918*, ed. J. Becker *et al* (Paris: Colin, 1994), pp. 91–102.

[32] Heinz Russe, in Werth, *Verdun*, p. 185.

[33] For a detailed analysis see Zabecki, *1918 Offensives*, pp. 97–112.

[34] Cf. Rupprecht, *Mein Kriegstagebuch*, ed. E. von Frauenholz, vol. II (Berlin: Deutscher Nationalverlag, 1929), p. 372; and Zabecki, *1918 Offensives*, p. 109.

[35] Jehuda Wallach, *Das Dogma der Vernichtungsschlacht* (Munich: Taschenbuch, 1970).

[36] Robert T. Foley, "Breaking Through: The German Concept of Battle in 1918," www.academia.edu

[37] Rupprecht, *Kriegstagebuch*, vol. II, p. 307.

[38] Hew Strachan, "Ausbildung, Kampfgeist und die zwei Weltkriege," in *Erster Weltkrieg, Zweiter Weltkrieg. Ein Vergleich*, ed. B. Thoss, H-E. Volkmann (Paderborn: Schöningh, 2002), pp. 276–278, makes the point that the retraining and reequipping were intended at least as much to restore morale as improve fighting power.

[39] Oberste Heeresleitung, "Der Angriff im Stellungskrieg," Erich Ludendorff, *Urkunden der Obersten Heeresleitung über ihre Tätigkeit, 1916–1918* (Berlin: Mittler, 1921), pp. 641–666.

[40] Alfoldi, "Hutier Legend," p. 73.

[41] Cf. Gudmundsson, *Stormtroop Tactics*, p. 145 *passim*; *Jäger Bn 3*, pp. 91–93.

[42] Zabecki, *1918 Offensives*, p. 125 *passim*, comprehensively and clearly surveys the German preparations at pp. 30–132.

[43] Among a literal library of relevant works, Greg van Wyngarden, *"Richthofen's Circus:" Jagdgeschwader Nr.1* (Osprey: Oxford, 2004), can be recommended as a reliable introduction.

[44] Zabecki, *Steel Wind*, pp. 63–78, is detailed, yet comprehensible to non-mathematicians.

[45] E. R. Hooton, *War Over the Trenches. Air Power and the Western Front Campaigns 1916–1918* (Hersham: Midland Publishing, 2009), p. 212.

[46] Samuels, *Command or Control*, pp. 198–229, describes the genesis of the "blob" defense.

[47] Martin Middlebrook, *The Kaiser's Battle* (London: Penguin, 1978), is a mine of examples reconstructed from interviews and war diaries.

[48] Holger Afflerbach, "Kronprinz Rupprecht von Bayern im Ersten Weltkrieg," *Militärgeschichtliche Zeitschrift*, 75 (2016), 21–54, is concise, perceptive, and persuasive. Crown Prince William awaits a counterpoint— though Jehuda Wallach notes that Ludendorff was at least considering forcing the kaiser to abdicate in favor of his son—who in that case would need all the warrior credit he could acquire (*Vernichtungsschlacht*, p. 190).

[49] For statistics on the manpower crisis generally see Herwig, *First World War*, pp. 422.

[50] Rupprecht, *Kriegstagebuch*, vol. II, pp. 402–403.

[51] Rupprecht, *Kriegstagebuch*, vol. II, p. 372.

[52] Lossberg, *Tätigkeit*, p. 321.

[53] Thaer, *Generalstabsdienst*, pp. 188, 196–197.

[54] Zabecki, *1918 Offensives*, pp. 311 ff.

[55] See Laparra and Hesse, *Sturmbataillon Rohr*, pp. 80–128.

[56] H. Oliver, "German Defeat in World War I, Influenza and Postwar Memory," in *Germany 1916–23. A Revolution in Context*, ed. K. Weinhauer, Anthony McElligot, Kirsten Hansohn (Bielefeld: Transcript, 2015), pp. 151–179.

[57] Stephen Badsey, *Doctrine and Reform in the British Cavalry 1880–1918* (Aldershot: Ashgate, 2008), p. 290 *passim*.

[58] For the eventual, reasonably successful, efforts to distribute captured resources fairly see Martin Kitchen, *The German Offensives of 1918* (Stroud: Tempus, 2001), p. 141.

[59] Zabecki, *Steel Wind*, p. 79.

[60] David Blanchard, *Aisne 1918* (Barnsley: Pen & Sword, 2015), is another of the combinations of history and guidebook published by this press.

[61] Cf. Edward Lengel, *Thunder and Flames. Americans in the Crucible of Combat, 1917–1918* (Lawrence: University Press of Kansas, 2015); and Robert Bruce, *A Fraternity of Arms. America and France in the Great War* (Lawrence: University Press of Kansas, 2003).

[62] Michael Neiberg, *The Second Battle of the Marne* (Bloomington: Indiana University Press, 2008), is an excellent analysis of this operation. Zabecki, *1918 Offensives*, 246–279, gives the German perspective.

[63] Lossberg, *Tätigkeit im Weltkrieg*, p. 351.

[64] Jonathan Bailey, "The First World War and the Birth of Modern Warfare," in *The Dynamics of Military Revolution*, ed. M. Knox, W. Murray (Cambridge: Cambridge University Press, 2001), pp. 211–128.

[65] See Edward Lengel, *To Conquer Hell: The Meuse–Argonne, the Epic Battle that Ended the First World War* (New York: Holt, 2008).

[66] Watson, *Enduring the Great War*, pp. 215–231.

[67] Zabecki, *1918 Offensives*, p. 307.

[68] Report of Hans von Below, commanding LXI Corps, Bundesarchiv/Militärarchiv Freiburg, Nachlass Otto von Below, N87/2.

[69] *Korporalschaften*—squads. *Kameradschaften*—affinity groups, friendship communities. *Kampfgemeinschaften*—fighting teams, "bands of brothers" more or less.

[70] Wilhelm Deist, "The Military Collapse of the German Empire: The Reality behind the Stab-in-the-Back Myth," *War in History*, 3 (1996), 186–207.

[71] Herwig, *First World War*, pp. 425–428; 444–447.

[72] See D. Scott Stephenson, *The Final Battle. Soldiers of the Western Front in the German Revolution of 1918* (Cambridge: Cambridge University Press, 2010).

CODA

[1] Michelle Moyd, *Violent Intermediaries. African Soldiers, Conquest, and Everyday Colonialism in German East Africa* (Athens: Ohio University Press, 2014).

[2] Eckard Michels, *Der Held von Deutsch-Ostafrika. Paul von Lettow-Vorbeck. Ein preussischer Kolonialoffizier* (Paderborn: Schöningh, 2014), goes beyond the myths without creating new ones.

BIBLIOGRAPHY

SELECTED SOURCES

Afflerbach, Holger, *Erich von Falkenhayn. Politisches Denken und Militärisschen Handeln im Kaiserreich* (Munich: Oldenbourg, 1994)

Bucholz, Frank, Robinson, Joe and Robinson, Janet, *The Great War Dawning. Germany and its Army at the Start of World War I* (Vienna: Verlag Militaria, 2013)

Chickering, Roger, *The Great War and Urban Life in Germany. Freiburg, 1914–1918* (Cambridge: Cambridge University Press, 2007)

Chickering, R. and Förster, S. (eds) *Great War, Total War. Combat and Mobilization on the Western Front, 1914–1918*, (Cambridge: Cambridge University Press, 2000)

Doughty, Robert C., *Pyrrhic Victory. French Strategy and Operations in the Great War* (Harvard: Belknap, 2005),

Ehlert, H., Epkenhans, M. and Gross, G. (eds), tr. and ed. by Zabecki, D., *The Schlieffen Plan. International Perspectives on the German Strategy for World War I*, (Lexington: University Press of Kentucky, 2014)

Feldman, Gerald, *Army, Industry, and Labor in Germany 1914–1918* (Princeton: Princeton University Press, 1966)

Foley, Robert T. *German Strategy and the Path to Verdun. Erich von Falkenhayn and the Development of Attrition, 1870–1916* (Cambridge: Cambridge University Press, 2005)

Förster, Stig, "Der deutsche Generalstab und der Illusion des kurzen Krieges," *Militärgeschichtliche Mitteilungen* 54 (1995)

Gudmundsson, Bruce, *Stormtroop Tactics. Innovation in the German Army, 1914–1918* (Westport, Ct.: Praeger, 1989)

Hässler, H. H., *General Wilhelm Gröner and the Imperial German Army* (Madison: University of Wisconsin Press, 1962)

Herwig, Holger, *The First World War. Germany and Austria-Hungary, 1914–1918* (London: Arnold, 1997)

Herwig, Holger, *The Marne 1914. The Opening of World War I and the Battle that Changed the World* (New York: Random House, 2009)

Janssen, Karl-Heinz, *Der Kanzler und der General. Die Führungskriseum Bethmann-Hollweg und Falkenhayn 1914–1916* (Göttingen: Musterschmidt, 1967)

Lossberg, Fritz von, *Meine Tätigkeit im Weltkrieg* (Berlin: Mittler, 1939)

Nebelin, Manfred von, *Ludendorff. Diktator im Ersten Weltkrieg* (Munich: Siedler Verlag, 2011)

Philpott, William, *Three Armies on the Somme. The First Battle of the Twentieth Century* (New York: Knopf, 2010)

Raths, Ralf, *Vom Massensturm zur Stosstrupptaktik. Die deutsche Landstreitkräfte im Spiegel von Dienstvorschriften uns Publiziztik, 1906 bis 1918* (Freiburg: Rombach, 2009)

Samuels, Martin, *Command or Control? Command and Tactics in the British and German Armies, 1888–1918* (London: Cass, 1995)

Sheldon, J. (ed), *The German Army at Ypres* (Barnsley: Pen & Sword, 2010)

Sheldon, Jack, *The German Army on the Somme 1914–1916* (Barnsley: Pen & Sword, 2005)

Sheldon, Jack, *The German Army at Passchendaele* (Barnsley: Pen & Sword, 2007)

Sheldon, Jack, *The German Army on Vimy Ridge 1914–1917* (Barnsley: Pen & Sword, 2008)

Sheldon, Jack, *The German Army at Cambrai* (Barnsley: Pen & Sword, 2009)

Sheldon, Jack, *The German Army on the Western Front 1915* (Barnsley: Pen & Sword, 2012)

Sigg, Marco, *Der Unterführer als Feldherr im Taschenformat. Theorie und Praxsa der Auftragstaktik im deutschen Heer 1869 bis 1945* (Paderborn: Schöningh, 2014)

Stachelbeck, Christian, *Militärische Effektivität im Ersten Weltkrieg. Die 11. Bayerische Infanteriedivision 1915 bis 1918* (Paderborn: Schöningh, 2010)

Ulrich, B. and Ziemann, B., (ed.), tr. by Brocks, C., *German Soldiers in the Great War. Letters and Eyewitness Accounts* (Barnsley: Pen & Sword, 2010)

Wallach, Jehuda, *The Dogma of the Battle of Annihilation: The Theories of Clausewitz and Schlieffen and their Impact on the German Conduct of Two World Wars* (Westport, Ct.: Greenwood, 1986)

Watson, Alexander, *Enduring the Great War. Combat, Morale, and Endurance in the German and British Armies, 1914–1918* (Cambridge: Cambridge University Press, 2008)

Watson, Alexander, *Ring of Steel. Germany and Austria–Hungary in World War I* (London: Penguin, 2015)

Wells, Neil J., *Verdun: An Integrated Defence* (Uckfield: Naval & Military Press, 2009)

Werth, German, *Verdun. Die Schlacht und der Mythos* (Bergisch-Gladbach: Lubbe, 1979)

Zabecki, David T., *Steel Wind. Colonel Georg Bruchmüller and the Birth of Modern Artillery* (Westport, Ct: Greenwood, 1994)

Zabecki, David T., *The German 1918 Offensives. A Case Study in the Operational Art of War* (New York: Routledge, 2006)

Zabecki, D. (ed.), *Chief of Staff. The Principal Officers Behind History's Great Commanders*, Vol. I (Annapolis: Naval Institute Press, 2008)

Zuber, Terence, *The Mons Myth: A Reassessment of the Battle* (Stroud: History Press, 2010)

INDEX